SURINAMESE MUSIC
IN THE
NETHERLANDS AND SURINAME

CARIBBEAN
STUDIES
SERIES

Anton L. Allahar and Natasha Barnes
Series Editors

SURINAMESE MUSIC
IN THE
NETHERLANDS
AND
SURINAME

MARCEL WELTAK
TRANSLATED BY SCOTT ROLLINS

UNIVERSITY PRESS OF MISSISSIPPI / JACKSON

The University Press of Mississippi is the scholarly publishing agency of
the Mississippi Institutions of Higher Learning: Alcorn State University,
Delta State University, Jackson State University, Mississippi State University,
Mississippi University for Women, Mississippi Valley State University,
University of Mississippi, and University of Southern Mississippi.

www.upress.state.ms.us

The University Press of Mississippi is a member
of the Association of University Presses.

First printing 2021

∞

Library of Congress Cataloging-in-Publication Data

Names: Weltak, Marcel, author. | Rollins, Scott, 1952– translator.
Title: Surinamese music in the Netherlands and Suriname / Marcel Weltak ;
translated by Scott Rollins.
Description: Jackson : University Press of Mississippi, 2021. | Series:
Caribbean studies series | Includes bibliographical references and index.
Identifiers: LCCN 2021015803 (print) | LCCN 2021015804 (ebook) | ISBN
9781496816948 (hardback) | ISBN 9781496834881 (trade paperback) | ISBN
9781496834898 (epub) | ISBN 9781496834904 (epub) | ISBN 9781496834911
(pdf) | ISBN 9781496834874 (pdf)
Subjects: LCSH: Music—Suriname—History and criticism. |
Surinamese—Netherlands—Music—History and criticism. |
Music—Netherlands—History and criticism.
Classification: LCC ML239.S9 S8713 2021 (print) | LCC ML239.S9 (ebook) |
DDC 780.9883—dc23
LC record available at https://lccn.loc.gov/2021015803
LC ebook record available at https://lccn.loc.gov/2021015804

British Library Cataloging-in-Publication Data available

CONTENTS

Translator's Notes to the Original Publication of 1990 VII

Surinamese Music in the Netherlands and Suriname,

   1990–2017—A New Introduction X

Foreword by Dr. Lou Lichtveld XXXIV

Introduction by Marcel Weltak XXXVII

I. Origins

1. Amerindian Music—*Marcel Weltak* 3

2. Afro-Surinamese Music—*Ponda O'Bryan* 10

3. Surinamese East Indian (Hindustani) Music—*Dr. J. Ketwaru* 25

4. Javanese Music in Suriname—*Herman Dijo* 30

5. The European Tradition 36

   Church Music, Choirs, and Bazuinkoor—*Marcel Weltak* 36

   Military Brass Band and Police Corps Brass Band—*Herman Dijo* . . 43

   Surinamese Classical Music—*Marcel Weltak* 45

II. Development

6. Bigi Poku and Kaseko—*Marcel Weltak* 55

7. Surinamese Jazz in the Netherlands—*Marcel Weltak* 73

8. Jazz in Suriname—*Marcel Weltak* 86

9. Contemporary Surinamese Jazz—*Marcel Weltak* 92

10. Pop 103

   Hindi-Pop—*Dr. J. Ketwaru* 103

   Pop-Jawa—*Herman Dijo* 104

Suripop—*Marcel Weltak* 105

Reggae—*Guilly Koster* 110

Hip-Hop—*Guilly Koster* 112

11. Surinamese Women in Music—*Marcel Weltak* 114

Acknowledgments (to the 1990 Edition) 117

Appendix 1: Selected Discography (to the 1990 Edition)—*Fer Abrahams* .119

Appendix 2: Content of the Music Cassette (to the 1990 Edition) 123

Appendix 3: Selected Discography to the Second Edition 126

Appendix 4: Filmography/Videography/DVDs, 1960–2021 136

Appendix 5: Sranan Song Lines and Titles. 139

List of Acronyms 141

Glossary of Musical Instruments. 142

Glossary of Musical Styles. 147

Sources and Bibliography 153

Contributor Biographies 158

Index 160

TRANSLATOR'S NOTES TO THE ORIGINAL
PUBLICATION OF 1990

When Marcel Weltak's *Surinamese Music in the Netherlands and Suriname* was published in 1990, it was the first time that a book had appeared that provided an overview of the music styles originating from the land that fifteen years earlier had gained its independence from the Netherlands. At the time roughly half of the population chose to emigrate to the Netherlands, where they have since settled and continued to develop and perform their music. The book also appeared just as the first two Surinamers took university degrees in ethnomusicology and Surinamers in general began to express the need to systematically document the development of various aspects of the music of their country. The Netherlands anno 1990 was also just beginning to add non-Western music at the Rotterdam conservatory as well as founding a world music school in Amsterdam in the wake of interest in the so-called "world music" movement. There had been a few monographs published in Dutch exploring the music of the Amerindians and maroons of the interior prior to the Weltak anthology, but no musical survey of the country as a whole.

Up until the 1990s, precious little had been published that dealt with the music of the country. That which did dealt with the music of the maroons in the interior of the country, beginning with the work anthropologists Melville J. and Frances Herskovits in the 1930s such as *Rebel Destiny: Among the Bush Negroes of Dutch Guiana*, 1934, and *Suriname Folk-Lore*, 1936; and *Creole Drum: An Anthology of Creole Literature in Surinam*, 1975, edited by Jan Voorhoeve and Ursy M. Lichtveld, with English translation by Vernie A. February. A series of publications on the Saramacca people in Suriname's interior by Richard and Sally Price began appearing in the 1960s, including their annotated notes for a record of their own recordings, *Music from Saramaka: A Dynamic Afro-American Tradition* (1977), and later book-length studies of the history of the people from the 1990s onward up until quite recently. Later still came work by Kenneth Bilby on the Aluka along the

Marowijne River, and a section on Surinamese African dance styles in Yvonne Daniel's *Caribbean and Atlantic Diaspora Dance: Igniting Citizenship* (2011). Apart from that, there was little that actually dealt with an overview of more contemporary music from Suriname other than Kenneth Bilby's section on Surinamese music in Peter Manuel's 1995 *Caribbean Currents: Caribbean Music from Rumba to Reggae.*

I myself read Weltak's book when it first came out, having gone to see a number of the musicians perform that were included in the book, and I was becoming personally acquainted with some of their experiments at mixing jazz and pop elements into their Surinamese roots and thinking how good it was that a book had appeared shedding light on the multicultural society the Netherlands was in the midst of becoming.

The large community of Surinamers who had settled in Amsterdam, in the district referred in Dutch as the Bijlmermeer, and later as Amsterdam Zuidoost (Amsterdam Southeast), was a spawning ground for talented musicians. Over time the first generation of musicians began organizing themselves to gain their place in the sun. One of the initiatives they undertook was to form the Surinam Music Foundation, whose goal was to promote both knowledge about and the interests of musicians of Surinamese descent in the Netherlands. They even founded a label (SME Records) and helped musicians professionally produce their music in the studio. At the time (in the late 1980s) they asked Marcel Weltak to edit and contribute to the anthology of music essays you have before you. The Dutch publisher engaged musicologist and composer Dr. Lou Lichtveld, the real name of the renowned grand old Renaissance man of Surinamese letters known as Albert Helman (1903–1996), to write the preface, the rationale being that his name on the cover would enhance its chances of being more widely read both in Suriname and the Netherlands. That said, Weltak stated that the publisher's brief at the time was to produce a book with a more popular "coffee table" feel to it, devoid of excessive footnotes and bibliography.

Reviews appeared following its publication, such as that by Professor Michiel van Kempen in the Dutch library review journal *Biblion*, who wrote, "it is a worthwhile introduction and hopefully a stimulus to conduct more exhaustive research," but criticized it for its lack of bibliographical or source materials. In the May 1991 edition of *Onze Wereld* (Our World), Harriet Kroon concluded her review by saying: "*Surinamese Music in the Netherlands and Suriname* must be viewed as the start of further research. Fortunately, more and more Surinamers realize the importance of documenting and recording musical developments. Recently, the first Surinamer received a degree in ethnomusicology, Terry Agerkop. He is specialized in the drum culture of the maroons. The transverse flute player Ronald Snijders became the second Surinamese ethnomusicologist in May 1991. He wrote his thesis on kaseko for the University of Amsterdam. . . . At present Marcel Weltak is conducting research in the interior of Suriname."

Since the book's first appearance, a new generation of musicians of Surinamese descent have carried on making music in the Netherlands and Suriname, while some of their elders referred to in the original edition have passed away. The catalog of recordings that have become available has also been extended, particularly in the areas of hip-hop, rap, jazz, R&B, and new fusions such as *kaskawi*. In the meantime, there have also been reissues of seminal works by the fathers of Suripop and jazz as well as some documentary films and television coverage of the music. This edition includes a new opening chapter by Marcel Weltak giving a historical sketch of Suriname's relationship to the Netherlands, updates on the popular music of second- and third-generation musicians of Surinamese descent in the Netherlands, and his own subsequent research into the Amerindian and maroon music of the interior.

Weltak's new introduction is followed by the integral text of the original edition except for a new, enlarged article Weltak has inserted on Surinamese classical music, replacing the original text. New appendixes have been added to this edition that include a bibliography and updated discography, a listing of films, videos, and DVDs on or about Surinamese music or musicians, concise alphabetically arranged notes on musical instruments and styles, as well as brief biographies of those authors who contributed texts.

To close, again with the words of Harriet Kroon's 1991 review: "Monographs are useful, but so are surveys. One can only hope that Weltak will go to the trouble of making a second revised edition. By crediting his sources, adding a bibliography and adding updated material." Here it is at long last.

Scott Rollins

SURINAMESE MUSIC IN THE NETHERLANDS AND SURINAME, 1990-2017—A NEW INTRODUCTION

Suriname was a colony of the Netherlands until 1975. In the seventeenth century, Suriname was traded by Great Britain for New Amsterdam. The exchange formally took place following the third Anglo-Dutch War of 1672–74, on February 19, 1674, at the Treaty of Westminster. At the time, the Dutch regarded it as a lucrative agreement because, in that historical period, Suriname was probably the largest plantation economy in the Americas. The principal crop on its thousands of plantations was sugarcane. According to historians, a highly significant proportion of Amsterdam's wealth was generated by agricultural products from Suriname. The Netherlands was the last European colonial power to abolish slavery.

After having been seized in the name of the Spanish monarchs by Alonzo de Ojeda, the ownership of Suriname changed hands several times. Great Britain, France, and the Seven Provinces of the Netherlands (later the Netherlands) became the new rulers of the land on the northeastern corner of South America in the wake of each war the European states waged among themselves.

At first Amerindians were used for the heavy work on the plantations. They were not used to such strenuous labor and died in large numbers or committed suicide. Following the declaration of Indians as "noble savages" by the Spanish Dominican friar Bartolomé de Las Casas, they were replaced by slaves imported from Africa.

The Amerindians of Suriname were divided into the *Kari'na* and *Lokono*. These groups lived predominately in the coastal regions. The Kari'na tribe formed part of the Carib group after which the island archipelago was named; the Lokono tribe were a sub-tribe of the Arawaks.

Beyond the great savannas stretching to the border of Brazil lived the Trio and Wayana. A few smaller tribes related to these two groups also lived there, who had originally come from Brazil and who led a more or less nomadic existence. The tribes from the coastal regions were converted to Christianity long ago. The Trio and the Wayana were converted at the end of the twentieth century through missionary work conducted by SIL International, formerly known as Summer Institute of Linguistics with its headquarters in Dallas, Texas.

The culture and religion of these coastal groups can be found in the African American *Winti* religion and in the form of music, dance, and musical instruments, and with such dishes and foodstuffs as *peprewata* soup, cassava bread, and the soy sauce–like *casareep*, that are staples of daily life.

Following the conquest of Suriname by the Dutch and their expulsion from Brazil, the Sephardic Jews who had originally fled Portugal because of the Inquisition in 1492 also came to Suriname. They had the most experience in plantation agriculture and the production of sugar. Suriname therefore became home to the first synagogue in the Western Hemisphere, followed by several others for both Sephardic and Ashkenazi Jews in the centuries that followed.

The Dutch West India Company (WIC) brought slaves from Africa to work on the plantations run by their Jewish and Dutch owners. The majority of Africans transported to Suriname came from the area later known as the Gold Coast (present-day Ghana), Dahomey (present-day Benin), and the area along the Loanage River in present-day Congo. The numbers of Africans transported are estimated to be between 500,000 and one million. There was a steady stream of supply because the life expectancy of laborers was so short. According to the Scottish mercenary J. G. Stedman in his *Narrative of a Five Year's Expedition against the Revolted Negroes of Surinam* in the years 1772 to 1777, life on Surinamese plantations was especially harsh and plantation owners exceptionally cruel, which resulted in a significant portion of slaves fleeing into the jungle shortly after their arrival. Anthropologists consider this a plausible explanation as to why older African culture in Suriname has probably been better preserved than in Africa itself. The social scientists claim that large sections of Suriname are more African than Africa itself.

The Surinamese Interior War in the remote inner regions of the country that was waged between 1986–92, and the flight of large groups of people to the coastal region, tore tribal connections apart and destroyed a great deal of their culture. Before the war, those people who originally hailed from several African regions formed close communities. The maroons or Bush Negroes were divided into an eastern and a western group.

The eastern group consisted of tribes of the *Aluku* (also called *Boni*), *Ndyuka*, and *Paramaccan*. The western group was formed by the *Saramacca*, *Kwinti*, and *Matawai*.

The eastern tribes speak a different language from that of those from the western and central regions of Suriname. *Sranan Tongo* (literally Surinamese Tongue), the Surinamese lingua franca, is used by everyone to communicate across ethnic divides.

Extensive studies were made of the Saramacca, initially by Melville and Frances Herskovits. This American husband-and-wife team published a few seminal works on them in the 1930s, including the standard work: *Rebel Destiny: Among the Bush Negroes of Dutch Guyana*. Richard and Sally Price began their exhaustive study of the tribe beginning in the 1960s. Their research among the Saramacca has yielded a vast amount of material on all aspects of this tribe's life and customs. They also went on to mount two separate exhibitions in the United States on the life of Saramacca.

Nearly a century earlier, at the International Colonial and Export Exhibition held in Amsterdam in 1883, part of the expo was devoted to the Dutch overseas areas. It included exhibits from the Dutch overseas colonies in the East and West Indies. The greatest attraction for the one million visitors were the "Surinamese savages." The Indians and maroons were put on display in the cold practically naked for Dutch people to look at. The exhibitions and books by the Price family were of a much different order; these anthropologists treated the objects of their study with great warmth.

A tradition of working with textiles developed right from the start of their culture, especially among the Saramacca. The use of patches and various sorts of weaving techniques yielded several different cloths. The *pangi* or loincloth is nowadays practically a national iconic symbol. New designs are introduced on special occasions.

Picasso and Dadaist artists were inspired by African sculptures. It appears that the great Piet Mondriaan switched from Impressionism to the geometric technique that was later to become known as *De Stijl* (The Style) after having viewed designs and motifs on the loincloths that were left behind in the Netherlands after the 1883 exhibition.

In the 1990s the American anthropologist and ethnomusicologist Ken Bilby conducted research among the Aluku along the Marowijne (Maroni) River. He writes in his dissertation that the Aluka were residents of French Guiana, although the inhabitants of villages along the Marowijne and Lawa reside both on the Surinamese and French banks of the rivers. In cases of illness they cross the river to go to Maripasoula, because the European hospital there is better equipped than the Surinamese medical posts.

Bilby's analysis of the differences in drumming techniques between the Aluku and the Saramacca is outstanding. Over the course of centuries the groups have grown apart, with their own languages and musical styles. What the Aluku *songé* and *susa* have in common with the *sekete* of the Saramacca is that they are both played on the *apinti* drum, even though the rhythmic patterns are quite dissimilar.

The Saramacca exerted a significant influence on Surinamese African dance music in the coastal regions from the 1980s onward. A fusion of *kaseko* with *sekete*, also known as *seketi*, became hugely popular.

After the abolition of slavery in 1863, African Surinamers had no desire to work on the plantations anymore. Since the work on the plantations had to be continued, the Dutch found the solution with the British to import contract laborers from British India to Suriname. The British colonies had already had experience with the hard workers from the north of India. By 1873, ten years after the mandatory, poorly paid work of freed African Surinamese slaves, the first ships arrived with contract laborers from Bihar and United Province (now Uttar Pradesh). *Lalla Rookh*, the name of the first ship on which the Hindustanis arrived, can still be found everywhere in Suriname and associations in the Netherlands.

In terms of language and culture, the same thing happened with the Indians in Suriname that had happened with the Africans. The policy in the British colonies was one of integration and assimilation, but the Dutch opted for the tactic of cultural apartheid.

The language and culture of Uttar Pradesh and Bihar had been preserved in Suriname along lines similar to that of African culture as scholars had noted. Hindustani Surinamers can travel to those two states from which their ancestors hail and easily communicate with the local inhabitants in Bhojpuri, the language that is spoken there. By contrast, Hindustanis in Guyana, Trinidad, and Jamaica must use English to be able to communicate in India. Surinamers have no need of English subtitles to follow the popular Bollywood movies. It is very lucrative for Hindustani Surinamese musicians to be able to speak the language of their forebears. Because of that, they regularly perform in countries in the Caribbean region as well as for an Indian population in the United States and Canada. Nowadays Kries Ramkhelawan can be heard more often abroad than in Suriname. But back in the days following independence, it was Surinamese singer Dropati, who was flown in to play at weddings in Canada, the United States, and Trinidad and Tobago.

Dropati was the queen of both *sohar* and *lava* songs. The latter is performed on *bhatwaan*, the day before a Hindu marriage. That is when the bridegroom is made fun of by the women from both families. There is a popular saying that goes that if Dropati had not played at the *lawa* (bridal ceremony), then the marriage would not be destined to last long.

Dropati is not known by any other name. Moreover, she is a talented composer in her own right. She knew the Surinamese-Hindustani music culture inside out, composing songs that spanned practically every Hindustani style that occurs in Suriname for her album *Let's Sing and Dance with Dropati*, on the Windsor label in Port-of-Spain, Trinidad. The sparse instrumentation of this music (harmonium, *dholak* drum, and the iron (*dhantal*) are excellently accentuated by her phenomenal melodic modulations.

The music played by this grand dame, who played the harmonium herself, is of exquisite beauty. Newspapers in Port-of-Spain wrote constantly about her hard work and talent and called her the Nightingale of Suriname. "If there is a singer who gets into the spirit of the song then it's Dropatri, who creates the mood with expert voice-controlled modulation that perfectly suits the particular song rendered. Dropati displayed a flair for music while still in her teens and of course her singing expertise grew from strength to strength as she gained maturity and popularity from country to country. The name Dropati has become a household 'Word' by 'Young and Old' not only in her native land Suriname but also in the Caribbean, and Trinidad & Tobago in particular."

In Guyana and Trinidad, Dropati is regarded the Godmother of Chutney. Thanks to her introduction of *baithak gana* with the local soca, she was able to conquer the world with chutney.

Droeh Nankoe came to the Netherlands at the age of nine. His Uncle Jaggan had been responsible for his primary music education in Suriname. His lessons continued in Holland in the Indian manner: the pupil sits with the pandit who sings and plays, after which the student repeats the lesson. He learned to play tabla, organ, and mandolin, and of course how to sing. In his day, Pandit Rambaran Jaggan was already a celebrated musician. His schooling had been so good that at the age of seventeen Nankoe was asked to sing and play in the Hindi-pop group Naya Roshini.

Nankoe quickly discovered that he wanted to do more than sing the same songs and make music for a group of dancers every night. That is why he began studying Western music at the Rotterdam Conservatory, followed by Indian classical vocal lessons with Ustad Mohammad Rasheed Khan. In the meantime, Nankoe toured half the world. He performed at the UN in New York and in practically every European country. In the Netherlands he has composed work for national television and radio.

Over the past few decades Nankoe has also collaborated with jazz, trance, and house musicians and sung in flamenco groups. But what he prefers most is singing the praises of his guru Sai Baba. In honor of this holy man he has released ten albums of music. Nankoe is currently a teacher at the Royal Conservatory in The Hague and in a few other European countries.

Droeh Nankoe's most renowned album, *Songs for Various Occasions*, was recorded in Mumbai. The song *Holi* on this LP sings the praises of the feast of the advent of spring in India and with the Hindustanis. Holi is a game between Krishna and the milkmaids in which they sprinkle one another with *abir* and other colorful agents.

Droeh Nankoe also released *Baithak Gana: Songs from Bihar, Uttar Pradesh and Surinam* on the Dutch label PAN Records. In contrast to most other CDs with Surinamese music, this album is something of a jewel in that it contains reliable liner notes with information about the origins of the songs such as the historical *Gana Nehi* (It is not a song) about the voyage of contract laborers and their subsequent heavy labor on the sugar plantations.

The career of Raj Mohan has followed approximately the same trajectory as that of Droeh Nankoe. He too came to the Netherlands from Suriname as a young boy. In contrast to Nankoe, Mohan began studying Indian classical styles such as *khyal enthumri* and light classical forms such as *ghazal*, love songs in Urdu or Farsi and bhajans, religious songs to raga melodies that exalt the Hindu religion.

Mohan later delved into the history of his origins; that quest was documented in his album and poetry collection *Kantraki* (Contract Laborer), written in Bhojpuri, the language of the Indian states of Uttar Pradesh and Bihar, from which the forbears of the great majority of Suriname's Hindustanis hailed, and in Sarnami, a creole language that arose in Suriname. When performing them he accompanies himself on the harmonium. What makes Raj Mohan's music so interesting is his successful, well-balanced fusion of elements of North Indian raga, modern Indian film songs (geet) with a recurring theme, and the Surinamese variant of Hindustani music, baithak gáná.

In the four-and-a-half-minute title song, Mohan sings of the history of the first contract laborers that left for Suriname in 1873. The first verse of the title song "Kantraki" runs: "tempted across the seven seas / showing us a dream of a new land / how deluded we were / taken to a place called Sarnam, across the seven seas." The song traces their state of mind with the passage of time: "residing in Sarnam we gradually / got used to it after a while / after putting in so much effort / how could we go back." Despite realizing their resettlement is probably permanent, many still believe "our soul says maybe we'll stay / now the state provides a plot of land / in the corner of our hearts / we still dream of going home, one day."[1]

Raj Mohan also composed music for the ballet *Aghori* and has become a sought-after singer in countries of the Indian diaspora.

When the supply of laborers from India stagnated, due to problems on the plantations and the British government putting an end to further transports, the Dutch government decided to import workers from its own colony in Asia, the Netherlands East Indies. The first shipload of Javanese arrived in 1890. They replaced the Hindustanis on the plantations.

The Javanese were needed to work, not make music. Therefore, they did not bring any music instruments with them to the New World, nor any paraphernalia for gamelan performances. The music, the form of the instruments, and the puppets necessary to perform the shadow dances were all stored in their memories. In Suriname, the new contract laborers did not find any bronze to make their *saron* and *bonang* gongs. Instead they used old train rails made of iron to fashion their sarons. Naturally, these metallophones sounded different from bronze instruments. In fact, the pitch and timbre were altogether different. It wasn't until after independence, when an Indonesian embassy was founded in Suriname, that the cultural attaché—who apparently was a music expert and aficionado, and had problems with that different sound—decided to donate new instruments to the Surinamese Javanese, and the authentic sounds of the Javanese *dessa* could again be heard.

Meanwhile, over the course of several decades those Surinamese of Javanese descent had become accustomed to the many musical influences that had crept into their version of gamelan. In the 1960s and 1970s gamelan concerts took place every weekend in Paramaribo that lasted all night. On Sunday afternoons there were performances of *jarankepang* (horse dances). Various radio and television stations made recordings. Unfortunately, all the reels were taped over at the next recording session.

An interesting development was the search by the younger generation for older musical forms such as the *terbangen*. This music form owes its name to the *terbang* drums. The terbangen was originally a Javanese Islamic form of song. Over the course of time it came to pass that at the end of an evening's performance the ensemble switched from playing sacred songs to secular music. The group was then further supplemented with modern instruments.

A sterling example of the fusion of gamelan with local music can be heard in the compositions of Lamie Larasatie. The opening strains of his song "Bakka Thalia," on the vinyl album released in Suriname by the formation of excellent musicians called Lamie and Tjondro Utomo, evoke memories of sultry nights in the Indonesian *dessa*. The bronze *sarons* produce sounds that resound and then fade. The *bonang* gongs keep the pulse of the music going. A female voice swirls into the air out of nowhere. She is singing in Javanese, but the lyrics soon switch to Sranan. She is singing about the strange situation that has befallen a woman behind Thalia, the national theater in Paramaribo. Not only have the lyrics switched to Sranan, the rhythm too lets us hear that the gamelan players have not closed their eyes to African Surinamese music styles. We hear snatches of kaseko being played by a gamelan orchestra.

Surinamese people of Javanese descent who emigrated to the Netherlands took their music with them. Efforts made by such gamelan professors as Orlando Kromopawiro ensured that Surinamese Javanese gamelan was included in the curriculum of a few North American universities, including Creighton University in Omaha, Nebraska. Interest in this form of gamelan is sadly absent in the Netherlands at present.

The most renowned exponent of pop-jawa (Javanese pop) who emigrated to Holland was singer and bandleader Ragmad Amatstam (1953–2011), the founder of the group Rupia. While living in Suriname he had not been conscious of his roots; such knowledge had not been necessary to advance in the world of local music. When he won the Surinamese National Song Festival, people from his ethnic background were quick to point out he was the first person of Javanese descent to have won this prestigious award. It was not until he was in the Netherlands that he began showing interest in his Javanese roots via the Bangsa Jawa organization in Amsterdam. In his subsequent songs, some of which were also sung in Sranang Tongo, we can clearly hear his Javanese roots. His greatest hit, "Mi Lobi Sranan" (I Love Suriname), is virtually the second national anthem and sung by everyone across every ethnic divide.

The third group of Asians who were brought to work on the plantations came from China. That too was not an unqualified success; the contract laborers from the southern province of Guangdong seldom if ever renewed their contracts. At the end of the term of their contracts, they stayed on in Suriname, setting up small retail businesses.

The colonial government then undertook several attempts to carry on work on the plantations by attracting Portuguese contract laborers from Madeira and Dutch colonists from the Netherlands. All these attempts failed. The heyday of the once flourishing colony with its thousands of plantations had come to an end.

To this day one can still see reminders of the wealth that was shipped from Suriname to the motherland in Amsterdam, and Middelburg, the capital city of the Dutch province of Zeeland.

DEVELOPMENTS IN SURINAME SINCE 1990

As described earlier, the maroon population was divided into tribes that lived in the east, Aluku (Boni), Ndyuka (Aucaners), and Paramaccan; and those who lived in the west, Saramacca, Kwinti, and Matawai. The language, religion, dance, and music of the two groups have grown further apart over the years. In the east there are such popular music styles as *aleke*, *songe*, *awasa*, and *susa*, while in the west the Saramacca play *adonke*, *seketi*, and *bandammba*. Elderly Saramacca claim that *adonke* is the only sort of American music taken directly from Africa. This adonke was played and sung at the funeral of Gaaman Aboikoni in 1992:

Botoman mi d'a y'anu

Botoman mi d'a y'anu 2x	Version 2
Tide mi jur' wan oso tamara mi e go na ini	*(Mi nene yuru wan oso,)*
Botoman mi d'a y'anu	
Te ya naki kapalesi yu say ere bori man tongo	

This song originally had to do with death. The bearers (boatmen) go by boat to a place where they dig a hole, performing all sorts of ceremonies. The dead person is then fetched and buried in the same ceremonious way.

Te yu naki kapalesi

This song has been added to the boto song. It originated from an *odo* (proverb) from a sugar plantation during slavery. *Kapalasi* is a large pan in which sugar is boiled. *Te ya naki kapalesi yu say ere bori man tongo* (If you want to know what really goes on at the plantation you have to be on good terms with the overseer).

Another example of *adonke* is about New Year's Eve:

Tide ja oo.	It is New Year's Eve now.
Adjemuna fiti Watjifolo.	Adjemuna and Watjifolo are a good match.
A taanpu waka fu ën sindo u, dee kijoo.	The one with the haughty bearing must sit over there.
Labatata wenze	Labatata, my wife.
Tide jai ee.	Today is New Year's Eve.
Tide jagi fiti Adjemuna ee.	Today all dignity befits Adjemuna.

Jai ee, jai oo, tide jai ee.	New Year's Eve, today is New Year's Eve.
Mujëë jagi fiti Adjemuna ee.	The dignified woman is a good match for Adjemuna.
Un ko mbei u go luku Watjifolo.	All of you come and look at Watjifolo.
A taanpu waka fu ën	The one with the haughty bearing
sindo u, dee kijoo.	must sit over there.
Labatata wenze.	Labatata, my wife.
Adjemuna fiti Watjifolo.	Adjemuna and Watjifolo are a good match.
Matunga maka.	Thorn of the *matunga*.
Tide jai ee.	Today is New Year's Eve.
Un ko mbei u go luku Watjifolo.	All of you come and look at Watjifolo.
Tide jai ee	Today is New Year's Eve
bika jagi fiti Adjemuna ee.	because all dignity befits Adjemuna.

On most occasions secular music forms are also played after the religious music for the *obia pre*. The clearest connections with Africa and African music can be found in *papa* or *vodu* music. The language of the inhabitants of the interior are tonal, as that of those living in coastal Ghana, and that is why the rhythms on the *tumaun* drum are broken down into fragments so they can be transmitted. But the different variations all originated in Suriname. The drums do, however, resemble those from Ghana and the Fon drums from Benin and have practically the same names as *apinti* or *dawra*. It is probably no coincidence that a village on the upper reaches of the Suriname River is called Dahomey. The gods and spirits of the maroons, but also those of the *Winti* found on the coast and in the city, can be traced back to Ghana, Benin, and Congo, such as *Anana Keduaman Keduampo, Kumanti Verekete, Legba*, and the use of the *mpemba* (white kaolin clay). Even maroons who were forced to migrate to the city because of the Surinamese Interior War have now grown closer together. In certain districts in Paramaribo such as Latour and Ramgoelamweg, members of several different tribes live together and engage in interpersonal relationships.

One of the best examples is the organization known as *Kifoko*. The concept of Kifoko comes from the Paramaccan language and roughly means "the corner of the house where things are stored that are not needed at present but may very well came in handy in the future."

Kifoko began as a workplace for the artist Kingbotho. It gradually grew to become a gathering place for visual artists and jewelry makers. As more and more musicians and dancers began frequenting Kifoko and music started being made, the Kifoko Houseband came in to being. A new style of music was generated based on the Ndyuka *aleke* percussion music.

The Paramaccan apinti master drummer Da Tipa Tojo taught youngsters to play the *awasa* and *songe* rhythms. After all sorts of ups and downs, the traditional music and dance group Kifoko was also formed. This formation went on to play throughout South America and the Caribbean region, and even performed in Moscow. Kifoko also generated such other music groups as that fronted by Anikel Awagi and the Masoewa Band.

Other musicians who operated independently from Kifoko modernized *aleke*, mixing it with other genres. The most important new element in *aleke* turned out to be *kawina*, after all. To music experts that was strange, since both were forms of percussion music. It is true, kawina did have other drums and drumming patterns. Still everyone thought that modernization would take place with modern instruments. That indeed has subsequently also come to pass. Aleke festivals now regularly take place in Paramaribo, where all forms of this Ndyuka music can be heard.

In eastern Suriname, Congolese *soukous* and French Antillean *zouk* are extremely popular among the youth, who regularly spend time in French Guiana. Besides zouk and soukous there were probably several variants of music styles from the Dominican Republic, Cuba, and Puerto Rico and Jamaica that were all the rage among singers who sold their music via Cayenne even to France. Two Surinamese maroon singers became popular beyond the borders of their own Surinamese communities. William Souvenir and Johan Misiedjan have attracted international fans abroad with their hybrid mix of soca, bubbling, and salsa with aleke. They sing in Aukan, the language of the Ndyuka. To most fans the lyrics are unintelligible, but the music is nonetheless highly appreciated. William Souvenir's family are Aucaners, though he was born in Paramaribo. While in French Guiana he came into contact with bands from Haiti (like Tabou Combo) and Guadeloupe. In the Netherlands, he played with Mighty Botai and released the albums *A Tin Télé* and *Na'f Mi Wang* in the 1990s on Dutch label MW Records. His sources of inspiration: mérengue, zouk, k-dance, cumbia, and a pinch of kaseko. The rock star among the Nduyka was Prince Koloni who, via Cayenne, French Guiana, built a large fan base in France. The best-known seketi kaseko bands of Ndyuka origin are Yakki Famirie, Ghabiang, and Cosmo Stars.

Scholars often claim that as far as culture is concerned, migrants are conservative. That applies in any case to the Surinamese maroons. Perhaps it is because certain groups needed more time to integrate into their new country. Sekete, the maroon variant of kaseko, arose in Suriname, was taken to Europe by people going on vacation there, and then perfected when they went back home.

By contrast, in Suriname maroon music has flourished like never before. The tribes in the west (Saramacca, Kwinti, and Matawai) are still experimenting with kawina and kaseko and with reggae and dancehall. One of the best exponents is King Koyeba, who has enjoyed success in Europe considering his tours of several countries.

In the eastern district of Marowijne, the largest tribe of Ndyuka still continue to undertake exciting experiments. In the meantime, Johan Misiedjan has become so popular in France that the famous Guadeloupian band Kassav' has contracted him to their record company. Yet other groups are blending aleke with Congolese soukous and French Antillean zouk. The musicians constantly shuttle back and forth from Moengo in Suriname to Cayenne in French Guiana and Paris itself, where they come into contact with modern African, Haitian, and Guadeloupian music.

Which direction Surinamese maroon music will take in the future is anyone's guess. The next source of musical inspiration might quite possibly be Brazilian music from the northeast of that massive country, since there is currently a considerable Brazilian immigrant group living in Paramaribo.

THE CONSERVATORY OF SURINAME

A major recent event to further stimulate the growth and professionalization of Surinamese music and musicians is the founding of the Conservatory of Suriname in 2011 by Dr. Ramon Williams and Albert Arens. According to Arens, one of the reasons it took so long for that to happen was the small population of the country (500,000) and the fact no one thought it was possible: too few students and a lack of qualified teachers and professional musical infrastructure. Still, in the words of the conservatory website: "The Conservatory of Suriname is a Higher Occupational Education Institution (HBO) with the mission to bring Surinamese music talent as well as the culture of Surinamese music to an international level." The lack of qualified teachers at HBO level is partly compensated for by classes on the internet. Curacaoan Dutch opera singer Tanja Kross, for instance, gives digital lessons from the Netherlands where she lives, and bassist Pablo Nahar, one of the founding fathers of the Afro-Surinamese Paramaribop style of jazz that mixes bebop with Caribbean and Surinamese rhythms, now resides in Paramaribo, and even during his frequent visits to Europe for concerts he is still able to still give lessons digitally.

The number of students has grown steadily since the first twenty-seven students were selected through auditions, climbing to sixty-five in 2015 with plans to double that number by 2017. In the meantime, the first foreign students from neighboring countries have come to Paramaribo to follow lessons in tabla and the Amerindian sambura drums. The first students have also recently graduated.

The young singer-songwriter sensation Jeangu Macrooy referred to earlier is perhaps the first student to have attended the Conservatory of Suriname who has become successful abroad. His debut album went gold in the Netherlands in a matter of weeks.

MAROON MUSIC IN THE NETHERLANDS SINCE 1990

Following a European tour, a few members of the Cosmo Stars settled in the Netherlands and founded the Ex(cos)mo Stars. Exmo Stars subsequently became a supergroup of musicians who had earned their spurs in various kaseko bands and the police brass band, such as saxophonist Ramon Laparra, Carlo Jones, and Onkel Seedo. The lyrics were in Saramaccan, with Jones and Laparra writing the melodies and harmonies. The band was a sensation and played throughout Europe.

Damaru and Kenny B(ron) are the two most renowned maroon musicians to make it big in both Suriname and the Netherlands. Damaru rerecorded his Surinamese hit "Mi Rowsu/Tuintje in mijn hart" (My Rose/A Garden in My Heart) with the popular Dutch singer Jan Smit and it became a smash hit on the Dutch pop music charts in the Netherlands.

Kenny B. had a megahit in the Netherlands with his song "Parijs" (Paris). The video clip was naturally shot in the City of Light and was subsequently covered by a host of other singers and even parodied by yet others. These pop songs had nothing to do with maroon music as such, but were pop hits sung in Dutch.

DEVELOPMENTS IN THE NETHERLANDS SINCE 1990

Since the publication of *Surinamese Music in Suriname and the Netherlands*, music of all ethnic groups, including all sorts of genres, continued to develop on either side of the Atlantic Ocean—not only purely in musical terms but in terms of the evolution of Dutch government funding policies regarding ethnic minority music.

At the outset of the 1990s, the Surinam Music Association (SMA), which ran the label of the same name, was forced to merge with the Moluccan organization Barak G if they wanted to remain eligible for government grants. The Multi Music Federation (MMF) came into being as a result. The next precondition laid down by the government was a merger between MMF with Stichting Scarabes (Scarabes Foundation), which had been entrusted with the promotion of performing arts by ethnic minorities, also for the same reason. The next stage was the liquidation of the new organization. The Dutch Stichting ter promotie van de popmuziek (SPN) (Foundation for the Promotion of Pop Music) and the organization for jazz musicians, BIM, would then promote the interests of ethnic-minority pop and improvising musicians. Both these organizations were unsuccessful in their efforts in trying to commercially promote their music, and not long afterward practically nothing remained of what had been a flourishing migrant music scene.

The Surinam Music Ensemble, who had experimented with bebop which critics hailed and dubbed as Paramaribop, ceased to exist. Franky Douglas's Sunchild also folded since there was scarcely any work for the band. Black Straight Music, the name of the band and record label run by the extremely active flute player and composer Ronald Snijders, leads a precarious existence. Fra Fra Sound and The Fra Fra Big Band perform every now and then thanks to the unrelenting passion of its founder and bassist Vincent Henar. Other Surinamese jazz musicians such as guitarist Arturo Castillion produce CDs every now and then, which they try and sell to their friends. There is very little left of the South American jazz scene in the Netherlands that began in the twentieth century with the likes of Kid Dynamite and Teddy Cotton, who had played with Coleman Hawkins.

In Amsterdam Southeast (also known as the Bijlmermeer) a group of Surinamers gathered around a local soccer field in 1975 where a game was being played. Everyone had brought food and drink, and refreshments were sold from the trunks of their cars. The following Sunday people brought their music instruments and began playing. By the 1990s Kwaku as it was known, had grown into a major Dutch summer event spread over weekends in July and August programming an entire range of activities that besides musical performances included sports, food, a beauty pageant, the presentation of a literary prize, debates, and lectures. The renaissance in kawina music could be heard there by Surinamers, the Dutch, and foreign visitors alike. Those first years an annual concourse for kawina bands was held. After several management changes, the current edition is now called the Kwaku Summer Festival and is held in the Nelson Mandela Park in the Amsterdam Southeast on weekends in July, featuring local music and two Friday evening concerts of major international bands.

In the 1980s Rotterdam experienced a similar event known as the Bakadjari (Backyard) Festival that was held over the course of five weekends in 1984. The house band each week was the Bakadjari Band whose cultural organization was known as the Federation of Music. Without any financial support from the city of Rotterdam, at the time their intent was to draw Holland's attention to the music potential in its own backyard. They instigated a music prize, the Masra Award, and a record label. Alas, festival, federation, and label were short-lived, along with the reggae bands Communication and Easy who had been affiliated with the festival.

The Bijlmermeer, where the Surinam Music Association was founded, was a hot spot for Surinamese music. The greatest kaseko singer of them all, Lieve Hugo aka Hugo "Iko" Uiterloo, used to live there. But other kaseko formations also arose there, including Rio Funmaster and later Iwan Esseboom. Practically every street was home to its own vocal choir or kawina band. The vast parking garages, underneath the apartment buildings of the borough, most of which were empty, turned out to be perfect rehearsal spaces.

Fortunately, young people were not the only ones to keep Surinamese music alive. The group Akrema played Winti music practically every week.

Women had gathered around Heloise Holband and were active with both Winti music from the plantations as well as such secular variants of it as *banja*, *laku*, and of course *lobisingi*. All these forms came into being in the nineteenth century. A salient detail in the Bijlmermeer was the fact that women began singing Winti songs; until then, Winti had been strictly a male preserve. The men did, however, continue to play the drums for them. But other strange things had earlier befallen Winti. Two of this synchronistic religion's best-known as well as most popular spirits underwent a gender change during the "middle passage." In Dahomey (Benin), *Legba* was a masculine Winti and *Averekete* a feminine one. Upon arrival in Suriname *Legba*, was now called *Leba* and had become feminine, while Averekete took on a masculine suffix. So the fact that women now perform Winti songs is in keeping with the established lines that sex changes are possible, as long as they are not rigid.

The passage to Europe did not result in intrinsic changes to the earth, air, water, and forest spirits of Winti. In the Netherlands, women sing to male spirits. The fact that women sing to the spirits was born out of necessity. The men now prefer to sing reggae or hip-hop. And the gods would rather be sung to by women than by no one at all. Since the 1990s, in Paramaribo *Winti-preys* (ritual dances) are frequented predominately by gays. These meetings are organized with music for *Aisa* (Mother Earth) played by *kopro 'tu* (brass, string, and big bass drum ensembles) and admission is charged at the gate.

Lobisingi was by far the most modern form of music performed by the group Abaisa, led by Heloise Holband. Holband was the *troki*, or precentor. She had a loud and powerful voice, perfectly suitable to sing African Surinamese songs in the absence of a public address system. Because of the way it was composed, the music lent itself more easily to the integration of new elements. Lobisingi can be most easily compared to European opera. It contains arias, choirs, and recitatives. There is an orchestral accompaniment. And last but not least, there is a plot.

Abaisa was a sensation in the Netherlands, especially due to the presence of Dr. Wilhelmina van Wetering. After completing her studies in Suriname, this cultural anthropologist became friends with Surinamese women in the Bijlmermeer and a member of their music group. Her presence at performances caused great confusion among white members of Dutch society, who did not know there were any other sections of the population not descended from African forebears. Van de Wetering's contribution was significant indeed, especially when it came to lobisingi, which arose from the "du" (the old Surinamese form of commedia dell'arte), a kind of poor man's opera. Oddly enough, the small brass band that accompanied the vocalists was termed a choir even though there was also a genuine vocal choir. Melville Herskovits referred to lobisingi as "an established form of social criticism by ridicule, bearing particularly on the reprehensible conduct of women." Lobisingi was employed by women to mock their rivals. Whereas lobisingi was initially intended for dishing out criticism, little by little the songs have become increasingly erotic. The lobisingi performance has recurring roles and lyrical passages. There is a musical leitmotif, but across the board there is plenty of room for improvisation. The music, dance, and choirs have not changed but the lyrics have, which now poke fun at contemporary political issues or love affairs.

Lobisingi in the Netherlands is now a thing of the past. Government funding has dried up; just as with Western opera, a song and dance company needs an entire orchestra to accompany it and a great deal of sponsorship. As the last form of secular music, lobisingi, along with the sacred Winti, formed the basis for practically all African Surinamese music that has followed. Kawina and kaseko lyrics nearly all stem from these two forms. What has changed over time are the rhythms; the various time signatures from Winti have now been transformed into a simple quadruple time.

On May 5, 2015, Heloise Holband, alias Queen of the Bijlmermeer, otherwise known as "Ma Hilli" left for what African Surinamers call *Yanasei*, the other side of life. As news of her passing went around, that day life simply stood still. It was not just a question of an old woman having died. It felt like a pillar had fallen out from under a whole building. As if the entire foundation of African Surinamese music in Amsterdam, or even the Netherlands had collapsed. Abaisa is no more. But Bethania, the name of the society for the bathing of corpses which Holband founded, still conducts the final washing of the dead body according to Winti rituals.

To celebrate the impending Suriname independence in 1975, impresarios organized parties practically daily, sometimes with as many as fifteen different bands on the bill. The parties were also meant to act as antidote to nostalgia. Upon arrival after a flight across the ocean that was also a flight to the unknown, people immediately felt homesick, missing the sun and laidback atmosphere.

The first dance parties were held on Saturdays. Later, Sundays were added, followed by the *mundedansi,* a dance that was held on Monday evening. Finally parties were dubbed with the names of every day of the week, and the Dutch began asking themselves whether anyone had any time to actually work for a living.

That was the heyday of kaseko. Each group had its hardcore fan base. Some groups broke through to the mainstream and regularly appeared on Dutch national television. At the time, Surinamese music could be heard at festivals in Belgium, France, Germany, Austria, and Switzerland. Albums by Max Nijman and the Caribbean Combo sold well on the west coast of Africa. Other bands had #1 hits in Holland, such as Boontjie Stars and Dutch Rhythm Steel and Showband's song "January, February." The Dutch sang along to Lieve Hugo's "Een Pot met bonen (Oh Marie)" (Jar with Brown Beans). The huge number of dance parties resulted in overkill. People soon tired of too much of the same.

The death of Lieve Hugo in 1975 heralded a decline in the popularity of Surinamese dance music. Lots of kaseko bands folded. Good musicians became street sweepers. Only the best, like saxophonists George Schermacher and Carlo Jones, were still asked to play as session musicians. Groups that made exciting fusions based on kaseko such as the almost punk rock Jongoe Bala or the funk kaseko of Kaseko Orkester unfortunately were not granted a long life.

A few years later Surinamese rhythms could be heard with such groups as Perikels, who began playing with Dutch saxophonist Hans Dulfer, or the Surinamese Dutch ensemble De Nazaten.

The Surinamese groups in the Netherlands who went on to replace the kaseko bands as purveyors of dance music were those who employed rhythms and styles from all over the Caribbean, such as La Rouge, South South West, Kasimex House Band, La Fiesta, and La Caz. They made use of melodies and texts from traditional songs, but the depth of meaning in the metaphors of the original lyrics often escaped them. These dance bands usually ended their songs with onomatopoeias.

One singer who did not fit this bill was the crooner Max Nijman (1941–2016). Nijman was initially a big fan of Brook Benton, and had performed as his support act. But he soon distinguished himself as a gifted lyricist and composer in his own right. A few of his compositions such as "Adjossi" and "Ai Sranang" have become part of Surinamese heritage. When he passed away in 2016, his body lay in state in an Amsterdam pop temple that was packed to the rafters. A huge crowd thronged the premises, surrounding the building after they were refused entrance by the fire department. He was then flown to Suriname where he received a state funeral. The burial service was broadcast on every radio and television station in the country.

A similar scene unfolded some forty years earlier with the passing of the King of Kaseko, Lieve Hugo, the stage name of Hugo "Iko" Uiterloo. He too died in the Netherlands, shortly before independence, immediately after having recorded the first song celebrating independence. His coffin was borne in a funeral procession in the city, with people dancing in its wake as is customary with African Surinamers.

Surinamers are immensely fond of their musical heroes. Even though it is true that Imro Belliot, aka P.I. Man (named after *pyjaiman*, the name for the Amerindian medicine man), did not get a state burial in the Netherlands following his sudden death on November 22, 2014, the church doors had to be shut at his funeral service because it was not safe to allow any more people to enter. More than a thousand mourners danced to *bazuinkoor* (small brass band) music behind the coffin at the graveyard. There was a time when P.I. Man was more popular outside the Netherlands than in his own country. He toured throughout Europe with his ingenious mix of Winti, kaseko, kawina, afrobeat, and calypso. His two albums are now highly sought-after collector's items.

It has been tough going for progressive African Surinamese music since the death of P.I. Man. "Odongo" Stanley Angel has not made any music since his brilliant album *Look Your Winti* in 1987. The gigs for his whirlwind performances of music dried up and so there was no money to support a touring band. And whenever Odongo had been able to get a booking somewhere after lengthy negotiations, he did not show up with the eight musicians as agreed but with sixteen, which meant the band members got half the fee stipulated in the contract. His hypnotic torrent of sound was a mix of free jazz, avant-garde rock, several Caribbean genres, and Winti.

Other interesting musicians such as guitarists Robbie Alberga or Arturo Castillion produce albums with a certain degree of regularity, but live performances seldom take place. They play in such other bands as De Nazaten or the Ronald Snijders Ensemble or are available for on-call work in dance bands that play on practically a daily basis.

Though the Surinamese element is still clearly discernible in the music of Robbie Alberga and Arturo Castillion, that is no longer the case with Surinamese female vocalists who play big halls for Dutch audiences. Ruth Jacott and Denise Jannah sing pop, soul, or jazz in large venues for predominately white audiences. Denise Jannah can still be heard in small venues for Surinamers. She tours Japan and the United States, playing at such venues as New York's Bottom Line, after having been signed by the famous New York label Blue Note.

Veteran musician Robert Harman Sordam, aka Robby Harman, released his first full-length album *Harmanized* in 2016. Under the name Robert Sordam he had been lead singer on several songs on albums by Fra Fra Sound; done backing vocals for Odongo (Stanley Angel) and The Spirits, and P. I. Man and Memre Buku; and had released several EPs. Harman was also a member of Milestones, an art collective of young Surinamers that produced most of the prominent Surinamese musicians of the 1970s and 1980s. In contrast to most of his friends, he had formal music lessons, taking lessons on accordion and trumpet, and in the 1970s was the only colored musician to play in the marching drum band Tubantia through the streets of Amsterdam. His musical education enabled him to make arrangements for compositions by his friends.

In the foreword to the book and CD *Harmanized*, Guilly Koster wrote that even though critics liken him to Al Jarreau, Robby Harman had already developed his own unique vocal style long before any of his Surinamese friends had even heard of Jarreau. Harman sings, scats, and breathes jazz and soul. He has also recorded several modern jazz arrangements of kaseko songs as well. On *Harmanized* he sings his own compositions in English and in Sranan Tongo. They mirror the wide range of musical styles he encountered over the years. Alongside kaseko and kawina we can also discern Dutch Antillean rhythms, jazz, and soul inflections. *Harmanized* has a stellar lineup of Surinamese, Dutch, and Curaçaoan musicians and marks a new direction modern Surinamese music will be taking. Robby Harman sadly passed away of cancer at the age of sixty-three in 2018.

A younger generation of Surinamese musicians has recently come to the fore. Many of them are male rappers or in hip-hop crews, brigades, and posses. One of the most popular is Typhoon, aka Glenn de Randamie. Born in the Netherlands to Surinamese parents, his first musical forays were in such crews as Rudeteenz, in which he rapped together with his brother Blaxtar, aka Kevin de Randamie. It was not until the release of his multi-award-winning album *Lobi da Basi* (Love Is the Boss) in 2014 that Surinamers recognized enough musical elements to regard it as something of their own. *Lobi da Basi* is a combination of kaseko, hip-hip, jazz, rock, and rhythm and blues. The album has been a huge crossover hit. Typhoon's swift rise to fame in the Netherlands has resulted in a high media presence in a relatively short space of time.

Typhoon was invited to perform live in The Hague for the Dutch King Willem Alexander and Queen Maxima and the Prime Minister during ceremonies to mark the two hundredth anniversary of the Netherlands as a republic. Together with his band he performed the song "Van de regen naar de zon" (From the Rain to the Sun): "From the rain to the sun / From the sky to the ground / From the rules, to the values / For the ships, for the water / From the rain to the sun and the other way around."[2]

Its lyrics contain his take on Dutch history: The land of coalitions and agreements / Alliances, charters, rules, treaties/ Big in setting trends and strategies / Haven for freedom seekers, mental and physical." The song identifies those who from the seventeenth to the twenty-first centuries have emigrated, settled in, and added to the Dutch nation: "Jews, Huguenots, Muslims, philosophers / Victims of war who arrive by the boatload / Surinamers, Antilleans, Turks, Moroccans, Poles by the crate, / It makes us colorful, makes us even greater." "From the Rain to the Sun" concludes taking a positive position on the question of diversity in the modern Netherlands: "We are determined by where we are going, not where we have been / Keep the power close to the people and fling fear to the wind."

A documentary on Typhoon's life and rise to fame called *Typhoon: Blues and Blessings* appeared on Dutch national television early in 2016. Filmed over a five-year period by his close friend and former housemate Hebert Alfonso, it is an intimate portrait of what makes the man tick and the influences that inform his music. It includes scenes from his trips to Suriname and New Orleans.

In 2018 Dutch national television broadcast a four-part series *Typhoon in Amerika*, in which the rapper interviewed members of Black communities in New Orleans, Memphis, Boston, and Baltimore examining what had become of the legacy of Martin Luther King fifty years after his death.

Yet another young talent is singer-songwriter Jeangu Macrooy, who was born in Paramaribo in 1993. After his move to the Netherlands in 2014, he enrolled in a Pop Music Academy in the city of Enschede. In 2016 he was nominated for a Dutch Edison Award in the category of Best Newcomer. Following national television appearances and extensive radio play, he is currently a much sought-after live artist at festivals. Macrooy's soul songs, gorgeous voice, and stage presence is giving goose bumps to a new generation of Dutch listeners both Black and white. Macrooy has since released four records in rapid succession. At the time of this writing, he is the official Dutch entry for the Eurovision Song festival of 2021 with the eponymous title song of his fourth album *Birth of a New Age*. This and the song "Gold" from his 2016 debut EP feature subject matter and musical styles of his Surinamese roots (see pages 129 and 137–38).

Just like the young Surinamese musicians with an African background on either side of the Atlantic Ocean, the original Amerindian inhabitants of Suriname modernized their traditional music, at first with Surinamese kawina. Lokono and Kalina migrants in the Netherlands took their cultural baggage with them and have conserved their traditional music, crossed with kawina. This form of music has been better retained in Europe than in Suriname.

In Suriname itself, Lokono and Kalina Amerindians, especially those living in the coastal areas, have succumbed to the temptations of mixing French Antillean zouk, Dominican merengue, Cuban son montuno, and Trinidadian soca into their *sambura* music. Other music variants such as *pyjai* and *krawasie* have remained unadulterated out of respect. What has clearly been retained is the sambura drum, the symbol par excellence of their Amerindian music. However, the various foreign influences have resulted in sambura music that is played at much faster tempos and as dance music for young people. Sambura music is quite possibly the clearest demonstration of the eclecticism of Surinamese music.

SURINAMESE WOMEN IN THE NETHERLANDS AFTER 1990

For several decades there has been an ongoing presence of Surinamese female vocalists in the Netherlands in the light music and jazz industry. In the 1930s there was Alma Braaf, aka Lolita Mojica. In the 1960s Millie Scott created a furor in Holland. Born on 1933 as Marion Henriette, Molly received a scholarship from the Amsterdam conservatory when her talent was discovered. She did not finish her studies there. She quit after being the butt of the umpteenth racist remark. Nevertheless, she was able to build an extremely successful show business career. She represented the Netherlands at the 1966 European Song Festival. She never read the newspapers and so she could travel to the festival with an open mind. It wasn't until afterward that the papers had written about her being the first Black female vocalist to participate in the competition. As a child from the middle class, Scott had received a quasi-white education and was shocked at being characterized as such.

Her heart lay with jazz, though to make a living she had to sing more light music. Concentrating on performing the music of Irving Berlin, Jerome Kern, and Cole Porter and others from the American Songbook enabled her to perform at several engagements in London as well as for the BBC. Her foreign performances made her famous in the Netherlands.

Ruth Jacott (b. 1960) was Millie Scott's successor. Like Scott she could have earned just as much performing jazz, light or serious art music. In the end she opted for a career in light music. She too represented the Netherlands at the European Song Festival held in Ireland. She traveled throughout Europe playing in Andrew Lloyd Weber's musical *Cats* and brought the house down with "A Night at the Cotton Club." Jacott performs in two thousand-seater theaters and stadiums and performs in English and Dutch.

Natascha Slagtand (b. 1974) enjoyed much greater fame outside the Netherlands than in her own country. At the time she was under contract for the Japanese label Avex, she was more popular in Tokyo than in Amsterdam. She later was under contract in the UK at Dom Records.

The music of Tasha's World, Natascha Slagtand's band, mirrored her musical interests: jazz, hip-hop, and neo-soul. Even though the singer won several Dutch music awards with Tasha's World such as the Zilver Harp (Silver Harp) and the Essent Award and performed at such prestigious festivals as North Sea Jazz and Lowlands, she still was more of a household name in the rest of the world than in the Netherlands, where her fame was mainly limited to the Surinamese and Dutch Antillean community.

Surinamese born Sabrina Starke (b. 1979) grew up with reggae, which was very big with young people of her generation. She was able to pull off what other young singers of her age were unable to do in the Netherlands. Her single "Do for Love" was a hit. It was widely heard on YouTube and used in commercials. She received the Dutch Edison award for Best Newcomer in 2008.

The American label Blue Note found her interesting enough to offer her a contract. This was followed by performances at New York's Apollo Theater. Starke's songs are strongly influenced by rhythm and blues, hip-hop, reggae, and other Caribbean styles. She has transferred the eclecticism of Surinamese music to the contemporary pop scene for young people.

Her 2013 album, *Lean on Me—The Songs of Bill Withers*, was chosen as best Dutch album in the category Soul and Jazz. The 2015 album simply titled *Sabrina Starke*, on which she sings funk and soul, features a photograph of thirty-seven prominent power ladies of Surinamese and Dutch Antillean descent in the music, entertainment, and media world. It was meant to encourage young Black women to pursue careers in the same industries.

Esperanza Denswil was born in Rotterdam in 1985 to Surinamese parents. Better known by her alter ego Pink Oculus, she is a recording artist, singer songwriter, MC, producer, and actress. Her motto is "let's have fun." Pink Oculus is one of the clear examples of the dichotomy that has arisen in Surinamese music: styles from back home and those from the diaspora. Young musicians in the diaspora call themselves Surinamese because they are regarded as such by others, they make music that is inspired by genres that come from the United States and call that Surinamese. Contemporary music styles in Suriname are more heavily influenced by those from the Caribbean region.

The music of Pink Oculus could have been made by a singer from New York who had listened to a lot of Surinamese music. It is jazz, soul, hip-hop in a superb mix with a hint of Surinamese influences. Pink Oculus is a gifted dancer and entertainer who can perfectly read the atmosphere of a venue and improvise from any preconceived set list at the drop of a hat.

CLOSING REMARKS

Since the publication of the first edition of *Surinamese Music in the Netherlands and Suriname* in 1990, several trends can be observed. The traditional kawina music, which arose at the start of the twentieth century and had practically died out, has undergone a renaissance. Now played with amplification and by using metal sticks instead of wooden ones, metal shakers instead of calabash maracas, and conga to replace the small *tum* drum, the sound has become more aggressive.

The *bazuinkoor* is now divided into the large and small brass ensemble. The large ensemble began with chorales and hymns and switched to Winti music for *Aisa*, the goddess of the earth. Jamaican dancehall exploded onto the Surinamese music scene and for a time was even more popular than kaseko.

There was a revival of *baithak gana* among Hindustanis. Singer and bandleader Kris Ramkhelawan was responsible for this. The charismatic

Ramkelawhan writes lyrics and composes his own melodies that greatly appeal to listeners and is a star not only in Suriname but also in the Netherlands and among Indian communities throughout the Caribbean, United States, and Canada.

Young Hindustanis attended Dutch conservatories and the Berklee College of Music in the United States and went on to play Indian classical and semi-classical music, though none of them achieved the level of Ramkhelawan's popularity.

In the Netherlands, Surinamese music was adversely affected by the downturn in world music programming and huge subsidy cuts in that sector. To survive, Surinamese musicians were forced to sing in Dutch or make North American music (soul, hip-hop, and rap). It is remarkable that the first popular rapper/hip hopper in the Netherlands was a Surinamer of Amerindian origin from the Lokono tribe with the stage name of Tony Scott (aka Peter van de Bosch). Tony Scott had several hits and has performed in New York and other locations in the United States. The same held true for the Urban Dance Squad with vocalist Rude Boy, who were members of the Black Rock Coalition from New York and who toured with Living Colour.

Contemporary Surinamese music is fanning out in all directions. In the meantime, the music played by certain ethnic groups has been well researched. This includes extensive publications by Richard and Sally Price on the Saramacca and Ken Bilby's study of the Aluku. The Amerindians of the coastal region have also been the subject of exhaustive research. The task of conducting further research into music of the Javanese and Hindustanis still remains.

Marcel Weltak

Notes

1. Lyric excerpts from Raj Mohan's "Kantraki" are quoted from his collection of poems *Bapauti/Erfenis* (In de Knipscheer Publishers, 2008), and appear on the CD *Kantráki* (Contract Laborer) (Pan Records PAN 213, 2005).

2. Lyric excerpts for Typhoon's "Van de regen naar de zon" (From the Rain to the Sun) are quoted from the album *Lobi Da Basi* (Love Is the Boss) (Top Notch/Universal, 2014).

FOREWORD

In order to avoid any misunderstandings, the following must be said: a clear distinction can be made between practicing music and musical life in Suriname, and that of those Surinamese native sons and daughters who engage in the same thing outside the borders of their country of origin. Precious little scholarly attention has been paid regarding the first aspect, which is largely the domain of ethnomusicology, and for reasons that can be easily guessed. It is all the more regrettable that—while making, composing, and arranging music (which, due to current circumstances, is greater in Suriname than elsewhere) has understandably resulted in its rapid spread outside the country's borders—there is still an especially fascinating (if not heart-rending) downside. After all, to a significant degree it has to do with practicing music in the diaspora and less so than ever before about making music for amusement, at least for those musicians involved. Homesickness, nostalgia, resistance, and self-awareness, manifestations as a minority and sometimes even as protest, play a greater role than they used to, when music was tantamount to having fun and engaging in an exotic pastime.

Very little has been written about the ethnomusicology of Suriname, the task of which ought to be to examine both the instruments and the ways in which they are played as well as the melodic and rhythmic components of the music produced by the country's Amerindian, African, Hindustani, Javanese, and Chinese inhabitants. Practically nothing is known, let alone researched or publicized about their mutual influences, about how despite their widely different origins, outside influences have affected them all. In a land that is so fascinating to scientists, this very broad terrain lies fallow and is—just as with spoken language—subject to continual change. Can we then speak here of musical "creolization"?

Moreover, in this connection such terms as "folk music" or "entertainment music" are of no use; after all, there is still not anything that can be regarded as a "folk," only a heterogeneous group of people who in historical terms were only recently brought together on a much too large patch of earth from four continents. To be sure, each group expresses itself in the universal language music is reputed to be by its very nature, in ways characteristic of their identity and origins, and their "languages" mutually influence one another probably more than their practitioners are aware of themselves. But it still remains an urgent task, even if only to make a start with a thorough examination of this area.

In this regard it is curious that "music by Surinamers"—all too carelessly referred to as "Surinamese music"—has indeed achieved a degree of fame and even popularity in the Netherlands as well. For most listeners it is only music for entertainment with a semi-exotic character, about which no inquiries are made. Therefore, it could still take a long time before those experts in the field referred to above, who at present are few and far between, will get around to publishing even the most necessary of preliminary studies. In the meantime, a great deal of data is being lost due to a lack of archives, to collections of relevant recordings and notes, as well as a lack of scientific expertise in music history and musicology by the researchers in question.

A few of those closely involved in this sector can no longer idly stand by and watch how year after year so many (ear- and) eyewitnesses disappear from the stages and society, whose observations and memories remain unchronicled and the results of their professional experience lost forever. That is, they want to save that which can still be saved. A younger generation, in search of its roots, in better times will be grateful for this, regretting that even more had not been recorded.

Accordingly, the somewhat archaic form of the Dutch adjective of *wachtensmoede* (tired of waiting) could be used as a motto for this collection of by-no-means-finished studies that were compiled though a great deal of effort about the practice of music in Suriname and by those born-and-bred Surinamers outside their country of origin. The pages that follow stem from the general human need to find one's not only biological but also cultural and in this case musical roots, as well as to save the remnants from oblivion—not in the least by manifesting itself in the international musical world, to determine its own characteristic place in it, to try and not be overlooked, and to make clear to others what that minority has in mind and for what reasons it considers itself to be of value with its own separate place.

"Tired of waiting" is therefore the phrase that accompanies this publication as well as serving as an apology for the sometimes fragmentary or incomplete contents of what is offered here. May it prove to be an incentive to further study of the components involved and, at the same time, provide evidence that it is in every way worth the effort to delve more deeply into the subject.

This commentary can serve as a general introduction for those who listen with pleasure in Suriname and elsewhere to the multifarious music that the sons and daughters of our country perform on every conceivable occasion, partly to demonstrate the fact that more is going on with non-European forms of music than listeners realize.

Dr. Lou Lichtveld (1903–1996)

INTRODUCTION

It is said that every country should have its own flag, national anthem, and airline. The newly independent Suriname has them all. However, another institute ought to be added to that list: a conservatory. While other South American countries often have had them at their disposal since the eighteenth century, Surinamers have had to do without up to the present day. That might account for the slow development of Surinamese music in the last couple of centuries. Most Surinamese musicians received their musical training from clergymen, in the army, or in the Volksmuziekschool (Folk Music School), which was founded in 1945. Ethnic diversity in Suriname has also proven to be a barrier: every community guards its own identity and therefore tends to hold on to the old musical traditions. This does not make musical development any easier.

In order to promote Surinamese culture, the Stichting voor Culturele Samenwerking (STICUSA) (Foundation for Cultural Cooperation) was set up in 1948. This, however, did not accelerate the development of Surinamese music in the way many had hoped it would. Indeed, there was the short-lived Surinaamse Filharmonisch Orkest (Surinamese Philharmonic Orchestra), and people in Suriname have been familiar with such excellent bands as the Militaire Kapel (Military Brass Band) and the Politiekapel (Police Corps Brass Band) for quite a while, but these ensembles only played European music for a long time. There was no shortage of European music elsewhere either. For instance, it was not until very late that experiments took place in the former center for European classical music in Paramaribo, known as Theater Thalia, with forms of symphonic music that integrated the sounds of Indian tablas and African drums.

Alongside these "official," European forms of cultural expression, Suriname is also familiar with many other musical forms, often hailing from other parts of the world. Besides the music of the indigenous Indians with their flute and sambura drum, there is the music of former African slaves with their Winti music on many different drums and that of the contract laborers (indentured servants) from India with their refined stringed instruments. In the nineteenth century even dances popular at European courts, together with tunes that had blown over from the American Civil War (e.g., "Yankee Doodle"), were given a second life in the Surinamese *set-dansi*, an idiosyncratic combination of music and dance.

Surinamers are multifaceted and inventive. The Javanese, who had been brought to Suriname after the abolition of slavery in 1863 together with the Hindustanis and Chinese to work in indentured servitude, quickly discovered the scrapped trolley rails on the plantations and used them to build their traditional gamelan ensembles. The Indian Hindustanis used the calabashes of the jungle savanna to make sitars. In the Surinamese jungle the West African slaves easily found the right trees to make their *agida*, a three-meter-long drum of African origin made from the trunk of a single tree. The sound of "talking drums" such as the *kwakwa* and *apinti* soon were heard in the Surinamese rainforest.

All these influences from Asia and Africa inundated the original Amerindian culture, which had already been heavily suppressed, first by the Dutch colonials and later by the American bauxite entrepreneurs. There is hardly anything left of the once-flourishing Amerindian music. Its influence can still be heard most clearly in the so-called *Indji Wintis*, because the Winti cult is a mixture of African and Amerindian religions. The Indji Wintis remind the listener of the manifold spirits and their power in daily life. Winti has been at the heart of much of the Afro-Surinamese music in the past hundred years.

Whereas the Amerindian culture was being suppressed, there was a steady increase of influence in the twentieth century from the Caribbean area and North America. Calypso from Trinidad, merengue from the Dominican Republic, and reggae from Jamaica all vied for top spot with Dixie, jazz, and soul. All sorts of Surinamese bands adopted these styles or used them as sources of inspiration. Hindustani music also underwent twentieth-century influences. Indian pop music reached its Hindustani audiences, and all kinds of groups that made a mix of Black creole and Hindustani music, through the movie house. All these cultural influences have made it difficult to define just what Surinamese music is. At present there is Afro-Surinamese dance music, Hindustani music, Surinamese jazz, Suripop, and classical pieces by Surinamese composers. This book is an attempt to shed some light on this kaleidoscopic whole.

Surinamese music does not fare well in most literature on the subject. Some "experts," for instance, regard *bigi poku* to be a failed imitation of European marching music. Others blame it for the exact opposite reason. In an essay dating from 1940, the Dutch musicologist Gilbert writes that "the

Dutch West Indies possessed no highly developed culture," in contrast to the Netherlands East Indies.

Gilbert is surprised at the "tenacity of such a primitive culture." In order to explain this rejection of European norms, the expert concludes: "The culture of the Surinamese native has no need of *art*."

Black Surinamese music is just as much art as any other music of the twentieth century. But most Europeans feel somewhat uneasy about serious Surinamese music. They would prefer to hear Surinamers playing superficial summer hits. It is quite telling that Dutch record stores still file the Surinamese jazz of Fra Fra Sound under "non-Western music," while such colleagues as the Cuban Machito are filed under jazz.

That is why the aim of this book is to view and listen to Surinamese music with other eyes and especially ears. *Surinamese Music in the Netherlands and Suriname* is the first book to attempt this. It is abundantly clear, however, that a final word on all of this is still not possible. Quite a few Surinamese musicians and groups are not included here, even though they may turn out to be just as important to the development of Surinamese music as those colleagues who are mentioned. When the Suriname Music Association, a society of Surinamese musicians, came up with the idea for this book, the first priority was to gather as much material as possible. There is still much to be done, seeing as how Schermacher, Blijd, Lokhin, and Suki Akkal and all the other great Surinamese musicians can still tell their story. Hopefully, this book will provide the initial impetus to conduct research on a much greater scale.

Marcel Weltak

PART I

ORIGINS

1

AMERINDIAN MUSIC

- Marcel Weltak -

The colonization of Suriname brought precious little benefit to the original inhabitants of the Surinamese jungle, the Amerindians. Of the original inhabitants there are now only twenty thousand left living in Suriname, divided among the members of the Trio, Wayana, Akurio, Kalina, and Arawak (Lokono) tribes. The first four groups are regarded as Carib Indians who inhabited northern South America. The fifteen thousand Kalina make up three quarters of Amerindian people living in Suriname, who live predominately along the coastal area.

The Trio and Wayana live in the southern Sipaliwini district, along the border with Brazil and French Guiana. The Arawaks, the only non-Carib Indians, inhabit the central savannas of Suriname.

Amerindian society has been under relentless external pressure for centuries. Wayana culture has nearly vanished, especially due to encroachment on their mode of existence by North American religious communities. The Americans allowed the Trio to play their nose flutes but not to make traditional music with them. The remainder, which repression did not destroy, was further wiped out by the ever-increasing dissemination of radio. A lot of young Amerindians came into contact with pop music as a result. In this way many Kalina in the east of Suriname were strongly influenced by the French Antillean cadence music. And *kawina* has essentially replaced original forms of Arawak music.

Conversely, the influence of the original inhabitants on Surinamese culture is minimal. Amerindian art never took a permanent place alongside the dominant Afro-culture. Only the Winti religion still bears Amerindian characteristics. Apart from that, and except for a few Amerindian words in kawina music, the precolonial culture of Suriname is practically extinct.

KALINA

The music of this largest group of Amerindians differs from that of the Arawak, Wayana, and Trio. The structure and organization of Kalina songs resembles that of the Yanomami Indians in the border areas of Peru and Brazil. In recent years the Kalina have been more successful at retaining their music culture; for instance, traditional music can be heard more often at their communal feasts. And in the meantime, organizations have been set up that promote listening to one's own traditional folk music. The culture of the Kalina appears to be out of the danger zone. The only thing that would mean the end of Kalina culture would be the disappearance of their villages.

Practically all Kalinas have converted to the Catholic faith. They did so because the Catholic Church offered them all sorts of facilities, such as schools for the Kalina children. Moreover, most priests sought converts in name only; they did not exert much pressure to become pious Catholics. As a result, the Kalina still resorted to the shaman for their spiritual salvation. Shamanism—the belief in spirits and forces of nature and the possibility of coming into contact with them when in trance—is a universal phenomenon with the Amerindian. All Surinamese Amerindians used to have a shaman, or *pyjaiman*; nowadays this wizard and guide is only to be found with the Kalina. The pyjaiman is a spiritual and cultural leader as well as medicine man, all rolled into one. He works in close contact with the Captain, the constitutional head of each Amerindian community.

Amerindians have a special reverence for musicians, especially the pyjaiman. He is the priest in a musical sense; the power of a song lies in his hands. He has to be a gifted singer and an expert at composition and lyrics. The words to a song often come to mind while he is in trance. Songs that come into being this way remain in the repertoire, which means new songs are continually added. In that sense the pyjaiman is still the guardian of Amerindian culture.

As a result of the double religion, the Kalina sing both about spirits and "God" (a concept that is a part of each person and of shamanism), but not about Jesus Christ.

INSTRUMENTS

According to Amerindian custom, all musicians must make the instruments they play. To this end, each village has a number of specialized instrument makers. The Kalinas' most important instrument is the big sambura drum.

The owner cuts this drum from cedar trees, because of the beautiful sound resonance of this type of wood. The preferred skin to stretch across it is that of the aboma snake (boa constrictor) or that of a deer. Attaching the stretched skin takes place in several different ways. The choice of stretching system and kind of membrane makes this drum resemble the Afro-Surinamese kawina drum. The musician often puts seeds inside the drum to give it a hissing sound. Finally, the tongue of the maripa palm is attached to the skin, which vibrates along when the drummer beats the drum with a short, thick stick.

The Kalina Indians say that the sambura must "boom." They often speak of "booming ground," by which they mean the wind that must carry the sound as far as possible. That is the only way to reach villages deep in the jungle. Kalina songs' first and foremost priority are to convey messages from tribe to tribe, not between individuals. That is why the Kalina say that you cannot make a celebration with just a single sambura. They would much prefer to play a dozen or twenty of them all at same time if possible. That is why during celebrations samburas must be struck as hard as they can be, all on the same beat. The only one who can deviate from playing the beat is the person improvising. This person must have mastered all the songs and know at which moments to add the syncopations to enhance the trance of the dancers. The leader of the group is usually the one who is responsible for these improvisations.

The sambura has two regular drumming patterns within four-four time. In the first pattern the even long beats are all given the same accent. The second drum pattern is built up from this form: *** * * ***. The Kalina in the west of Suriname play the first series of beats all at one time, followed by a series of triplets. They play the sambura songs more slowly than in the east of the country.

The *krawasie* often takes the place of the sambura. A krawasie consists of a rattle with the seeds of the poisonous krawasie tree in a basket of braided warimbo palm leaves. During the songs, the Kalina hold the krawasie in their hand or attach it to a stick, which they stomp on the ground. When more than one krawasie is played, they all play the same pattern. Krawasie songs are sung faster in the west than in the east of the country.

The Kalina also make music with maracas and flute beside the big sambura and krawasie. These flutes are cut from kwama bamboo and have a maximum of four holes.

Maracas (or pyja-rattles) are made by putting seeds of the paracua plant into a calabash, supplemented with *tawono* pebbles from a riverbed. The village women then paint the rattle with natural dyes. The maraca is played with a rotating motion.

SONGS AND CELEBRATIONS

The sambura songs of the Kalina have a festive character, and are quite lively. But there are also songs for religious feasts, devotional songs, and laments. These are separate from the songs of the pyjaiman; they are called *oremi*. They consist of séance songs that are sung in a deep throaty voice, and of songs accompanied by maracas. The pyjaiman sings the songs *parlando* style, which is more speaking than singing. Songs such as these are in a minor key.

The Amerindians often use the pyjai-songs as bridges between two pieces in the sambura and krawasie-cycle. The krawasie songs are played when a person dies, at funerals and the lifting of the period of mourning (*kodono* after a month and *omangano* after a year). No drum is used here, which is an instrument that inherently lends itself to expressing joy. During the ending of the mourning ceremony, women sing krawasie-laments and the men indulge themselves in the joyful sambura songs. Finally, there are also work songs for Kalina women, which they sing especially when they are weaving or cooking. The women do not sing when they are outside working the land.

For the Kalina, the text of the song determines the beat. Pyjai songs are in three-quarter time with the accent on the first beat. During séances, the pyjaiman ends each song with a prayer. After the prayer he begins playing a musical introduction with the maracas, after which the singing commences. There are no prayers in the maracas songs. In both cases the pyjaiman sings alone.

Laments begin with humming, after which the krawasie comes in and the solo singing begins, which is then joined by a choir. Sambura and krawasie songs can be played both in three-four and two-four. One of the musicians leads off playing the drum for the joyous sambura songs and is then joined by all the others. There is a precentor for these songs. Following the drum introduction, he looks for the right tone and the right song. This search for the right tone usually sounds like the beginning of making guttural sounds: "*A tere tere . . .*" The musical themes of the sambura and krawasie songs also originally came from the pyjaiman. They can be improvisations on an actual event, songs of praise to the ever-rotating celestial bodies, songs about God or the summoning of good spirits. The emotional life of an individual is a constant source of new songs, like everywhere else in the world. Kalina tribal members in Paramaribo have sung songs about being homesick. During his travels studying the Kalina, the researcher Nardu Aluman heard them singing the praises of the artistic merits, power, and inventiveness of Kalina women.

Songs, for Surinamese Amerindians, and especially for the Kalina, are not just an accompaniment to dancing, but also a means of communicating with other tribes. A tribe who is busy singing for two days is mostly occupied by conveying messages. The messages may convey warnings not to approach a certain territory, or the opposite, inviting other tribes to enter into friendship.

The Kalina still organize sambura and krawasie celebrations, which often go on for days at a time. When a person has died, the rituals began at the crack of dawn, such as cutting off the bangs of hair on the forehead and painting the body. By 9:00 a.m. the musicians commence singing laments, which goes on until sunset. If there is enough liquor and food left over, the Kalinas prolong the mourning an extra night. That is because the feast to end the mourning goes on all night.

During the Kalina celebration those in attendance do not sing along. Anyone wanting to sing must join the circle of dancers or take part playing a sambura. The dancers stand in semi-circular rows, one after another. During krawasie and pyjai songs, they sing while dancing and stomping the ground, to the sound of flutes that are played synchronously.

The purpose of the music is to send someone into a trance. This is reached especially through the uniformity of the songs. The simultaneous beating of the samburas and the synchronous playing of the flutes at first sounds quite monotonous. But anyone dancing for half an hour in a group loses all track of time. Hours seem like days, and vice versa. Aluman fell asleep during one of the Kalina celebrations because he did not participate.

WAYANA

Both the Wayana and Trio tribes inhabit the southern borderlands of Suriname. As a result, their music sounds pretty much the same, especially the flute playing. The two tribes are clearly related in terms of clothing and the like.

Until recently the music of the Wayana could not be heard in Suriname. In their zeal to convert the native population, the Catholic and Protestant churches had forbidden them to play their traditional music. And the North Americans finished off the job when they practically wiped out their culture for the purpose of mining bauxite. In order to celebrate a traditional feast with *kasiri*, the beer brewed from cassava, the Surinamese Wayana have to cross the Maroni River into French Guiana. Young Wayana Indians want to take up the music of their ancestors again, but this is a laborious process. The Wayana observe a longer period of mourning than the Kalina; they play and drink for three days and nights in a row. Then they sleep for a week and resume the music for the next three days running. Like the Kalina, the

Wayana have maracas and krawasie. For their krawasie, however, they lash together several small baskets filled with seeds and bind them to their ankles. This way they can play this rattle when stamping their feet. An impressive Wayana instrument is the two-meter-long bamboo flute with its oboe-like sound. The Wayana have several different kinds of flutes, made from animal bones, bamboo, plastic, or metal. As rhythm instrument, the Wayana use a slit drum that lies on the ground from a hollowed-out trunk. The characteristic hollow thudding sound results from banging on it.

THE ARAWAK

According to the Surinamese music researcher Nardu Aluman, the Arawak have a more strongly developed sense of rhythm than the Carib Indians. This is especially audible in their singing. And their extremely melodic playing on the *jankabuari* (transverse flute) is more highly developed than other Surinamese Amerindian people. At Arawak feasts the flute can play both a primary and secondary role, where the singing takes over the function of filling in parts where they are not played. Nowadays, guitars often also accompany Arawak songs along with the jankabuari. They once used maracas, but this instrument has fallen into disuse.

THE RISE OF KAWINA

The Arawak relinquished their culture at an early date, or were "too loyal with regard to other cultures," as Aluman euphemistically put it. The other cultures were the North American popular music and Afro-culture, from which kawina ultimately emerged. Under the influence of kawina, the original music of the Arawak in Suriname has practically died out. Their kawina ensembles are in no way inferior to the Black African ones, and often no difference can be discerned. In some villages, the Arawak play kwatro (four-stringed guitars), a typical kawina instrument, and sometimes self-made violins.

The introduction of modern instruments did not essentially change the structure of Arawak music. Only tone color and interpretation had to be adjusted. The pentatonic character of Arawak music has been retained to this day.

The music made on modern instruments strongly resembles that of the *altiplano* music of the Amerindians in the Andes, who in Suriname are often regarded as being related to the Arawak. The melodic structure and flute technique of the Arawak bears a slight resemblance to that of the Peruvian Quechua Indians.

Young Arawak musicians in search of their "roots" even use electric guitars nowadays in order to spruce up and make acceptable the remnants of their traditional music. Yet other Arawak youths try to reconstruct the traditional music using authentic instruments and playing techniques.

The Wayana and Trio do not play—still do not play—kawina music, but the Kalina do. The Kalina run kawina workshops in their villages of Bigi Poika and Bernard-dorp. However, there are no kawina songs that are completely sung in an Amerindian tongue. The Kalina and Arawak sing their kawina in Sranan Tongo, with only a few words in their own language. Nonetheless, in a number of Indian kawina groups one can still hear the stately sambura rhythm resound.

In both the Netherlands and Suriname, Amerindians are trying to keep their culture from vanishing. In the Netherlands, the Arawak group Wayono in Rotterdam and the Kalina song and dance ensemble Yamore in Amsterdam are actively keeping their traditions alive. In Suriname plans are being worked out to found an Amerindian cultural company for theater and music. Unfortunately, the pieces they will produce will be in Dutch and Sranan Tongo, albeit with elements from four Amerindian tribes in Suriname.

2

AFRO-SURINAMESE MUSIC

- Ponda O'Bryan -

There is no getting around Africa to understand the music of Afro-Surinamers. Practically all music, dance, and theater is dominated by the culture of the Black continent on the other side of the Atlantic Ocean. Of extreme importance is the Winti religion, on which nearly all Afro-Surinamese music is based.

The African slaves who were brought to Suriname in the seventeenth, eighteenth, and nineteenth centuries originated from powerful people who at the time were endowed with a rich culture. These people from the African Gold Coast (now Ghana), the Slave Coast (Togo, Benin, and Nigeria), Ivory Coast, Guinea, and Congo all had cultures based on oral traditions; there was no written language to any large degree. However, this did not mean in the least that there was a homogenous African culture, which people in Europe thought at the time.

The great differences that had characterized those African peoples, all melted away when they were slaves in Suriname. Nonetheless, the Afro-Surinamese culture that grew from this was anything but uniform. To be sure, the slaves were spread across the plantations, without regard to their country of origin, but they in turn were extremely isolated from one another. In this way, for instance, each plantation had its own Winti songs, which were later named after the plantation where they were created. And soon thereafter, small groups of runaway slaves were formed, who all created their own music.

MAROONS, PLANTATION CREOLES, AND URBAN CREOLES

After the deprivations suffered on the crossing on the slave ship, African slaves were introduced to the harsh regime on the plantations. Soon many attempted to run away and disappeared into the rain forest. The Surinamese rainforest strongly resembles the African jungle; the runaway slaves could not only survive but also organize a guerrilla campaign against the slave owners of the colonial regime. The maroons, the honorary sobriquet accorded to the runaway slaves, gathered in the rainforest and in the course of time formed their own tribes. They became so powerful in such a short space of time that in the seventeenth and eighteenth centuries the colonial rulers were forced to negotiate peace agreements with them. The great maroon leaders—Joli Coeur, Baron, and Boni—are now often referred to by name in Surinamese music. Deep in the Surinamese rainforest, maroon communities arose who were reasonably successful at retaining unadulterated African culture. In this way, certain customs that no longer exist in Africa have been retained in Suriname. To this day, deep in the interior of Suriname, drums still send messages from tribe to tribe. The maroons have been divided into the following groups:

1. The Ndjuka or Aucaners along the Maroni, Cottica, and Commewijne rivers
2. The Saramacca along the Suriname River
3. The Paramaka on the Maroni and Cottica
4. The Kwinti on the Saramacca River
5. The Aluku or Boni along the Lawa River
6. The Matawai on the Saramacca

The Afro-Surinamese community also had the so-called plantation Creoles, who lived on the various plantations:

1. Commewijne and Cottica (along the banks of the river)
2. Upper-Suriname (along the Suriname river)
3. Para (along Para creek)
4. Saramacca (along this river)
5. Coronie (along the coast between the Saramacca and Nickerie rivers)

The plantation Creoles maintained contact with the maroons, who had often fled from the same plantations. There was a continual stream of runaways who joined the ranks of the maroons. Moreover, the maroons regularly raided the plantations to reduce their shortage of women. This practice ensured that the cultures of the maroons and plantation Creoles were not too far apart.

Finally, there were also the urban Creoles in Paramaribo, the majority of whom were made up of city slaves; but there were also a few Creoles who had been set free by their masters. This manumission (the freeing of the slaves) took place occasionally. After the abolition of slavery in 1863, many former plantation slaves migrated to the city, a process that is still ongoing.

MUSICAL INSTRUMENTS

Just as in Africa, Afro-Surinamers had appropriate music to suit all kinds of occasions, often corresponding to the Winti gods, who played an important role in them. The colonial rulers forbade some of these forms of music, out of fear that the "talking drums" could foment revolution. Other forms were allowed to be sung—for the entertainment of the white masters. Despite this arbitrariness, Afro-Surinamers still have music for death and bereavement, births, religious ceremonies, and so forth. These forms of music will all be dealt with after a discussion of the most used instruments.

Shakers and Drum Instruments

Sakka: a cleaned-out calabash gourd filled with seeds through which a stick is inserted. Both the Amerindian and African cultures possessed these instruments. The sakka has both rhythmic and sacred significance for either the *bonuman* or pyjaiman (traditional medicine men of the maroon and Amerindians, respectively).

Siksak (sek-seki): an iron tube filled with pits or seeds. This shaking instrument is used in kawina music and in Brazil is known as *ganza*.

Dawra: iron cowbell of African origin (from the Akan tribes in Ghana: *dawura*). In Suriname it is sometimes replaced by a hoe head (*tjapu*). The dawra plays an important role in traditional music.

Godo: two calabashes, the larger of which is filled with water and the smaller is turned upside down to float on the surface of the water. It is played with sticks.

Grumi: wooden washboard that is played with two thin sticks as a scratchboard, akin to the North American washboard.

Djendjen: cowbell in the shape of a clock to summon the gods.

Mata: wooden mortar, the stomping of which can create rhythmic accompaniment to work songs.

Kwakwa: hollowed-out tree trunk with a slit drum that is played with two sticks. Besides its rhythmic function it also has a role as "talking drum," that is, to convey messages. Derived from this is the:

Kwakwa-bangi: a wooden bench that is played with two sticks, probably hailing from Africa (Congo: *nkpokpo*).

Benta

In Suriname this refers to various stringed instruments and thumb pianos. These instruments have largely fallen into disuse. The **papai-benta** is a thumb piano (Africa: *sanza, likembe, mbira*). The **golu-benta** is a hollowed-out calabash gourd with strings stretched across it. In Africa, such instruments are still quite popular (Sierra Leone: *congoma*; Ghana: *primprimsua*).

Wind Instruments

Pakrotutu: horn made from a shell to summon the gods.
Kawtutu: cow horn with the same function.
Bototutu: iron horn for communicating between riverboats, especially on the Maroni, nowadays largely replaced by the radio or megaphone.
There used to be several kinds of flutes, such as the odd **nose flute**. They have practically all died out.

Drums

Apinti: the national Afro-Surinamese drum, used to communicate with the gods and send messages. This "talking drum" (forest telephone) is originally from Ghana (Akan tribes: *apentema*, other names: *apretia, oporenten, atumpan*). The apinti has a conical shape about 50–100 cm high, and a diameter ranging from 30–40 cm. It is usually played by two hands or with one hand and a stick. The drumhead is stretched with wooden pegs that are knocked into the drum. The Saramaccaners also call it *tumao*.

Dutch plantation owners were scared to death of the apinti, and severe punishment was meted out to anyone who played one, such as hacking off the hands and even arms—for fear that the apinti would incite a rebellion.
Agida: the largest Afro-Surinamese drum. It is two to three meters long and 40–50 cm across, fashioned out of the single trunk of a tree. This drum is especially reserved to communicate with the gods of the earth and is played with one hand and a stick. Before playing it is sprinkled with beer and white earth and covered with a special cloth (Ghana, Togo, and Benin: *atsigo, atsimevu, asafo, fonfonfrom*).
Mandron: just as the agida, made from a hollowed out single trunk of a tree, only shorter, about 150 cm and a diameter of 25–30 cm. The mandron is played by both hands and stretched with the help of pegs (a stretching system used primarily by the West Bantu and Ibo). During a celebration in

the *banja-style*, the mandron is also sometimes referred to as *langadron* or *langaudu*.

Pudja: short, hollowed-out tree trunk about 50 cm long and 25–30 cm across. It is played and stretched with a skin like the mandron and always played in ensemble with the mandron. The Saramaccaners also sometimes call it *deindein*, and sometimes play it with either two hands, two sticks, or one hand and one stick.

Apukudron: hollowed-out tree trunk about 130 cm long and a diameter of 20–30 cm. It tapers, getting narrower toward the bottom and has the same stretching system as the mandron. The Saramaccaners use it to call *Apuku*, the forest deity, and play it with two hands. In some areas it is also known as *luangadron*.

Kawinadron: short, cylindrical hollowed-out tree trunk, about 45 cm long and 25 cm in diameter, stretched on both sides with a system of cords. The drum is laid across the lap and played on one end with a stick and the other by hand. Its origin is difficult to trace, because it is known in both Amerindian and African cultures (in the Netherlands Antilles and Dominican Republic) as the *tambora* drum, used especially to accompany merengue. In Suriname, this drum only really became popular in kawina music.

Bongo: short, cylindrical hollowed-out tree trunk about 40 cm long and a diameter ranging from 20–25 cm. Just like the mandron a skin is stretched and held in place by wooden pegs. In Coronie the bongo is used to play kawina music, where it is played with two hands. The instrument is not related to the modern Cuban bongo. In Cuba, however, there is a sacred drum (*bonko enchemrya*) whose shape and system of stretching the skin is related to the Surinamese bongo.

MAROON MUSIC

Like Africans, the maroons made ceremonial music for most occasions: when someone dies, or to enhance fertility, at births, initiations, and so forth. Naturally, there is also religious music. Peculiarly enough the maroons do not have a specific word to denote "music." When drumming they refer to "playing Ashanti" (after the tribe of the same name in Ghana). In his book *Musique de l'Afrique*, Francis Bebey writes that "music is so strongly connected to man himself; he did not find it necessary to give it a name." In this respect the maroons do not differ very much from most African peoples.

The maroons sometimes accompany themselves with hand clapping or benta instruments; sometimes they sing a cappella. Most music styles however are a combination of instrumental music, song, and dance. There are several variations, also within the same tribe. The Saramaccaner *seketi* and the *awasa* and *songé* of the Aucaners are virtuoso dances in which the dancers add rhythmic accents to their steps with rattles attached to their ankles and wrists. But just as in Africa, by far the most important role is played by drums—together with other percussion instruments in ensemble form. This all has to do with polyrhythm; several instruments play rhythms over and against one another, the combination of which is the actual rhythm. Some instruments play an accompanying role (the so-called *hari*) and there is always a leading, or solo drum, the "master drum" or kot'dron. A sakka usually keeps time, and a dawra plays the key rhythm or clave: the basic rhythm by which the entire ensemble is driven.

Afro-Surinamese percussion music is a fusion of two African styles: the West Bantu and West Sudanese ensemble forms. The Bantu usually play clave on the slit drum or on the body of another drum. West Sudanese ensembles almost always use metal bells and rattles on which clave is played alongside a battery of different drums, and the slit drum is absent. Metallophone bells are less important to the Bantu, but small rattles are sometimes attached to wrists to produce extra sound. In Suriname, the drum that produces the deepest sound is almost always the one on which to play solos, just as in the two African styles; the other instruments support the rhythm. In Suriname, where the Bantu style is in use, the form of the song is determined on the slit drum, the kwakwa. In other regions, just as with the West Sudanese, a metal cowbell (dawra) is used to play clave. There are also hybrid forms in which both the bell and slit drum are used.

Woodcutting and engraving play a significant role in Afro-Surinamese culture; drum makers are also woodcutters. Just as in Ghana most of them are made of tweneboa, a kind of cedar wood. To begin with, certain rituals are observed when felling the tree. The trunk is hollowed out and stretched with a skin. If it is a sacred drum, it is ritually initiated and is sometimes even given a name. The playing of the drum is strictly a male affair: it is taboo for women. In Afro-Surinamese culture, particularly that of the maroons, quite a few African taboos still exist. There are food taboos, and sleeping with a woman who is having her period is forbidden. These taboos are often broken in Africa itself.

RELIGIOUS MUSIC—WINTI

The Winti cult was born out of African religions with Islamic elements, and in Suriname it has even undergone Christian and Amerindian influences. For instance, a person who has gone into trance during an *indji-Winti* dances with buckled knees. This is a typical Amerindian way of dancing.

In his book *Winti, een Afro-Surinaamse godsdienst in Suriname* (Winti, an Afro-Surinamese religion in Suriname), C. J. Wooding defines the Winti faith as follows: "An Afro-Surinamese religion whose central tenant is the belief in anthropomorphic supernatural beings, that can take possession of a person and take over their consciousness and heal sickness of a supernatural order." At its core is the belief in a supreme being (the Creator Anana Kedua-man Keduampon) and the individual spirits (the Wintis). The realm of the gods is usually subdivided into water, forest, earth, and air, and the Wintis themselves are subdivided into the places from which they originate or the power they exert. Incidentally, experts can tell from which region of Africa the Winti hailed by virtue of its name.

The Winti cult, however, is more than just a religion. It is a way of life in which music plays an important role. Specific songs, dances, and rhythms belong to each Winti, sometimes even a special form of ensemble and special sort of drums. The master drummer who plays the lead drum (kot'dron) plays the Winti in question in drum language. That is why all Winti rhythms have their own character and color. Certain Wintis only manifest themselves when called upon in song and dance. Winti drummers often have yearlong training behind them to learn all the various songs and rhythms. These musicians are sometimes specialists on a certain drum, such as the agida or apinti.

During a Winti ritual (*Winti-pré*) the order in which the songs are played depends on the location, the choice of the medicine man, and the reason for the ritual. All Winti-prés begin with songs dedicated to *Aisa* (Mother Earth). Schematically, a normal song cycle looks something like this: first songs for the earth (*prisdoti*), then for the water spirits, and finally a series for the spirits of the forest. A Winti-pré usually starts at ten in the evening and ends at the crack of dawn. Songs are played to the air gods usually between twelve and five in the afternoon.

MUSIC ON PLANTATIONS: TUKA AND OTHER STYLES

Religious music was also the most important kind to the plantation Creole, but there is not a single plantation style due to the fact the plantations differed so much from one another. In principle, when it comes to religion, there is not much difference between maroons and plantation Creoles, but there are differences in drumming techniques. Another difference was that most of the social dances were forbidden on the plantations, which resulted in their total disappearance.

Nowadays, most of the plantations have been abandoned. Quite a few people have migrated to the cities or the Netherlands. That migration resulted in a new sort of drumming style coming into being: the *para-pas'dron*, mostly played in the religious music that arose in Paramaribo and other urban areas.

The disappearance of the plantations also meant the disappearance of the *awasa* and the *sekete* (sekete for the Saramaccaners) as specific, separate forms of dance: they were absorbed into the so-called *tuka*, a style in 4/4 that is played during a Winti-pré to alternate with the 12/8 beats or as a transition to another style. Other styles besides tuka exist or used to, which we will now deal with in succession.

Sokkos or *sokko songs* (also sokko psalms, because of their religious meaning) are sung in an African language during worship of ancestors. They are almost impossible to translate into Sranan Tongo. There is no instrumental accompaniment; the songs consist solely of introductory hymn and chorus. Sokkos usually initiate the ceremonies, even if there is a switch to other styles. The sokkos probably originate from Ivory Coast (from a tribe by the name of Sokko) or Guinea, where the Sosu (or Susu tribe) live. The Sosu are also referred to in Suriname by the name Sokko.

Krioro-dron literally means Creole drum, but there are no drums involved. Krioro-dron songs are sung a cappella, just like sokko psalms. They are only about social events, and they are critical of certain situations. In contrast to sokkos, they are not religious; moreover, they are sung in Sranan Tongo, which indicates their Surinamese origin.

Besides sokko, the *banja* style is the most important form of dance and music within the cycle of ancestor songs. Those present during a banja session (or pré) can be possessed by the spirit of an ancestor. In Africa the banja already played an important role, just as do the *laku*, *susa*, and *kanga*, which will be discussed later. Except for the plantation Creoles, only the Matawai maroons know the banja dance, although with a slightly different character.

Every banja pré begins with songs to Mother Earth (Aisa) to honor the location or ground where the pré is being held. The ensemble consists of one each of the following: kwakwa-bangi, dawra, sakka, pudja, langadron (mandron), djendjen, and godo. The banja is in 4/4 meter. The songs consist of introductory hymn and a choir, out of call and response. The tension between the melody and the rhythm makes the songs difficult to perform

and are reserved for experienced singers. The old dance is a gorgeous sight.
It is predominately danced by women, and at some plantations was even
allowed to entertain the masters.

There are several sorts of banja-prés:

Prodo-banja, in which certain people or situations are criticized. In this
form of music it was possible to express feelings about the oppression
of the slaves, just like the blues. What sometimes happened was that
the white master allowed himself to be entertained by dancing and
singing slaves, while their words announced the flight of those very
same slaves, without the whites understanding.

Baka-futu-banja or *notu-banja* is a form of banja that was forbidden
until after the abolition of slavery, since the slaves venerated their
ancestors and Wintis. The banja for the ancestors is also referred to
as *jorka-banja*. Winti-banjas are named after the respective spirits
involved, such as Aisa-banja or Ingi-banja.

Lanti-banja, played specially for a certain location, for instance a plantation or a market, is usually performed at regular intervals.

Borgu-banja, in which a symbolic boat that transports African slaves to
Suriname, plays the lead role.

Partij-banja or *banji-banja*, performed by song and dance companies
who organize one or more large-scale banja-prés annually. These
companies are known as *du-groep* or *partij*. They put on full-length
dramas with a fixed theme and cast of characters such as Afrankeri,
Aflaw (the woman who faints), Sisi (the female ceremonial leader),
Moi-Moi (Beautiful), Boketi (Flower bouquet), Tanta (Aunt), and
Datra (the doctor). A fixed part of the group was a *banji-banji*, an
African altar that belonged to a certain du-groep or plantation. Somewhere around the middle of the eighteenth century these groups were
tools in the hands of the slave owners. They were often members
themselves, a situation comparable to the samba schools in Brazil.
Internal conflicts among slave owners were fought out through the
du-groeps, because during the drama persons could be insulted. The
du-groeps were later banned. It was not until the twentieth century
that they were known by the name "partij." There are still a few partij groups in Suriname, and also one in the Netherlands, the group
Abaisa. However, the altars have practically all gone by the wayside.

The *laku* is a dance spectacle in drama form, related to the banji. It is not
clear when it originated. According to some it was around 1860, but banja

expert Alex de Drie places the first lakus in the so-called indentured servant period, starting from 1873. The contents make clear why.

The laku makes use of the same figures as the partij-banja, but the symbolic African boat is replaced by one of the Asian indentured servants, and a few figures have been added, such as Snesi (Chinese), Kuli (Hindu), and Kuli Konstro (British Consul).

Just like the banja, the luku is in 4/4 meter. The songs often criticize certain persons and situations and make use of featured singers and choruses. The ensemble consists of the following: kwakwa-bangi, pudja or apinti, langadron (mandron), dawra, sakka, and possibly one skratyi. A well-known modern laku female singer was Nelly Slagtand, whose song "Mi na kakafowru, mi kroon da mi ede" (I am the rooster, my crown is on my head) was a hit in Paramaribo. At the request of the Dutch professor Voorhoeve, together with Fransje Gomez, she performed a laku-pré, but after she died the entire laku-pré tradition was buried.

The *susa* is a play in dance form that is mainly performed by men. The ensemble is comparable to that of the laku but without the skratyi (bass drum). It was known by both plantation Creoles and maroons and was of African origin. In West Africa and the Congo especially, such dances are still known. Two men dance opposite one another. It concerns the movement of their feet: at the beginning of the dance an agreement is made as to how they should move. Whoever moves his leg the wrong way loses and immediately makes way for the next contestant. Susa can be compared to Brazilian capoeira. Susa contests used to be organized in which teams from several regions and plantations competed. Susa was then regarded as a sport.

Kanga is a collective term for all sorts of children's games, most of which were of African origin. One or more songs are associated with each game. To the beat of the song the children imitate certain movements. Kanga songs can be either in 12/8 or 4/4 meter and are accompanied by hand clapping and sometimes two drums (apinti and/or pudja). Kanga is played especially at night during full moon on the plantations and in the jungle interior.

Anansi-tori are stories about the spider Anansi. These stories also occur on Curaçao and other Caribbean islands, but especially in Ghana, from which they originally came. Each—mostly humorous—story contains a moral, which is expressed at the end in a song usually accompanied by hand clapping and possibly with one sakka or sometimes two drums, just as in the kanga.

Lobisingi (love song) is the Afro-Surinamese form of comic opera. The first version of this style was most likely to have been played on kawina instruments. Later, brass instruments were introduced, together with stringed instruments and skratyi drum. Lobisingi originated from the *du* (the old Surinamese form of commedia dell'arte) and can be considered a beggar's comic opera with recitatives and arias, accompanied by a small brass orchestra, the so-called "choir." Herskovits in his 1936 book *Surinamese Folklore* typified the lobisingi as "an established form of social criticism by ridicule bearing particularly on the reprehensible conduct of women." The lobisingi as an art form was almost always performed only by women. During slavery, a planter's wife took her own, or a group of hired slaves to the house of a rival, where the female slaves put on a play to ridicule the rival in front of her own home. It has several fixed characters from the partij-banja and laku, such as Afrankeri, Aflaw (someone who always faints from the Dutch verb to faint—*flauwvallen*), and Datra (doctor). There is invariably a policeman and a nurse. Someone faints, a doctor is called and the person in question is revived.

The intro, in which the story of the song is summarized, is called the *langa-singi*, which is a cappella. It is followed by the *kot'-singi*, in which the moral of the song is sung, accompanied by an ensemble consisting of European brass, percussion, and possibly string instruments. However, the music has an African feel to it. The music is in 4/4 time and has a kind of oom-pah-pah rhythm, in which the participants engage in forced laughter after each solo sung, the choir sings, and the crowd can dance. There are several different texts and only a limited number of melodies, such that different lyrics are sung to the same melody. Seeing as how lobisingi are always about the vicissitudes of love, emotions sometimes ran high. The genre was even forbidden at one time, due to fights.

A typical example of a standard part of each performance is the following song that translates as:

How can you still dare to say I am not beautiful?

Two flowers have conceived me
My mother is a rose
My father is a bachelor button (*Stanvaste*, a Surinamese variety of *Gomphrena globosa amaranthaceae*)
How can you still dare to say I am not beautiful?

After slavery women began to sing about one another—at first critically, then later erotically. Lobisingi sometimes took on the allure of being a ritualistic public display of lesbian love. In Suriname lobisingi lives on as a form of oral culture that is sporadically performed among working-class women. In the Netherlands lobisingi has largely lost its function as a mocking form of music theater and lesbian love ritual. In modern-day performance (still all women) soloists take turns singing songs that ridicule and poke fun at the love affairs of famous people and historical or topical events in Surinamese and/or Dutch society.

The musical accompaniment of lobisingi by a song and dance company accompanied by a brass band has not changed in the Netherlands, but the song lyrics have. In the 1980s there were still regular performances of lobisingi in Amsterdam at the Vereniging Ons Suriname (Our Suriname Union) house in Amsterdam. One of the most famous modern lobisingi singers was Heloise Holband (1925–2015).

Nowadays lobisingi is seldom performed, owing to the high costs of hiring a song and dance company as well as orchestra. And a good performance necessitates a great deal of rehearsal.

Kawina music, known to Surinamers simply as *kawina, kawna,* or *kauna,* came into existence at the end of the nineteenth century, just after the abolition of slavery on July 1, 1863. Ever since, this music has grown to be the most popular form of traditional Afro-Surinamese music, with influences from banja, laku, and tuka. Various theories exist concerning the precise origins. In any case, the name has to do with the river Commewijne, situated in the district of the same name. In Sranan Tongo both music and river are called Kauna. Some people think that kawina originated in the upper reaches of the Commewijne, where Creoles, under the influence of Amerindians, created the music. Others claim that this music was originally called *mabu-poku* and was later named after a talented singer from the Commewijne district. Yet another theory postulates that it was developed as a form of relaxation and recreation by the gold diggers and rubber tappers working in the jungle.

At any rate, kawina is Creole. Its function is practically the same as traditional West African recreational music. Other similarities with West African music are that the key rhythm or clave (the kwakwa-bangi) plays an African key rhythm, the liberal use of metaphors, and the fact the lyrics are often about male-female relations.

Kawina is played in 4/4 meter, with the fourth beat getting the accent through the heaving rhythm of the *timbal,* the old name for the conga in Suriname. A well-known kawina singer is Big Jones.

There are two kinds of kawina. The *prisir-kawina* is the oldest: not religious but a kind of social music people could relax to, played on a sakka, two kawina drums, and a *reson* or *kwatro* (four-stringed guitar). Over the course of time, each plantation developed its own style.

A former custom was to compose—often on the spot—new numbers to record certain situations or events; moreover, banja, tuku, and laku songs

were sung to the streamlined kawina rhythm. That is how the Winti-kawina
arose: Winti songs, that were mostly in 12/8 meter, were transposed to 4/4
meter. Due to their religious content, the Winti-kawina was played at a faster
tempo. The solo drum has to perform more variations in order to be able to
communicate with the various Winti spirits.

These days, the kwatro is hardly played anymore. The kwakwa-bangi and
the pudja, and sometimes the conga, are permanent parts of the kawina
ensemble. In recent years musicians have added iron shakers and an iron
cowbell and some groups, especially in Paramaribo, even play the skratyi.
Vocals resemble most other Afro-Surinamese music: featured singers and
chorus who complement one another, such that call and response take place.
Kawina is mostly danced in a circle, counterclockwise.

Until roughly 1965, it was forbidden to play the sacred apinti in the towns.
Alternatives were sought at the turn of the twentieth century, and people
began playing Winti music on European instruments. In that way, *Winti-poku* arose with its most prominent style *indji-poku*. The kwakwa-bangi
was replaced by the snare drum, the agida and apinti by the skratyi. The
sung Winti melodies were performed on wind instruments. In fact, little
change occurred with regard to the traditional form. Both the melody and
meter of the rhythm were maintained: Winti-poku still makes use of 12/8
and 4/4 meter and is still danced in a circle. The places where it became
most popular were in Paramaribo and Coronie district, where it is loved
even more than their traditional forms of drumming, and the same holds
true for The Netherlands.

Finally, two more styles used to play a modest role in Afro-Surinamese
music but nowadays have (virtually) disappeared: the *bal-masque* and *kursow*.

The day slavery was abolished, July 1, 1863, became a national holiday for
Afro-Surinamers. Ever since, on the first of July all kind of parties are held
and music played in such styles as banja, laku, susa, and bal-masque (masked
ball). For quite a long time the bal-masque was the only form of celebration
where European instruments were played. For many Afro-Surinamers this
ball had significance within the rites to venerate their ancestors. On some
Caribbean islands there still exist related styles that use masks, such as John
Canoe in Jamaica and *diabolitos* in Cuba.

Both in Sranan Tongo and Papiamentu, *kursow* is the word for Curaçao.
The kursow was a dance performed only by Curaçaoan male railroad workers in Suriname, and their Surinamese or Curaçaoan wives. The culture of
Curaçao is more traditionally oriented toward Spanish America, and that is
the reason it never had a prominent place in Afro-Surinamese music. As far
as can be ascertained, kursow has disappeared altogether.

TRADITIONAL AFRO-SURINAMESE MUSIC
IN THE NETHERLANDS

Surinamers that emigrated to the Netherlands brought a lively music tradition with them to Europe. The many Creoles among them succeeded in maintaining the customs of Afro-Surinamese culture in the Netherlands. Because many of them still practice the old Winti religion and the music that is closely related to it, a number of the styles just discussed are still played in the Netherlands. Of all genres, kawina is probably the most popular.

Some groups play only kawina, while others play various styles. Winti-poku is currently very popular. Whenever a *bazuinkoor* (choir of brass instruments) performs, after the Christian section, Winti-poku often follows. Maroons also have a few groups in the Netherlands; one of the most renowned is Dufini. Unfortunately, this population group have very few traditional drummers in the Netherlands.

Cultural societies are important for Surinamese music in the Netherlands, seeing as how they engage in playing several different styles. In Amsterdam-Zuidoost we find, among others, the group Baisa, who still regularly play banja, laku, and lobisingi. That also holds for the group Afu Sensi based in The Hague. Other cultural societies are Koafi in Rotterdam and Abeni in Amsterdam. Furthermore, there are (usually small) groups of traditional drummers and singers who dedicate themselves to playing Winti drumming. These ensembles are mostly invited to come and play during rituals. As a rule, the older drummers among them are often capable of playing old drum styles for hours on end. Traditional drum ensembles are Akrema and Blaka Buba in Amsterdam and Asanti Buba in Rotterdam.

CONCLUSION

In the face of all prohibitions in the past and current lack of interest, the African legacy, which arrived on the shores of Suriname four centuries ago, has nonetheless been excellently conserved. Nowadays Africans in Suriname and the Netherlands can once again be introduced to the drums of their native land that have fallen into disuse. The research conducted by the American Herskovits shows just how African Surinamese music still is. With a special scale that ranged from A(frica) to E(urope), he tested aspects of Black cultures in both Americas, such as religion, language, and social organization. Suriname continually scored the highest A and the United States a high E—one more argument to view Suriname as a piece of Africa in the New World. The unique Afro-Surinamese music plays an important role in that regard, and it is to be hoped that this culture, in all its facets, will continue to exist.

3

SURINAMESE EAST INDIAN (HINDUSTANI) MUSIC

- Dr. J. Ketwaru -

We must look to India, the cradle of most Surinamese of East Indian descent, for the origin of Surinamese East Indian music, alternately referred to as Sarnami-Hindustani music.

Their ancestors who arrived in the later part of the nineteenth century, came predominately from the northern part of India (Uttar Pradesh). Nowadays Indian music is divided into northern Indian (Hindustani) and southern Indian (Carnatic) streams. The latter form belongs to the more orthodox musical stream in India that strongly emphasizes fixed compositions, with a great deal of space for rhythmic accompaniment. In Hindustani music, on the other hand, improvisation plays a prominent role. By Indian music in this chapter we are referring to northern Indian, i.e. Hindustani sounds: the origins of Surinamese-Hindustani music.

HINDUSTANI MUSIC

Hindustani music, with its refined tonal ornamentation, primarily serves to express moods. The core of this is *raga*, a basic melodic pattern. The mood of the raga is not only determined by the notes used, but also by the way the performer approaches them. In addition, the amount of characteristic sequences of notes helps make clear the meaning of a raga. The mood is often romantic and varies from sad to joyous. There are special ragas for every hour of the day and for every season of the year. Nonetheless, a great deal depends on the frame of mind of the performer. To convincingly be able to play a raga, three elements are indispensable: talent, a good guru or teacher, and years of intensive study. Each performance of a raga is therefore a fascinating mixture of age-old traditions and the ideas of the guru.

A performance of Hindustani classical music often begins restrained, to build up the tension. This is the so-called *alaap*, an arhythmic, step-by-step exploration of the notes and mood of the raga. This is sometimes followed by a rhythmic piece, *djor*. It is subsequently followed by *gat*, in which players begin improvising to *tabla* accompaniment. To this end, this instrument plays a *tala*, a rhythmic pattern in a certain cycle. The improvisations are characterized by a strongly accented first beat of the cycle, after which the rhythm is whipped up to a climax on the final note, usually the most important note of the raga.

Westerners often find Hindustani mood to be plaintive. This is especially because of the use of microtones (*sruti*), which are about half as big as a minor second in western music; twenty-two such sruti form an octave.

Indian music changed significantly during Mongolian rule. The dominion of the Mongolian emperor Akbar the Great brought Indian cultural life to a high level. The marvelous edifice that was built during his regime, the Taj Mahal, among other things, attests to this. But several strange instruments also made their first appearance at that time in India. They were imported by the many artists that the emperor brought from his vast Mongolian empire. A famous court musician at the time was Tan Sen, whose musical abilities afforded him a prominent place at the imperial court. A great many contemporary performers of classical Indian music lay claim to a blood relation with this legendary figure.

INSTRUMENTS

Two instruments introduced in India during the period of Mongolian rule were the sitar and tabla. The names derive from Arabic. Sitar means "three-stringed," but at present the instrument has thirteen main strings and eleven or thirteen drone strings. Tabla, roughly translated, means "something flat that produces sound." It consists of two separate drums that are completely covered. They are stretched with either calf, sheep, or goat skin; for purity of sound a mixture of ingredients is added to the skin, called *masala*. Both instruments have a prominent place in classical Indian music and therefore influence Surinamese-Hindustani music.

A harmonium resembles a small organ. The *dholak* is a kind of drum, and the *dandaal* consists of a long metallic bar, on which the player indicates the beat with a small V-shaped rod. The *dhapla* is a large drum that is played deep into the night at Hindustani weddings. On calm, sultry Surinamese nights the thudding sounds of the dhapla carry quite far, such that any guest without a map can find their way to the Hindustani wedding celebration.

SARNAMI-HINDUSTANI STYLES AND FORMS

Fortunately, our ancestors, the Indian contract workers who came to Suriname starting in 1873, were not lacking in spiritual faculties. Because of this they were able to further develop Indian music on their self-made instruments in their scarce free time. As a child I watched how in the Surinamese jungle my father sought the right kind of wood and a calabash to make a true-sounding sitar. After many experiments with several materials, he finally made a sitar that could not be distinguished from the original Indian instrument. With it, he gave a great many musical performances of Saranami-Hindustani.

Surinamese-Hindustani music is characterized especially by the fact that it arose in a country of several different ethnic groups, and therefore can be considered a small world of its own. In the music of Surinamese Hindustanis, there are emotions and musical patterns from other people such as the Dutch, the African Creoles, and the Javanese. These influences do not play a role in India. To clarify the matter, we will limit ourselves to a discussion of a few of the most common musical forms and styles of Surinamese-Hindustani music.

Baithak gana as a musical form is a typical slice of Surinamese culture, especially since the influence of the other people in Suriname are clearly audible in it. Despite the great stimulus that emanated from *qawwali* and *bhadjan* groups, which will be discussed later, baithak gana has a style of its own, especially developed by a second generation of Surinamese Hindustanis.

Musicians sit on the ground during baithak gana. They make use of simple texts and a sober musical accompaniment, which usually consists of harmonium, dholak, and dandaal. Texts are in the Surinamese-Hindustani language. A well-known performer is Eddy Jankipersading.

When performing qawwali, musicians also sit on the ground. They are mainly Surinamese East Indian Muslims who perform this musical form. They sing all sorts of devotional songs in Urdu, to praise Allah and his prophet Mohammed. Subjects from the Quran are also sung about. Qawwali mostly consists of the interplay between call and response in which two vocalists participate. They are usually accompanied by a harmonium and one or more percussion instrument such as dholak, tabla, *naal*, or *mridang*.

Bhadjans are religious songs of the Surinamese Hindus. They too have as minimal accompaniment a harmonium and one of the percussion instruments referred to above, and the musicians also sit on the ground.

Ghazals are usually about the fairer sex. They are often romantic songs of a nonreligious nature, usually sung in Urdu. Here too, the musicians often sit on the ground, although it is not required. The main instrument in ghazal, harmonium, is supplemented with one or more percussion instruments (tabla, naal, and/or dholak). In addition to this, the musicians can make use of mandolin, sitar, guitar, or tambourine. Sometimes ghazals are performed by entire orchestras.

Nadjams or *nazaams* are religious Islamic songs in which texts from the Quran are sung. The most important difference with qawwali is that there are no musical instruments involved. The nadjam or nadaam ensemble consists solely of vocalists, in which someone performs as a lead or solo singer. These songs can be heard on special Islamic holidays (Maulads) such as on the birthday of Mohammed (Milad-U-Nabi).

Chautaals are sung especially by Hindus in connection with Holi-Phagwa, a Hindu celebration to mark the transformation of nature in spring. Chautaals praise all the gods of Hinduism, such as Brahma, Krishna, Shiva, and Vishnu. They are sung to the accompaniment of bells and *madjieras* (tambourines). Holi-Phagwa is a colorful, festive occasion; visitors spray paint one another while dancing and make music with coloring liquids and powder. Chautaals resound during the spring feast from dawn until late at night.

Birahas originally belonged to the category of lament and funeral music, sung after the loss of a loved one. According to many scriptures, this arose from the Vedas, the ancient religious texts of Hinduism. Birahas that are now heard in Suriname can be about all sorts of situations or persons. During the call-and-response form, singers try to outdo one another. Whenever there is singing during the *ahirwa ke naadj* (see below), it is mostly biranhas.

Sohars are not attached to a certain religion. Women ensembles sing these romantic songs at weddings. They sing all kinds of comic texts that poke fun at the bridal couple and their respective parents. The accompaniment is usually a harmonium and dholak.

Paturia ke naadj is also known as *ganika*. With this, one of the men in the ensemble is dressed as a woman and imitates typically female (dance) movements. In so doing, he is trying to mainly entertain the male portion of the audience. These ensembles are hired to play at weddings. They consist of a minimum of four artists: a sarangi (Hindustani violin) or harmonium player, a dholak player, a singer, and a dancer.

Ahirwa ke naadj also has to do with a combination of music and dance. The difference with paturia ke naadj is that it is not about graceful feminine dance; the dance movements take place to the rhythm of the accompanying percussion instruments. The most prominent instrument here is the *nagara*, two drums that are played with two sticks. The men performing the dances during ahirwa ke naadj almost always depict religious Hindu stories. This is often done to the accompaniment of birahas.

REVIVAL OF CLASSICAL MUSIC

In the 1960s a great many young people started to take an interest in Indian cultural life. Indian grand masters (Ustads and Pandits) regularly performed at Indian concerts. This brought mainly the third generation of Surinamese Hindustani back into contact with heavily Indian classical music. Some of them got themselves a sitar or tabla and went to study with the Ustads and Pandits in India. They then reintroduced Indian classical music to Surinamese Hindustani life. Ragas were the basic compositions in this regard, in which a great deal of free and structured improvisation can take place. In the case of the latter form, the musicians must stay within the bounds of the raga and tala, while in the free improvisation several melodic and rhythmic variations and patterns from other music cultures are available, such as Creole, Javanese, and European music. This marks the greatest difference between Surinamese-Hindustani and Indian classical music.

Nowadays the sitar and tabla can be heard across the entire spectrum of the world of Surinamese music. A beautiful example is the integrated Surinamese music, in which the audience is treated to the interplay of tabla, the Creole apinti drum, and congas.

4

JAVANESE MUSIC IN SURINAME

- Herman Dijo -

One of the most characteristic sounds in Javanese music is that of the gamelan. It includes the ideal instruments to convey the Javanese tradition. The Surinamese Javanese have always striven to retain this inheritance for the next generation. Culture is vitally important because it gives content to the Javanese sense of insight and feeling. Whenever this traditional culture is absent, there is often tension among the Javanese community.

The sound of gamelan can make a confusing impression because of the tonal system in which gamelan is tuned. There are two separate tonal systems, *slendro* and *pelog* (not to be compared to major and minor). Slendro is closer to the Western whole-tone scale, while pelog more nearly resembles the pentatonic scale. But in both cases the length of the intervals deviates strongly from that to Which western ears are accustomed. A slendro and pelog set are never played simultaneously; they are not complementary in terms of sound.

Anyone listening attentively to gamelan music played by people with a Western-oriented sense of hearing quickly discovers that the terms "insight" and "feeling" do not mean the same for everyone. The idiomatic sound of gamelan does not correspond to their expectations. And quite a few Surinamese Javanese have their hearts set on gamelan without being capable of practicing this form of art. To be able to play gamelan well, the musician must constantly be conscious of the specific demands that insight and feeling impose. It is this fact that also makes other Javanese musical forms in Suriname so special.

SURINAMESE GAMELAN

Much Javanese music in Suriname came with the first group of Javanese who arrived in 1890. They began as indentured servants for the sugar company

Nederlandsche Handelsmaatschappij at Mariënburg plantation. Quite soon there was a need for entertainment to break the drudgery of the heavy work in the fields. At first they sought relaxation in the traditional culture that was so important to them, but the original music instruments were largely absent. The music instruments and kinds of instruments that followed were, therefore, largely produced in Suriname itself.

The Mariënburg plantation owned an extensive set of instruments for a gamelan ensemble, so many Javanese at Mariënburg sought diversion in gamelan. They had often played gamelan in the past on occasion, but none of them had really studied it. Books about *gending-gending* (songs) and *wayang* (shadow puppet plays) were available, but most of the Javanese indentured servants could neither read nor write. Even today, most lessons in gamelan take place orally, which fosters a good transference of emotional meaning of this traditional music.

A single gamelan set was soon not enough for the Javanese community in Suriname. The set of instruments was far too heavy to move around and remained at the same location both day and night, in the *kampong-gede*, what people these days would call a multifunction building, with large spaces where just as large parties were held with gamelan music. But not everyone could afford such a party, especially since the expensive musicians had to be paid. And if someone else wanted to throw a party somewhere else, the Nederlandsche Handelsmaatschappij would certainly refuse permission to move the only set of instruments.

As creative as the Javanese were, they started building their own gamelan set of instruments. The first problems were quickly overcome. The *bonang* (a gamelan instrument with a pan-shaped sound source made of brass) was replaced by bars of an iron sound source with a bulge on them. The material for them came from scrapped iron factory plates and metal cross ties underneath the train tracks.

In sonic terms, this gamelan had less of a ring to it than its Javanese example. However, there were not enough experienced musicians among the Suriname Javanese to maintain the original lineup. This forced them to experiment, and as a result the existence of Surinamese gamelan was now a fact. The lineup was drastically reduced to five persons. They were divided over the following instruments:

- the extensive *saron* with fourteen sounding bars (replaced the *bonang*), which in turn was eventually replaced by the *penurus*, with seven sounding bars.

- the *demung* with seven sounding bars (replaced the *ketuk* and *ke-nong*).
- the *gong set* with three big sounding bars (*kempul, suwu-an,* and *kenong*).
- the *kendang* (one drum, remained the same).

If five instruments or players were not available, sometimes they got by with four or even three people making music. In a lineup of four people, one of them would double up on the demung and penurus, while in an ensemble of three people the penurus was left out altogether and someone played both the gong set and demung at the same time.

Apart from being music to listen to, gamelan also served to accompany theatrical performances. The most well-known are *wayangwong* or *Rama-yana* (shadow plays with actors), *ludruk* (farces), *ketopak* (Arabic-tinged theater), and *wayang-kulit* or *wayang-lulang* (shadow puppet plays). An important role for contemporary gamelan is still *tajuban*, a dance celebration in which one or more female dancers sets the tone.

Ever since the arrival of the consulate (and later the embassy) of the Republic of Indonesia in Suriname, gamelan music has undergone strong development. Regularly held courses are available in gamelan and classical Javanese dance, in which practitioners can avail themselves of a set of gamelan instruments especially imported to that end. All this attention has partly contributed to the founding of the gamelan society Krido Suoro.

STEEL-GAMELAN

Gamelan in Suriname also came under the influence of nearby Caribbean music, especially steel bands from Trinidad. The cultural society Krido Rini in the town of Dijkveld in the Para district built a gamelan that looked a great deal like the set of instruments to be found in a steel drum orchestra. In this way Surinamese gamelan underwent a new transformation and steel-gamelan was the result. Not only was the resemblance in form striking but the traditional costumes are typically South American. This unique steel-gamelan is in *slendro* tuning; the membranophones of a genuine steel band (drum set and congas) have been substituted by the *kendang*. It is worth the effort to keep following the development of steel-gamelan, a rare example of Indonesian music on instruments from the American continent.

TERBANGEN

The Javanese Islamic faith provides many Javanese in Suriname with something important to hold on to. Their religious songs are often accompanied by a *terbangen* ensemble, of which there are two kinds. T*erbangen-cilik*, or *terbangen-kencring*, consists of kinds of tambourines and a *bedug*, which resembles a large Turkish drum. *Terbangen-gede* or *terbangan-maulad nabi* *is* a typical Surinamese formation in which many hand drums and a *kendang* are the main elements. The songs performed by terbangen ensembles are based on the so-called "solo-tutti" concept: a single cantor or precentor begins and the rest follow. The texts come chiefly from the Quran, the Islamic holy scriptures, and are intended to honor the prophet Mohammed.

One name that is inextricably linked to terbangen-gede is Bapak Masekan, *pengulu* in the village of Tamanredjo in the Commewijne district. The pengulu is a religious functionary, charged with blessing marriages, in which the terbangen-gede plays a central role.

KRONCONG

Opinions differ as to the origin of *kroncong* music. One interesting theory was put forward by the Portuguese, who say that kroncong arose from the *saudade* of the Portuguese colonists. The Portuguese music expressed melancholic, nostalgic longing for folklore and feelings of love. The word *kroncong* is an onomatopoeia of the strumming of strings on the ukulele. The "crong" sound of this four-stringed plucked instrument from Hawaii is characteristic of this music. And characteristic is the prelude in most of the songs that resembles that of the *bebuka* (intro) in gamelan music. Other characteristics include going from the tonic to the dominant; ornamenting or playing around the melody line on the melodic instruments violin, flute, and six-stringed Hawaiian guitar; and the sensibility of the music that is dominated by gamelan.

In addition to the melodic instruments, a Surinamese kroncong ensemble mostly uses three or more acoustic guitars, a ukulele (sometimes a banjo), a double bass (or bass guitar), and a cello. However, cellists are scarce, which means the *gedugan* (kendang-like playing) is usually taken over by a guitar.

Besides gamelan, kroncong flourished among the indentured servants at Mariënburg. Indo-Europeans and Ambonese (Moluccans) were the main players of kroncong, even though the music was loved by practically everyone. Kroncong was quite suitable as listening music and as musical framing of *bangsawan* performances (a type of theater). The language used in kroncong and bangsawan was Malay, what is now referred to as Bahasa Republik Indonesia. A few kroncong songs that used to be popular in Suriname are "Bandung seletan di waktu malam," "Bangawan Solo," "Terang bulang," "Meratap hati," and "Di bawah sinar bulan purnama."

Di bawah sinar bulan purnama
Di bawah sinar bulan purnama, air laut berkilauan
Berayun-ayun ombak mengalir, ke pantai senda gurauan
Di bawah sinar bulan purnama, hati duka jadi senang
Gitar berbunyi riang gembira, jauh malam hari petang
Beribu bintang taburan, menghiasi langit biru
Menambah cantik alam dunia, serta murni pemandangan
Di bawah sinar bulan purnama, hati sedih tak dirasa
Si miskin pun yang hidup sengsara, semalam itu bersuka.

Under the Beams of the Full Moon
Under the beams of the full moon shines the water of the sea
The waves surge forth, poking fun at the shore
Under the beams of full moon, the sorrowful heart is content once more
Guitars resound with joy, from day unto deep into the night
Myriads of stars are scattered that ornament the blue sky
They bestow charm on nature and purity on the panorama
Under the beams of the full moon you do not feel your sorrow
Even the poor man who lives in misery enjoys such a night.

Most of the established kroncong vocalists in Suriname at one time or another sang in Mata Hari, an extremely renowned kroncong orchestra. Mata Hari was instrumental in promoting kroncong music outside their own Javanese audience. The leader of the orchestra, "Uncle" Ramin, played violin. His wife, "Aunt" Anna, sang in the orchestra; a woman in those days needed a great deal of courage to do so. Because Mata Hari played so often at Surinamese dance parties, percussion needed to be added to the band. The official language of most of the Javanese in Suriname was Javanese, not the Malay used in kroncong. Kroncong with lyrics in Javanese therefore soon became all the rage. A few titles of kroncong songs in Javanese are "Putri Solo" (the Princess of Solo), "Bocah gunung" (the Child from the Mountains), and "Suwe ora ketema" (Long Time No See).

CONCLUSION

Surinamese-Javanese music contains more variants and styles that can be covered in such a brief chapter. What you may have missed is *anklung*, which is played on rattles made of bamboo, and *kotek-an* (music made with a rice stamper). Furthermore, we briefly mention the fixed songs of the Islamic *angguk*, the religious *menor* theater, and *jarankepang* (trance-inducing horse dancing). Hopefully this chapter has been able to stimulate the reader enough to discover for himself the Javanese musical tradition in Suriname.

5

THE EUROPEAN TRADITION

Traditional music in Suriname was nourished from many continents of the world—including (directly and indirectly) from Europe—and just like the African, Indian, and Javanese, the European musical contribution has been extremely varied: religious and worldly, classical and "light," vocal and instrumental. In this chapter we review the most important facets.

CHURCH MUSIC, CHOIRS, AND BAZUINKOOR
- Marcel Weltak -

Whenever the church is referred to in Suriname, one is immediately reminded of the Moravian Church,[1] a Protestant order from the village of Herrnhut in Germany known in Dutch as the Evangelische Broeder Gemeente (EBG)—a translation from the Latin *Unitas Fratrum*, meaning "Unity of the Brethren." Many members of the well-to-do Surinamese citizenry and its political organizations, such as the NPS, are members of the EBG. Surinamers also use relationships built in church outside it as well. The "anitri kerkie" (Moravian church), as the EBG is referred to in the vernacular, therefore, dominates a large segment of the population, even though in terms of numbers it is less than the East Indian segment, for instance. It shall therefore come as no surprise to anyone that the EBG dominates church music in Suriname.

Tempo

The biggest difference between church music in Suriname and that of the Netherlands is the tempo. The Dutch drag the music along, while Surinamers find that God must be praised with fire. In the Netherlands, long notes are popular: half and quarter notes. But even during funerals, Surinamers still play eighth and sixteenth notes. The lively Surinamese choirs were therefore a handful for the Dutch Moravian Brothers. Whenever a Surinamese organist accompanied the songs, he often got ahead of the Dutch church members who were singing.

"Praising God with cymbals" is how Rudolf Adamson uses a Biblical quote to illustrate the tempo. As a celebrated church organist, he is one of the most experienced people in Surinamese church music. He was once the second organist in the Grote Stadskerk (Moravian Main City Church) in Paramaribo. Moreover, he has played practically every church organ in Suriname. In 1967 he received a scholarship from STICUSA to further his organ studies in Amsterdam's Westerkerk, under the supervision of organist Simon C. Janssen.

Adamson was born in Nickerie in 1918. In the district with the same name, he began as a drummer in the jazz band Waterloo. Adamson also played swing and ragtime with saxophonist Anton Budel on the Bronsplein in Paramaribo. He became a member of a youth choir at age fifteen. A year later he was playing the church organ in Nickerie. This was thanks to the maroon teacher Adolf Jonathan Egbert Libretto, a man whose musical name betrayed his talent, and who tutored Adamson in the rudiments of church music. Besides drumming, singing, and playing organ, Adamson also played French horn in the Suriname Philharmonic Orchestra. He left the Maranatha choir in 1948 and founded the choir called Centraal (Central). He later went on to conduct the Maranatha choir for two years.

According to Adamson, the difference in tempo also is due to the fact that Germans are originally a "cadence folk." There is a steady kind of rhythm in their music, and in that of their church. The tempo of German songs was adapted by Surinamers "because you have to enjoy music," in Adamson's view. That is also the reason why Surinamese churchgoers prefer simple arias as preludes to works by Bach. Adamson: "The people often hum along to an aria, and which Surinamer does that to Bach or Händel?"

Adamson also sees a fundamental difference of approach in playing between organists in Suriname and the Netherlands. "Dutch organists like to show off their prowess. Surinamers don't, they play for the benefit of the churchgoers. The churchgoers often thank the organist after the service, whenever he plays an aria during the prelude or collection." Another characteristic includes the EBG organist's consulting with the minister as to what melody to play for the scripture of the day. The organ is accompaniment and not dominant over the congregation. In that way the congregation can keep itself under control. Adamson: "In The Netherlands you can often not hear what the congregation is singing; the organ is much louder than their voices. But then in The Netherlands the faithful are less familiar with the hymns." The Moravian Brothers have an intensive musical culture. "When housewives are doing the ironing they sing, and then not kawina but church hymns," Adamson tells. "Nowadays, even in the Roman Catholic churches they sing 'anitri' [Moravian Brother] hymns so as not to miss the boat. People no longer want to hear about misery." In the old days there used to be EBG hymnal services without sermons. The minister would then just read the daily scripture from the Bible, followed by a number of hymns, six or seven chorales one after another. There was prayer in between. The renowned ministers Polanen and Belfor often organized evenings in which unfamiliar chorales could be rehearsed. That facilitated a rapid expansion of the repertoire. The popular *Koraalboek* (Hymnal) in which all these chorales were included also had a supplement with mainly English hymns, once intended for the ministers in Nickerie. The "balata-bleeders" (rubber tappers) from neighboring British Guyana had to be able to follow the service in their own language. In the district of Coronie along the Guyanese border, the sermons and hymns were held in Sranan for the same reason. The Surinamese music of the EBG has not been adapted to modern times: the German system still holds sway. The *Ariabuku*, a book filled with standard arias, originally came from the Germans. Some even believe that German music has become so established in Suriname that it has become an authentic part of the country.

The hymnal was revised recently. A complete white Dutch commission that includes Professor Jan Voorhoeve and minister Legene compiled the new hymnal. They have combined Moravian, Lutheran, Dutch Reformed, and Protestant hymns into the *Liedboek der Kerken* (Church Hymnal). As far as Adamson is concerned, church music does not need to undergo a "renaissance." For him it remains an orthodox form of music and will remain so. "The pattern of the Germans can stay if you ask me; after all they are our forefathers as far as church and school is concerned." Only in the Netherlands have attempts been made to introduce changes to Surinamese church music.

Church Organs

Some information about the organs can be found in the churches of Suriname. The oldest organ used to be in the Grote Stadskerk, located at Steenbakkerijstraat in Paramaribo: a so-called double Schittmeyer clavier. The Noorderstad church had a pedal organ with tongues instead of pipes. The Lutheran church at the Waterkant had an 1842 German Bätsorgel with a single register—regale—with sublime voicings. The trumpet on that organ really sounded like a trumpet. In the cathedral is a mechanically operated concert organ, just as in the Reformed church on the Kerkplein. This latter model, a Dutch Flentrop organ, is probably the finest of them all. It certainly has more facilities than its colleague at the cathedral, partly owing to its two keyboards.

Suriname is too small for an organ builder. Yet the country used to have an excellent repairman for these instruments in the person of "baas" (boss) Messas. He was a furniture maker who tuned the organs and was able to restore them with scissors and twine. In 1973 and 1974 he restored and tuned the Flentrop organ referred to earlier. A few of them were in really bad shape; the pipes were left intact, but the organs were fitted out with the latest electronic devices.

Choirs: Maranatha

Besides singing during church services, Suriname also accommodates three major choirs, in the order of their founding: Harmonie, Maranatha, and Centraal. All three were founded following World War II. Certainly most renowned, if not the best, is Maranatha, which from its inception in 1946 (with interludes) was conducted by Walter Leerdam and for which, in its initial period, the likes of Lou Lichtveld (Albert Helman) composed pieces. The male choir of eighty voices has won prizes in quite a few concourses around the globe. With their gorgeously intonated choral singing and great dynamism, the Maranatha singers often surpass professional choirs from the United States and the (former) Soviet Union. The cause of this musical success presumably lies in the difference in tone color between the Surinamese choir and most Western choirs. European and American choirs use more vibrato in their voices than Maranatha and other Surinamese vocal societies. The singers conducted by Leerdam make greater use of the natural timbre of the human voice. What is of course special is that the majority of the choir are not classically trained voices; they sing, after all, for pleasure. The only training the choir receives is in the principles of breathing and formation of tones, and before a concert begins, they do voice exercises.

The choir is usually comprised of fifteen first tenors, twenty second tenors, twenty first basses, and twenty second basses. The simplicity of these voices and the pleasure they radiate is one reason why a Maranatha concert is such a special experience. Maranatha achieved greater fame than other choirs from Suriname and the Caribbean region, even though they too may not produce a Western timbre. The important difference is in their repertoire. Other Caribbean choirs sing less often, and then mainly church hymns and sometimes gospels and spirituals. At first Maranatha limited themselves to this as well, but currently the choir also sings German chorales, English hymns, Surinamese folk songs, Spanish and Caribbean songs and evergreens, and such classics as *Te deum laudamus*, Mozart's *Die Zauberflöte*, or Gershwin's "Summertime."

Conductor and arranger Walter Leerdam received a STICUSA scholarship to study choir conducting at the Amsterdam Conservatory. Before that he accomplished a great deal with choral music through self-study. An example are his arrangements of the song "Prijs Jehova" (Praise Jehova) from the Moravian *Koraalboek* (Hymnal).

Maranatha only sings existing songs. They are rearranged to be performed for an audience for which they were not originally intended. An example of this are the folk songs that Walter Leerdam and Maranatha have dressed up in new attire. This can sometimes be a big hit when touring abroad; during a tour in Germany he was asked for a copy of the musical score of his arrangement of (the Surinamese folk song, trans.) "Min, mini, kon njang." Maranatha often exchange arrangements in this way.

The choir realized at the right moment that the time was ripe for folk songs. Despite violinist Arnold Juda's failed attempt to adapt for choir the song "Mis 'Elena, Mis' Elena, trin tran tring, mi na moni masra," Maranatha still continued down this road. Whenever they performed their folk song arrangements, the singers were practically received with shouts of jubilation. However, despite the efforts by Leerdam and the Police Corps bandleader John Nelom, the repertoire of folk songs is not that extensive.

The Maranatha repertoire still does not contain any songs by the Javanese, Hindustani, or Amerindians. According to Leerdam, this all has to do with ongoing integration and could take years, something Leerdam wants to start with Winti songs. He considers Winti a form of folklore and different from merely singing folk songs. The Dutch chapter of the Maranatha choir has no difficulty performing Winti songs. In the future, they want to add an apinti drummer as accompaniment. Besides the Winti songs, the Maranatha-Netherlands choir have also taken over many songs from the repertoire of the chief choir in Suriname. The Dutch chapter of the Maranatha main choir is conducted by Stan Lokhin, who has also attended the Amsterdam Conservatory. Most of the members of the choir came from Maranatha-Suriname. Maranatha-Netherlands has a lineup of six first tenors, six basses (baritones), six second tenors, and six second basses. The group is accompanied by Glenn Gaddum on piano.

Other Choirs

The strong presence of the Moravian church in Suriname has contributed greatly to the development of such choirs as Maranatha. It also has a strong song tradition at schools. Although they had gone through a rough patch, singing lessons are on the increase again on curricula of Surinamese school-children. Of course, there is always the Catholic church, where young people begin singing at mass at a young age. School choir festivals are regularly held around the country. Even though there are quite a few church choirs in Suriname, their goal seldom reaches further than adding luster to a church service. This is more the case with the Catholic choirs than the Moravian ones, who are more flexible in this regard.

The Bazuinkoor[2] (Choir of Trumpets)

At Surinamese birthday celebrations you stand a good chance of hearing something that resembles church music: a *bazuinkoor*. The bazuinkoor is a rather unique phenomenon, that except for Suriname, only exists in Germany. Despite what the name suggests, there are no human voices in a bazuinkoor. It is instrumental music that is played especially at birthday celebrations, based on German chorales and English hymns that through the church are familiar to many Surinamers.

The name bazuinkoor refers to the instruments: a *bazuin* is a kind of large trumpet, and a bazuinkoor consists predominately of brass instruments. The bazuinkoor came into being after the Christianization of Suriname by the German *hernhutters* (or Moravian church), still one of Suriname's largest church communities. Old Surinamers still talk about chorale music, a term that was born when these orchestras only played German chorales. When the "balata-bleeders" (rubber-tappers) and gold diggers (from British Guyana) arrived in Suriname they brought English hymns to the repertoire of the orchestras from their Methodist, Anglican, and Pentecostal churches, which gradually became known as bazuinkoor. At the very outset, toward the end of the nineteenth century, bazuinkoors still made use of such stringed instruments as mandolin and kwatro. There were also bazuinkoors with strings; violin, cello, and double bass were the main instruments. But with the introduction of brass wind instruments at the beginning of the twentieth century, bazuinkoor music only made use of trumpet, cornet, tuba, althorn, and euphonium. The trombone followed later, and in the last twenty-five years the saxophone. Nowadays alto and tenor saxes play the alto and tenor parts respectively, and the baritone sax increasingly replaces the tuba.

Bazuinkoor music is mainly concerned with harmonies, in this case four-part harmony. Which instruments you use or how you play them is not crucially import, just as long as the soprano, alto, tenor, and bass parts are covered. The starting premise of the bazuinkoor is tightly played homophonic music. With homophony there is a chord behind each note in a melody. The slow and stately bazuinkoor music lends itself well to this system.

The German chorales are generally solemn and static, while the English hymn-tunes are usually joyous with gorgeous twists of melody. The chorales often make use of other chords and the hymn-tunes. The music essentially has not changed over the years. The subdominant following on from the fundamental chord is very popular, which in turn is followed by the dominant and the fundamental chord.

The structure of bazuinkoor music looks like this. Much use is made of standardized chords from the diatonic scale. This practically always involves the cycle (fundamental chord C), a major chord (F), followed by a dominant seventh chord (G7), and finishing on the fundamental chord. The cycle repeats itself for each stanza of the song. In Surinamese chorale music, more use is made of seventh chords than in the German version.

The hymn-tunes make more use of the supertonic (d) from the scale, but quite a few seventh chords can still be heard. The hymns sound richer and fuller than the German chorales, and because of the quicker tempo, more cheerful.

In the 1980s the bazuinkoor underwent a major change. Because some bazuinkoors included a rhythm section, there was a split between the large and small bazuinkoor. The rhythm section was added so that people could dance to the music. The large bazuinkoor now plays the same devotional songs, but now to the rhythmic accompaniment of drums. That could include a complete drum set or sometimes only snare and bass drum. There are often also a bass and rhythm guitar. The big advantage of large bazuinkoor music at parties is that after the opening solemn and formal section the music often switches to ordinary dance music.

A large bazuinkoor without the rhythm section, however, is not automatically a small bazuinkoor. The large bazuinkoor is more high-spirited. Rhythm, tempo, and often also harmonies have been altered from the original bazuinkoor arrangements to make them suitable for dancing. Given that they are well-known church songs, the guests can sing along if they desire. On the other hand, the small bazuinkoor remains more church-like and because of that only plays listening music. Currently, Bazuinkoor music is rarely played in an authentic manner. Most groups do not play harmonies of the chorales according to the rules, but only in the kaseko way. Musicians such as alto saxophonist Jopie Vrieze (b. 1914), who plays in one of the last small bazuinkoors, always performed instinctively but following all the rules. Vrieze: "You blow bazuinkoor music differently than kaseko, more softly." And Vrieze should know; he has played bigi poku, Winti poku. and set-dansi.

Nowadays, bazuinkoors also play secular music and songs from the Winti cycle. John Nelom, the composer and conductor of the Politie Kapel (Police Corps Band), sees a strict distinction: "The chorales are spiritual songs, Winti-music is worldly." Not all religious music is appropriate for bazuinkoor. Gregorian chant is too static for Surinamers. Catholic liturgical music does not lend itself to be played with swing in a bazuinkoor. Attempts to play Catholic church songs as bazuinkoor music have foundered because of the different chords and the many brusque turns of melody of those songs. In Dutch church music (especially in the Reformed churches), much use is still made of old modes such as Doric and Phrygian church scales. The harmonies and turns of melody of these songs lend themselves less readily to the bazuinkoor than the German and English church music do. For that matter, not even all chorales are suitable for bazuinkoor treatment. That depends on the character of the melody. The North American Pentecostal church, in contrast, often accompanies church song with the rhythmic clapping of hands and drums. The music is joyous, invites one to dance, and therefore lends itself excellently to the bazuinkoor.

All in all, bazuinkoor music can be considered the legacy of the European church that took its definitive shape in Suriname.

MILITARY BRASS BAND AND POLICE CORPS BRASS BAND
- Herman Dijo -

Only a few people are members of the three brass fanfares of which Suriname can boast. The continued existence of the Militaire Kapel (Military Brass Band), the Politie Kapel (Police Corps Brass Band), and De Trekkers brass band therefore is dependent on the fortunes of a few individuals. Just what can happen is illustrated with the experience of the Surinaamse Filharmonisch Orkest: when its conductor Wessels died, the orchestra was disbanded.

When it comes to the Military and Police Corps Brass Bands, the government authorities of Suriname have a great deal of say. They can exempt people from their duties to rehearse. The government also makes it possible for members to take educational courses in the Netherlands.

The Military Brass Band's repertoire contains many European and American pieces. Alongside pieces by Boedhijn, Glenn Miller, and Sousa there are quite a few Creole folksongs, adapted by conductor/composer Eddy Snijders. They are beautiful pieces with such titles as "Komisi da botri" (The cook is in the kitchen) and "Poeroe foetoe" (Move your feet). In the period before independence, the Militaire Kapel, also known by the name TRIS—brass band (Tropical Armed Forces in Suriname), was made up of a select group of musicians. Many of them had outside jobs as teachers at music schools or evening educational courses. Others were busy playing dance music or in the so-called bazuinkoor. Despite this demanding existence as military musician cum choir leader or private teacher, these musicians could hold their own with their colleagues in the Netherlands. This was abundantly clear when the band attended the 1969 Taptoe (Military Tattoo) Delft festival in the Netherlands. The Dutch audience was extremely taken with their great dedication, carefully worked out performance, and high-quality musical interpretation. Until independence in 1975, the directorship had been in the hands of a Dutchman. Only in the final phase of the preparations for independence did the military make a scholarship available to a Surinamer to study in the Netherlands. Alfred Liew On was appointed conductor of the Military Brass Band after independence.

Until independence the military musicians were in the service of the Dutch government. They were then given the choice to go the Netherlands or stay in Suriname. Almost half the brass band left; part of them went to the Netherlands to retire.

Of the group that went to the Netherlands, only a few found employment again in the music world. This was because practically all the musicians in the Military Brass Band were autodidacts; they had learned music by playing it. A few dogged individuals were able to acquire a conservatory diploma, but the majority did not get far in the Dutch "paper society" without a diploma, no matter how beautifully they played.

There were hardly any new musicians to compensate for those who left the Military Brass Band. That is why it merged with the Police Corps Brass Band; the new ensemble was called Staatskapel (State Brass Band). The agents rehearsed together with the military men, each in his own uniform, in the Memre Buku Armory. To breathe new life into the brass band music, some pensioned military musicians were asked to teach the young. Apparently the initiative paid off, because since 1984 both the military and the police have had their own music corps.

Nevertheless, one of their traditional performances will no longer be able to be seen: the long parade after the march past dignitaries on Koninginnedag (Dutch Queen's Day). Hundreds of people used to dance along the route to the Prins Bernhard Kampement (Prince Bernhard Barracks), now (the Memre Buku Armory). Later in the evening on Koninginnedag, Politie Kapel and Militaire Kapel together played the military tattoo on the former Oranjeplein (Orange Square), now Onafhankelijkheidsplein (Independence Square). The brass bands were always at their best at these sorts of special occasions.

Good musicians often left the Politie Kapel for the Militaire Kapel, as they had better terms of employment. The police allowed you to perform music outside the official band without having to get permission from the top brass. The military applied Dutch norms: shorter working hours, a good salary, and nearly all work time devoted to music. In contrast, at first the police musicians only had time off from their normal duties to rehearse at one two-hour session per week. Out of fear of the power of attraction to the Military Brass Band, the police leaders changed this to five two-hour rehearsals a week. From 1958 to 1963 there was even a musically experienced military man who conducted the Police Corps Brass Band: Eddy Snijders, the same man who would later also conduct the Military Brass Band. Whenever he was absent, the band was led by the next highest-ranking person—a procedure that did not always work well in practice because the next highest-ranking person was not always next in terms of musical quality. To partly solve this problem, a police officer was given a scholarship to study conducting at a Dutch conservatory: the tuba player John Nelom, who became conductor of the Police Corps Brass Band in 1970. During his course of studies, which lasted nearly six years, one of the other musicians had to take over the baton. His replacement changed the repertoire. For the first time, the Police Corps Brass Band began playing Hindustani and Javanese music alongside the familiar classical and religious works. This considerably enlarged its audience. At the military tattoo, for example, the policemen played a potpourri of Hindustani, Javanese, and Creole music. Well-known Creole folksongs that were adapted into marching music are "Komisi da botri" and "Mini mini kon njang" (Min mini, come and eat). During the Devali celebration—the Hindu Feast of the Lighting of the Lamps—on the Onafhankelijkheidsplein, the police played appropriate Hindustani music. During the parade, the brass band even played a Surinamese march, which was something totally unusual.

SURINAMESE CLASSICAL MUSIC
- Marcel Weltak -

In the case of Suriname, when we refer to classical music, we do not mean European music from the period of 1750 to 1810, the era of such great European composers as Mozart, Beethoven, and Haydn. We are referring to art music that is rooted in Western church and vernacular music traditions.

The earliest Surinamese art music dates from the end of the nineteenth century. However, the most important Surinamese classical composers lived in the twentieth century. Even though most of these composers studied at Dutch, French, and German music institutes, and were thus familiar with the work of atonal composers, no such influences can be found in their work.

Though situated in South America, Suriname has little in common with the rest of the continent, and not merely because of the language. Together with its neighbor to the north, Guyana, they are the only two countries in Latin America without a Romance language. This is clearly discernible when it comes to the influence of European classically composed music. To this day, there is still an ongoing and vigorous tradition of baroque musical culture in various South American countries. It is even regularly maintained that baroque music, and especially that from Italy and Spain, has been better conserved in South America than in those countries themselves. By contrast, European classical music in Suriname was dominated by German composers, especially Johannes Sebastian Bach. The most plausible explanation for this can be found in the largest European religious denomination to be found in Suriname: the Moravian church. Although its current-day principal seat is in the Dutch town of Zeist, it was founded in the Moravia region of the former Czechoslovakia, hence the name Moravian.

The works of Bach landed in Suriname thanks to this church movement. Songs can be heard daily on Surinamese radio. *Jesu Joy of Man's Desiring*, the last part of the cantata *Herz und Mund und Tot und Leben* (BWV147), is used to announce obituary notices. There was even an amphitheater built in Paramaribo to perform a Surinamese version of the *St. Matthew Passion*, which was performed on two occasions over the years. Lou Lichtveld (alias Albert Helman) and Majoie Hajary composed work for the Heilige Week (Holy Week) based on the *St. Matthew Passion*. Hajary's composition is aptly entitled *Na Pina Wiki* (The Poor Week).

Bach's *St. Matthew Passion* was composed as an oratorio and in Suriname was performed as an opera. It wasn't until many years later that something similar took place in the Netherlands. And Surinamers always referred to Matthew as a passion play.

The influence of the *St. Matthew Passion*, and Bach in general, seeped into the folk culture. All elements of *the St. Matthew Passion*, for instance, can be heard in lobisingi. This form of Surinamese music makes use of an orchestra. Recitatives and arias abound. And just as in *Matthew*, there are passages for choir and chorales. Bertolt Brecht and Kurt Weill called their

Dreigroschen Opera (*The Threepenny Opera*) a poor man's opera. Lobisingi can also be seen in this regard. The border between high and low culture is quite arbitrary in this form of music and easily transgressed.

Due to the dominance of the Moravian Church on Surinamese cultural life—church music is almost completely German, Calvinist, and Lutheran—and although the largest church that dominates the Paramaribo skyline is the Catholic cathedral, most composers are influenced by Johann Sebastian Bach.

Another influence on Surinamese classical music stems from English church music that dates back to the time of English rule. English hymns, together with German chorales, were played by the bazuinkoor small ensembles of brass instruments, becoming vehicles for the composer's repertoire. The earliest song forms were almost purely European. Gradually, however, popular local rhythmic patterns increasingly became part of compositions.

Johannes Nicolaas Helstone (1853–1927)

Johannes Nicolaas Helstone, born in the village of Berg en Dal, eighty kilometers south of Paramaribo, is considered the most important composer of Surinamese classical music. As a boy, Johannes received his first music lessons from a German couple, the Willigers, who had gone to Suriname as missionaries. When they decided to return to Germany after years of working in Suriname, the Willigers took Helstone with them to their fatherland. In Germany, Helstone underwent instruction in music theory and on the harmonium. Because of his talent, Helstone entered the conservatory in Leipzig despite his deficient preparatory training, where he studied piano and organ. He graduated cum laude. In 1892 Helstone again went to Leipzig and two years later took a PhD in music.

Helstone was not only a composer. Apart from composing mazurkas, fugues, toccatas, and setting Psalms to music, in Suriname he was even more well known as a conductor. His most important work is *Het pand der goden* (The Premises of the Gods), a musical drama for choir, piano, organ, and orchestra that was first performed in Paramaribo in 1906. The magazine *Oost West* (East West) wrote on May 5, 1906: "It is a major work, beautiful and sublime. The music is exquisite and affords great pleasure to music lovers. The scenes make such a profound impression on the audience, that everyone is totally engrossed in the spectacle. The costumes and scenery are designed by the artist Rustwijk. The compiler and composer of all this is Helstone. Oh, what greatness he exhibits with this piece. It is masterfully put together, gloriously adapted."

Besides being a musician, Helstone was also a linguist. In 1903 he wrote a grammar for Sranan Tongo entitled *Wan spraakkunst vo taki en skrifi da tongo foe Sranang* (One Grammar for Talking and Writing in the Surinamese Tongue). Some of his other publications include *De Griekse muziek in 't licht der moderne toonkunst* (Greek Music in Light of the Modern Western Music) and a textbook with the title *Muziekschool* (Music School).

In 1899 Helstone had the great misfortune of having both his pianos as well as all his manuscripts and musical scores go up in flames during a major fire. His opera *Het pand der goden* was performed in Berlin, where it was reported to have been a sensation.

In 1944 a committee was formed in Suriname to honor Helstone with a monument, and four years later the Helstone monument was unveiled behind the Centrumkerk (Downtown Church) on the Kerkplein (Church Square) in Paramaribo.

Johan Victor Dahlberg (1915–1946)

Dahlberg left his native Suriname with his mother at the age of one in 1916 for the Netherlands. After attending music school, he went to the Amsterdam Conservatory, where he studied composition and piano. In his brief thirty-one-year life Dahlberg composed works for orchestra, choir, trio, string quartet, piano, organ, violin, and cello.

In the Netherlands Dahlberg compositions have been performed by, among others, the Utrechts Stedelijk Orkest (City of Utrecht Orchestra), Radio Blazers Ensemble (Radio Brass Ensemble), the Brabants Mannenkoor (Brabant Male Choir), and Koninklijke Zangers (Royal Singers). Dahlberg's concert for orchestra and male choir *Ciconna di Chiesa* received a rave review form his colleague, composer Herman Strategier: "this piece for male choir and orchestra is a work of surprising beauty, replete with salutary earnestness, dramatic in impact but never pathetic, fiercely expressive but not grim, vocally quite sonorous and most certainly equally well orchestrated." Strategier's notes on Dahlberg's *Symphonie Macabre opus 7* are well documented by several sources. This symphony was awarded the Alphons Diepenbrock Prize. Dahlberg's work has also been on the repertoire of various chamber music ensembles.

Majoie Hajary (1921–2017)

Majoie Hajary was born August 15, 1921, in Paramaribo. After graduating from secondary school, she went to the Amsterdam Conservatory to study piano and composition under, among others, Hendrik Andriessen. She received several accolades for her piano playing. Hajary left Amsterdam for Paris, where she studied composition under the famous Nadia Boulanger.

She has given concerts on every continent. With her Hindustani roots, Hajary preferred dressing like an Indian woman in a colorful sari. The places where rave reviews and articles were written about her concerts include Vienna, Berlin, New York, Caracas, and Tokyo.

Hajary is the probably the Surinamese composer/musician with the most LPs to her name. She was under contract to CBS. She made records with Indian raga music and even wrote a book on this Indian concert form. Hajary composed an opera, *La Larme d'or*, that has been performed in several European countries. For CBS she also recorded *La Passion selon Judas*. Her oratorio *Da Pinawiki*, inspired by and comparable in popularity to *St. Matthew Passion* in the Netherlands and Germany, was performed over an extended period during Holy Week celebrations in Suriname. CBS also recorded her *Requiem for Mahatma Gandhi*. Even though she presented herself as an Indian in a sari, her compositions were full of allusions to motifs and melodies from Surinamese folk music. She incorporated elements of African, Asian, and Latin American music into the European art music she had studied. She also contributed to the soundtrack of the Surinamese feature film *Wan Pipel* (One People) that appeared shortly after Surinamese independence.

Hajary also wrote a textbook for piano instruction, *L'art du piano*, as well as *Yoga voor de pianist* (Yoga for the Pianist). She also translated into French the great nineteenth-century anti-colonial novel *Max Havelaar* by the Dutch author Multatuli, which dealt with the Dutch East Indies (present-day Indonesia), as well as work by Jan Tinbergen, the Dutch economist awarded the Nobel Memorial Prize in Economic Sciences in 1969. The pianist/composer lived in Paris and was married to Roland Garros of the renowned French family. This together with her charismatic presence, undoubtedly contributed to her renown and popularity.

Richenel Edgar "Eddy" Snijders (1923–1990)

Snijder's current fame is in large part due to *De man met de piccolo* (The Man with the Piccolo) , the title of the biography written in Dutch by his son Ronald Snijders, himself renowned as flutist and composer throughout Europe.

Eddy Snijders was flutist in the Surinaams Filharmonisch Orkest (Surinamese Philharmonic Orchestra) and became the first conductor of the Police Corps Brass Band he helped form, and then as concertmaster of the Military Brass Band and finally the State Military Band.

Snijders received his basic musical training at the Patronaats Harmonie (Catholic Youth Group Brass Band) of the Catholic church. He transformed the small brass ensemble De Trekkers, which he conducted, into a full-fledged brass band. He played trumpet in several groups such as Sonora Paramarera.

As a composer, Snijders was completely self-taught. His compositions—such as the music for ballet *Anansie Torie* (Anansie Tales); *Eerste Surinaamse rhapsodie* (First Surinamese Rhapsody), derived from Surinamese folk songs and commissioned by the Surinamese Philharmonic Orchestra; and several art songs based on African Surinamese tunes, with Caribbean and Latin American rhythms—all bear the hallmarks of an extremely talented composer. He also excelled as an arranger.

Snijders performed with the Surinamese Philharmonic Orchestra on several islands in the Caribbean region. There are reviews of concerts in Trinidad and Tobago, Curaçao, and Guyana. Snijders and the Military Brass Band also recorded tracks in 1961 for the North American movie *Spiral Road*, starring Rock Hudson.

Lou Lichtveld (1903–1996)

Of all Surinamese classical composers, Lou Lichtveld is the most well known in the Netherlands. But not so much as a composer: Lichtveld was an extraordinarily prolific writer. Under his nom de plume Albert Helman, his publications could fill an entire bookcase. His early works especially were critical of the Dutch colonial presence, while at the same time possessing exquisite literary beauty.

Lichtveld was a war correspondent and fought, as did Ernest Hemingway, on the Republican side during the Spanish Civil War. In World War II he was a member of the Dutch resistance. After the war Helman returned to his native Suriname in 1949, where he was appointed Minister of Education and Health until 1951. He later held a number of positions in the government and diplomatic corps, which included posts in Washington, DC, and New York.

Lichtveld always kept his two most important activities strictly separate. In the world of letters he was Albert Helman; in the music world he was Lou Lichtveld. His chamber music, songs, chorales, and oratorios were performed in Amsterdam's Concertgebouw and the Beurs van Berlage. He composed musical scores for cineaste Joris Ivens's early films. In Suriname, his oratorio was performed annually in a theater built especially for Holy Week.

Dario Saävedra (1876–1909)

Dario Saävedra, born Daan Samuels, was invited to study in Leipzig at the recommendation of his teacher Helstone. He studied in Berlin and Leipzig and did so well he became a professor at the conservatory there. Saävedra was an immensely successful pianist. He was known as one of the best interpreters of Beethoven's music for piano.

Saävedra composed songs, choral works, sonatas, and variations on Surinamese songs.

Eddy Renada (1913–1983)

While in the Netherlands Eddy Renada made his living playing piano and making arrangements for the jazz band of saxophonist Kid Dynamite (Arthur Parisius). To be able to make art music he had to move to Brussels, Belgium. There one his serious works, *Sinfonieta*, was performed by the Radio Philharmonic Orchestra of Norway.

The Radio Nederland Wereldomroep (Radio Netherlands World Service) has recordings of his piano sonatas. Manuscripts of his musical scores are housed in the Gemeentemuseum (Municipal Museum) in The Hague, where an exhibition of his work and concerts were once mounted and performed.

Alma Kensmil (1892–1985)

Alma Kensmil composed music for the Nederlands Philharmonisch Orkest (Netherlands Philharmonic Orchestra). Her *Praeludium Pacis* from 1946 was last performed in 1996. Her neighbors rescued for posterity musical scores that had been put out with the trash after her death. They included piano concertos, works for choir, orchestra, and songs.

A new generation of classical composers is currently active. The most well-known among them is probably **Christoffel Snijders** (b. 1953). Like most Surinamese musicians and composers, he received musical instruction in the Netherlands, where he studied trombone and conducting. When he returned to Suriname, he became director of the Nationale Volksmuziekschool (National Folk Music School) in Paramaribo.

Snijders conducts a brass band, plays trombone, works at the university, and composes. His work covers a broad spectrum of music. He has written works for brass band, guitar, and chamber music.

One of his best-known and greatest works is the *Mass in F major* for soloists, mixed choir, and brass band orchestra. His works have been published
in Vienna, where his *Mass in F major* has been performed.

A rising star in the Netherlands is **Yannick Hiwat** (b. 1988). Hiwat studied
violin at the Rotterdam Conservatory and graduated cum laude. Even though
the violinist had a classical education, like many of his contemporaries he
does not limit himself to playing only the kind of music he had to play
during his studies.

Hiwat has accompanied the famous North American soprano Renee
Fleming but enjoys playing rock and jazz equally as well. He was also artist-
in-residency at the Concertgebouw De Doelen in Rotterdam. In his composition *Kodjo's Spirit*—a musical odyssey from the beginning of the transatlantic
slave trade to the present-day, inspired by the death of 664 Africans in the
Dutch slave ship *De Leusden*—he was inspired by European, African, and
Surinamese music.

In his work with the Doelen Ensemble, he plays with the famous mez-
zosoprano Nora Fischer. He also leads a jazz quartet.

Surinamese musicians and composers usually are jacks-of-all-trades. **Rudi
Bedacht** (b. 1932), better known as the poet Corly Verlooghen, is a talented
guitarist and composer besides being a professor in Sweden and Panama.
Flutist Ronald Snijders plays jazz, Surinamese folk, pop, funk, as well as
classical music and has written quite a few compositions in all these genres.
Alongside their work in music schools and conservatories in the Netherlands,
guitarists **Robert Faverey** and **Stanley Noordpool** have played all over the
world as a duo or separately, where they have performed works of modern
European, Caribbean, and South American composers. This has unfortunately not allowed them much time for composing themselves.

Notes

1. Moravian missionaries were the first large-scale Protestant missionary movement.
They sent out the first missionaries when there were only three hundred inhabitants in
Herrnhut. Within thirty years the church had sent hundreds of Christian missionaries
to many parts of the world, including the Caribbean, North and South America (see
Christian Munsee), the Arctic, Africa, and the Far East. They were the first to send lay
people (rather than clergy) as missionaries, the first Protestant denomination to minister
to slaves, and the first Protestant presence in many countries.

2. Typical Surinamese brass religious music.

PART II

DEVELOPMENT

6

BIGI POKU AND KASEKO

- Marcel Weltak -

Opegooie, bungu bungu, motjo poku, badji, bigi poku, kaseko: those are some of the monikers Afro-Surinamese dance music has had. The several variations usually differ very little. Two of these styles appeared on records and therefore have become the most well known: *bigi poku* and *kaseko*. Until the end of the 1960s, bigi poku was the most important Afro-Surinamese dance music. The music then changed through all sorts of influences and received a new name: bigi poku became kaseko.

BIGI POKU

Bigi poku probably came into being around the turn of the twentieth century, but it is not entirely clear how it happened. Surinamers were surrounded daily by their dance music and had absolutely no desire to study it. The Dutch colonial administrators viewed the people and their culture with scarcely concealed contempt; to them Suriname was only a colony in which to make money. It was not until 1929 that the first study of Surinamese dance music was conducted. In their book *Suriname Folklore*, the North American husband-and-wife authors Melville Jean and Frances Herskovits provided a summary presentation of *lobisingi* (love songs), which together with kawina and bazuinkoor, among other things, was presumably responsible for the inception of bigi poku.

Incidentally, the wealthy colonials did contribute to this twentieth-century form of dance music. It came into being in the nightlife of the turn of the twentieth century: in the brothels, nightclubs, and bars of Paramaribo, where the rich came to be entertained. They asked for different, "more modern music" and they had the money to pay the musicians. What Surinamese dance music had in common with American jazz, Cuban habanera, and Argentinian tango was that it was first played in brothels.

The name bigi poku is probably a corruption of English "big" and Dutch "pauk": music of the kettle drum or timpani. The big drum in the bigi poku is the *skratyi-dron* (skratyi drum) or bass drum. This drum owes its name to the trestle that supports it while playing it on stage. During marches and processions however, the skratyi is hung from a strap on the belly of the player.

The rhythm in bigi poku no doubt comes from kawina. The improvisational role of the kwakwa-bangi and the two small drums in kawina are taken over in bigi poku by skratyi and snare drum respectively. Besides the percussion section, the oldest form of bigi poku also included trumpet, tuba, and flute. Later, this would change into trumpet, cornet, banjo, and vocals, and the tuba was replaced by the string bass.

In kawina the lowest-tuned drum (the *pudja*, and later the congas) always marked the basic rhythm, also known as *hari*. The highest-tuned drum plays *koti*, or improvisations. In bigi poku, the tuba took over the function of the pudja to indicate the rhythm. The kotis came from the skratyi—which is therefore sometimes also called *kot dron*, which accounts for the other names bigi poku is known by such as *skratyi poku* or *kot poku*, after the bass drum that determines the beat of this music.

Influence of European Music?

Various theories exist when it comes to the origin of the snare drum, the small drum in the percussion section. One of them is that Surinamers in the nineteenth century had adopted the classical music of European court dances of the time. Together with such folk tunes as "Yankee Doodle" from the United States, Surinamers made *set-dansi* out of them. Those Surinamese dances and their music were one of the sources for bigi poku. We can see the influence of European dances throughout the Caribbean area. In this way the danzón came into being from the contradanza, a Cuban version of the French and Spanish contredanse. The beguine in the French Antilles and Haiti is of similar origin, while in the Netherlands Antilles one finds dances derived from the polka and the mazurka.

English dances were adopted in Suriname, possibly through neighboring British Guiana and through the growing influence of the United States in the bauxite industry. To be sure, such dances as the *carré*, the *caledonia*, the English and French *lancer*, and the quadrille are today only played as examples of folklore, but the ensembles who accompany such folkloristic performances always have a snare drum alongside the violins. Chorales are also included in the bigi poku repertoire alongside English melodies. The song "Lele sina go" was originally a Bach chorale. The slaves heard it being sung by the plantation owners during church services. The solemn chorales were given a new rhythmic basis in bigi poku, while the melody line of the chorale was left intact.

The army is another possible source of the snare drum. That instrument had been used for centuries to sound roll call and play at funeral marches. The army traditionally did not have a bass drum; the infantry used trumpets or bugles or drum rolls as a signal to attack or for reveille.

The army also influenced bigi poku in another way than just such instruments as tuba and snare drum. Surinamese musicians became proficient at playing marching music in the army; most musicians in Suriname came from or are from military brass bands. The very tight drum roll in bigi poku is due to the influence of military marching music; however, this does not mean that it is derived from marching music—or, as some Dutchmen have claimed, that bigi poku came into being because Surinamers could not play the march correctly. Bigi poku does resemble marching music due to the instruments, but the rhythm is of a totally different origin. The so-called marching rhythm that can be heard in bigi poku (and currently in kaseko) consists mainly of beats in the performances of old (Afro) music forms still played on the kwakwa-bangi, and we have seen that this originated from kawina and not European marching music.

Clave

One of the clearest characteristics of Afro-Surinamese music is the clave rhythm. The word is an old Spanish form of *llave*, which means key. Clave is indispensable to Afro-music. It is more than just a key motif, but practically the key to the music itself. The clave determines not only the rhythm of the music but the way it feels as well; the color of the music depends on the staccato. So that is why everything is geared to the clave. Both the rhythm section and the melody instruments that play rhythmic phrases must be "in clave." Thanks to the clave there is an interlock of rhythms in bigi poku. It is the polymorphic tempo of the basic patterns and figures that makes this music so rhythmically strong. In both Ghana and the Congo—two African countries from which many slaves in Suriname came—the concept of polyrhythm is quite well known. In Ghana use is made of the *dawura* or cowbell to indicate the beat of the clave. In Suriname too, the dawra is used for the key rhythm. The same clave can be found in the music of the French Antilles and Trinidad. The Cuban clave deviates from this, although bigi poku is strongly influenced by it.

The Role of the Tuba

Over the course of time, tuba took on a freer role in bigi poku. The instrument was now allowed to improvise (*koti*) and no longer just had to "pull" (*hari*). The actual koti-instrument, the skratyi, laid down the beat, alongside its normal improvisations. The skratyi began to improvise around the hari-beat, after which it can freely continue for a couple of bars. After all, the skratyi always comes back to the beat.

Instruments like the tuba were not intentionally included in bigi poku. Musicians discovered automatically while playing that certain instruments were better able at carrying out given functions. In this way, in the first bigi poku ensembles the *kwatro* (four-stringed guitar) were used, though this typical kawina instrument later disappeared. Other instruments kept being used to make harmonies. As has already been stated, the tuba came to replace the pudja. But in the meantime, the tuba has been replaced as a hari-instrument, first by the double bass and at present in kaseko by the more modern and handsome bass guitar.

All these changes in the bigi poku lineup resulted in a rhythm section with as its most important instruments the bass, the big (hari) drum, and the snare drum (kot-dron). The complete rhythm section is often set up the same for the audience: to its left the *sek-seki* (derived from kawina), with the cowbell, aka *agogo*. To the right is the bari-dron and in between the kot-dron, which could be a skratyi or snare drum. The snare drum always plays a figure over two measures, while the tom-toms play the basic patterns. There is little variation in the snare drum figure: it is the kawina bell pattern. However, bigi poku is based strongly on counterpoint; the many contra-figures give the music its power.

Badji and Motjo poku

Kawina was not the only forerunner to bigi poku. Other styles also made their contributions, such as the badji, the chorales, lobisingi, and motjo poku.

Practically no horn players were living in Suriname at the beginning of the twentieth century. But suddenly there was a large influx of wind instrument players with the arrival of the rubber tappers and gold diggers from neighboring British Guyana; with its calypso-like badji music, Guyana was long familiar with wind instruments. These Guyanese badjis were incorporated into bigi poku, which swelled the ranks of wind players. The best Surinamese wind players, except George Schermacher, hailed from the western district of Nickerie, close to the border with Guyana: Tjen A Tak, Thompson, McBean, and others. Kaseko, the successor to bigi poku, still bears a strong resemblance to badji played at a faster tempo.

Jazz critic Rudy Jong Loy calls badji the only genuine Surinamese dance music. In his opinion, bigi poku and kaseko have too many foreign elements, such as Western marching music and chorales. An example of an English song that ended up in Suriname through badji music is "Watra e long na mi ai" (Water flows from my eye, i.e., I am crying).

Motjo poku is not only regarded as a forerunner, but also as part of bigi poku. Motjo poku still retained the tuba as hari-instrument, and there are always vocals in motjo poku. For motjo poku sprang from a "civilized" music style, the lobisingi, but the character and structure of motjo poku is much rougher. The lyrics often are about sex and in general are quite obscene and coarse. In this regard motjo poku resembles calypso, which later on would strongly influence kaseko.

Baas Adriaan, George Schermacher

Bigi poku had its big stars, one of the most renowned of which was Baas Adriaan. He is practically a myth—partly because there were no recordings made in Suriname in his day—and all kinds of stories are doing the rounds, such as the tale of the train.

Somewhere in the mid-1930s Baas Adriaan was playing non-stop trumpet with his band on the train between Valiantsplein in Paramaribo and Lelydorp, twenty kilometers down the line. Whenever the guitar player or banjo player wanted to take a break, Adriaan screeched at the musician: "Boi, was' a te, was' a te!" (Boy, keep going on your string, keep going on your string). He played whatever came into his mind, one song after another, against the noise of the train. The engineer provided rhythmic accompaniment for Adriaan on his steam whistle. Adriaan's music was dubbed "opegooie," with such folk tunes as "Konu Oloisi lassie, mi jere a bubu tekin." There were not many solos, and the banjo played harmonies. Surinamers became acquainted with such American instruments through the westerns playing in the movie theaters in Paramaribo.

There are recordings of another bigi poku star: saxophonist George Schermacher. His style of playing was instantly recognizable from thousands of others: quavering and full of ornamentations. In contrast to his jazz music, his big-poku and kaseko renditions contained hardly any improvisations, he preferred to play variations on the melody to get more swing out of the music. "People want to dance, you shouldn't bother them with all kinds of ideas," according to Schermacher. Jong Loy doesn't actually consider Schermacher to be a jazz musician, more like an exceptional sax player, but doesn't see much difference between jazz and kaseko, except in terms of rhythm. "In fact, they are two forms of the same African music," according to the jazz reviewer. In the Caribbean region and Africa, all music with modern rhythm sections was consistently referred to as jazz.

Bungu

In the 1950s Surinamese dance music was known as bungu bungu. The name came from the sound of horses made on the carousels at fairgrounds. They creaked loudly while moving up and down, because there was no money to lubricate them: "bungu . . . bungu. And so, the carousel was called the bungu bungu, and later the music as well.

The bungu bungu lineup was simple: a single trumpet or stringed instrument, accompanied by a roll on a snare drum. The most famous bungu bungu players were the brothers "Noso ka" and "Flenflen" Gilhuis. One was deaf and played the banjo, the other was blind and played the snare drum. To be sure, the banjo player only knew how to play chords, but he played the rhythm and set the tempo for his blind brother on the snare drum.

KASEKO

No one knows exactly where the word kaseko comes from. The Surinamese musicologist Herman Dijo heard it the first time at a party where his group was playing. Someone asked him to play a "kawina a la secco." Secco was the name of a famous record label that at the time released music that included the Cuban singer Celia Cruz and the Sonora Matancera. This music was hugely popular in Suriname in the 1950s and 1960s.

Another possibility is that kaseko is a corruption of *kase le corp*, Patois for "break the body" (Patois is the creolized French spoken in neighboring French Guiana). In general, dance music in that country—and in the Lawa region of eastern Suriname—is also referred to as kaseko. A third possibility is that the word derives from the African language (presumably Ashanti) *kaiso*, which means both "shake" and "bravo." In that case, kaseko would then share the same root of the name with calypso.

The Influence of Caribbean Music

The resemblance with calypso goes beyond the word. This Caribbean dance music was certainly the most important source of inspiration for kaseko at the outset of its development. The clave of kaseko and calypso are closely related indeed. Calypso infiltrated Surinamese music through the "kon'frijari" (fair). Such calypso greats performed there as Calypso Rose, Lord Kitchener, and King Fighter.

Another Caribbean influence came from the South American dance music played in the heyday of bigi poku by the so-called *conjuntos*: copies of Cuban orchestras with bongos, congas, and other percussion. The conjuntos played mainly for the well-to-do citizens, who found that the skratyi was only suited for the crude motjo poku.

The conjuntos accordingly regarded their music to be a higher order and only regarded the big drum as suitable for some whorish street market surrounding. However, in the 1960s Surinamers had had enough *Spanjoru poku* (Spanish music) of the conjuntos. People wanted to be able to understand the lyrics again. To remedy the situation, a great many conjuntos switched to playing Surinamese music at the time. Cuban *guaracha* and *bolero* rhythms were retained but lyrics were now Surinamese. In terms of the way in which it was built up—intro, solo, chorus, improvisation, and close—the song "Poeroe foetoe" (Move your feet) by Eddy Snijders is more of a Cuban *son* than a bigi poku song. Just like the bigi poku bands, the conjuntos too started playing badjis and waltzes with other instruments. This genre was developed further in the Netherlands by bands such as Twinkle Stars and Happy Boys. The band Sonora Paramarera also had a Cuban conjunto lineup without the popular percussion that become popular later.

Apart from the demand for Surinamese lyrics, the Cuban revolution was also responsible for the disappearance of the then popular Cuban music in Suriname. Many Cuban artists settled in the United States in the 1960s, such as Celia Cruz and Sonora Matancera. The first thing calypso did was make the kaseko sound lighter: the skratyi disappeared from the stage. In its place came Cuban maracas, which together with the cymbals on the drum kit played the syncopations (syncopations are the connections between weak and strong beats, whereby that which first was strong now sounds weak and vice versa). Congas appeared in kaseko practically simultaneously with the disappearance of the skratyi. Earlier on it had been noticed that the double bass increasingly replaced the tuba from bigi poku. The maracas had already appeared in the first bigi poku ensembles, but they were not played as a kawina instrument, but in the Cuban style.

There were yet more influences on Surinamese music. The dropping of Cuban music provided the impetus for other Latin American styles to come to the fore; into the limelight came the music of Shleu Shleu from Haiti, Mighty Sparrow from Trinidad, and the renowned bossa nova from Brazil. The influence of the Caribbean region on kaseko had mainly to do with harmonies. The brass arrangements underwent a complete metamorphosis. In bigi poku the core of the brass section was focused on counterpoint, which made the music sound a great deal like Dixieland from New Orleans. The harmonies in the brass charts for kaseko are much busier and fuller. Staccato playing with its many riffs was introduced as well as licks from calypso and son montuno from Cuba. Kaseko equaled calypso in terms of the number of riffs employed. The music got rougher at the edges and in general the brass playing was more direct.

The transition from bigi poku to kaseko was complete when the skratyi-dron was replaced by the modern drum kit. However, the arrival of the drum kit meant that the instruments took on another task. There was much more room for the double bass, which had taken over from the tuba. The kaseko took over various guajeos (bass runs) from Cuba and Trinidad. The tuba in bigi poku had played its part much tighter than the double bass, and later electric bass guitar, in kaseko. Surinamese musicians now refrained from adding practically total copies of foreign styles into kaseko. They also made more discriminating use when citing other musicians. In that way the influence of other music styles remained limited to solving harmonic problems in the same way it did with other styles.

Lieve Hugo; Winti kaseko; Washboard

Vocals were also accorded a more prominent place in kaseko. Musicians in bigi poku formations played more instrumental music; they could only be heard in choir as it were. The soloist paraphrased voices with his instrument. The development of vocals in kaseko is mainly thanks to Lieve Hugo, the stage name of Hugo "Iko" Uiterloo. This kaseko musician was able to write catchy lyrics on pretty melody lines. On top of that he had magnificent stage presence and a fine voice. Uiterloo was also the source of another trend: Winti songs and kaseko songs inspired by calypso. Well-known examples of Winti kaseko are the Kromanti song "Kodokoe" and the Loeango songs "Mi bébe" and "Lekefiye." The secularization of kaseko had a somewhat banal effect on the Winti song lyrics. Songs about the spirits used dirty language and were danced to in a similar fashion.

One of the first groups to play kaseko in the mid-1960s was Washboard, one of whose members was Lieve Hugo. In fact, this band was responsible for bringing about the transformation from bigi poku to kaseko. The horn players in Washboard had grown up as children with bigi poku and played kaseko as adults. There was still plenty of bigi poku on Washboard's first records, but kaseko could readily be heard as well. The rhythm, lyrics, and vocal phrasing of music on the first LPs were borrowed from calypso.

Just as with other groups, there was a great deal of coming and going of musicians, who brought with them a different influence (from the USA, Cuba, and Trinidad). The Washboard LPs clearly display the transitions between the several styles. In the number "Tai na boeriki" a solo can be heard, followed by the band playing mambo riffs from the well-known evergreen "El Manicero." After the mambo section the band then reverts to kaseko.

The rise of calypso in Suriname also left its mark on Washboard. In the piece "Gang" (Journey), the band allowed itself to be influenced by the French Antillean and Haitian beguine. The rhythm came from the French Antilles, but the bass runs and percussion gradually morphed into calypso. During the beguine section the high-hat and guitar were already playing calypso. The horns and especially the trumpets were clearly oriented toward Cuban music with an Andalusian background.

Several Washboard musicians came from the Winti scene. The *Spirit* LP is a good example of how Winti songs were given a modern sound with the help of calypso. "Aje ajo" is an example of Amerindian Winti. The snare drum plays the Amerindian Winti extremely tight. It is based on the same scheme as "Mi sjie deng jonkuman," with an Amerindian *tuka* (intermediate beat). The *indja-tuka* can easily be transposed to the kawina, and from there it is a short way to kaseko. The words "sjarwa sjarwa" sung in "Aje ajo" are an Amerindian greeting, a memory of the practically extinct Amerindian culture.

"Wayambo," from the same album, is also an Amerindian Winti originally with a 12/8 beat, which also existed in a kawina version. Kawina musicians made the work for kaseko musicians hugely easier. They were the ones responsible for changing the 12/8 back to 4/4. And a kawina song in 4/4 meant it was no longer a headache to keep straight. Finally, "Malango" is a Loeango song (Winti) in 12/8 with a lovely improvisation by the singer Mighty Power.

The band Washboard came to perform in the Amsterdam Concertgebouw during the Holland Festival in the early 1970s. One of the members of the very famous brass section was the trumpet player John Gietel. Gietel was actually a thoroughbred set-dansi and motjo poku musician. The other trumpet players were Os and Plato.

Lieve Hugo, who at the time was a member of the Washboard orchestra, stayed behind with other members in the Netherlands. Stan Lokhin subsequently produced Lieve Hugo's first record for EMI Bovema. That was possible because Washboard's LP *Spirit* had sold more than 17,000 units. At the time, the Netherlands dictated Surinamese dance music: kaseko with Cuban guaracha on the conga.

Stan Lokhin (1947–2010)

There were three leading groups in the 1960s: the Swingmasters, Koele Koele, and the Rhythm Makers. All these bands had a "civilized" Latin lineup: bongos, congas, maracas, bass, guitar, and horns. There were musicians in the Rhythm Makers who were to set the trend for the next twenty years in the Netherlands. Names such as Carlo Jones, Cabenda, Ewald Krolis, Eugene Bonam, Stekkel, and Stan Lokhin.

"With the Swingmasters we were the only band who could read and play sheet music," trumpeter, arranger, and producer Lokhin proudly told me. "We accompanied foreign artists such as Doris Troy, Jackie Opel, and the Bluesbusters." In contrast to many of his colleagues who had learned to play from priests, Stan Lokhin developed his music skills in the Salvation Army. At the end of the 1960s, Lokhin began arranging music that could be called Latin kaseko. The founder of this form of kaseko was William "Wilmo" Kambel, from the group Koele Koele. Kambel arranged in the Cuban style, and by doing so began to modernize Surinamese music. He wrote such songs as "Piau piau" (the name of a Chinese gambling game). However, Kambel's approach toward doing business was one that made him unable to hold on to his musicians for very long. For instance, he felt he was entitled to be paid for his arrangements; after all, payment had to be made for arrangements from the USA as well.

In the 1970s Lokhin began producing records and forming bands in the Netherlands. That resulted in the inception of, among others, Happy Boys, with René van der Lande on trumpet, singer Botai Felter, Eugene Bonam on drums, Cabenda on guitar, and Layo Gilles on bass. The name Happy Boys was coined only after Cabenda had been replaced by Harold Biervliet and Botai Felter by Lieve Hugo. The Twinkle Stars, already known for their experiments with conjunto lineups, had by that time already recorded their orchestral kaseko LP *Trotyl*, with three saxes and three trumpets.

Lokhin's productions for the Twinkle Stars, Lieve Hugo, and Happy Boys displayed a clear unity. His arrangements needed little or no tinkering; they were set in every detail. Though Lokhin extended the number of chords from those used the 1960s, people could still dance to his music. In 1972 he got a scholarship from the United States to do a six-month course in pop arrangements and producing. Four years later, EMI paid for a study tour to the United States following his having produced the Billy Jones LP *Birds of the Sea* with strings, and in 1976 he recorded a kaseko record there with a big band.

De Vrolijke Jeugd

An extremely renowned ensemble that played kaseko, among other things, was the choral and theatrical society De Vrolijke Jeugd (The Merry Young-sters), founded in 1942 in Paramaribo by René Waal. When Waal was a child himself, there was a lively choral tradition in Suriname. The lessons at school always began with an hour of singing. After school Waal sang in various men's choirs; the repertoire was made of mainly of such Dutch religious hymns as "Prijs de Heer" (Praise the Lord). With the children's choir Waal sang devotional songs in Sranan Tongo and North American spirituals. He wrote his songs predominately in kawina or kaseko style and had them accompanied by a ukulele or *kwatro* (four-stringed guitar). A fixed part of the repertoire was Winti songs. Waal himself had no technical musical training, but by means of a simple solfege technique he notated the music he played on the kwatro; he worked out all the vocal and instrument parts in the same way. A phenomenal feeling for music saw him through any technical difficulties.

The second arm of De Vrolijke Jeugd is theater. Members of the society performed Waal's plays. His most famous piece was *Kwasi, da lobi fu Jaba*. The Dutch university professor Jan Voorhoeve, who toured the interior of Suriname with the group, was impressed by his achievements. In his trav-elogue he writes: "A few hours before the performance in Phedra a new idea emerged for a play, which was performed that very evening with great success. The reactions to this hilarious comedy were so enthusiastic, that the piece was included in the regular repertoire." In Phedra that evening there were an estimated one thousand people in the audience.

De Vrolijke Jeugd was a mixed ensemble from its inception: boys and girls. Almost all its members (including many of the Waal family) came from the capital. The choir began with performances at birthday parties, at first even for free. They sometimes gave four or five concerts a day. To reduce the number—the members did not have any time for their normal work and rest—after a while the choir asked a small fee. The low fees were not very attractive to the choir and the fee was subsequently doubled.

Age determined the circulation of members in De Vrolijke Jeugd. Children left the group; years later their own children became members. In the
1950s De Vrolijke Jeugd became quite famous thanks to the performance of
"Little Marlène" Waal. The group became the house ensemble of the Nationale Partij Suriname (NPS). This creole political party under the leadership
of the legendary Jopie Pengel used the choir especially during elections. At
mass meetings in the capital and during the campaign in the countryside
the group served as claque during the speech of the great leader, and his
speeches were preceded, interrupted, and followed by singing from De Vrolijke Jeugd. Pengel's career had a stimulating effect on Waal's children's group.
Waal: "Pengel had a shrewd grasp of cultural (musical) affairs." At the time,
De Vrolijke Jeugd recorded an LP on which fragments of Pengel's speeches
were alternated with songs. Wealthy NPS members supported the group in
various manners. For example, the movie theater owner Emile de la Fuente
let the group perform regularly in the theater in his Palace Hotel or Theater
Star. Waal: "Vrolijke Jeugd never received a penny from the NPS." But the
party did pay for the children's outfits, printed the programs, and organized
the group's annual tour of the Surinamese interior. They also subsidized
traveling abroad (twice to the Netherlands, Curaçao, and Germany). Shows
on Surinamese television came about through mediation by the party.

De Vrolijke Jeugd was politically popular because they did not resort to
slanging matches with other groups. Waal had too much love for community
to sow dissent through music: "With my music I always tried to get voters
to come to the polls instead of trying to brush them off." The group happily
went from one of their NPS performances to play at a party of the boss of
a rival political party. Renowned political songs by the choir are "Tai hori,
brada naga sisa," "Te mati e kori, a no e lafu," and "PPB [Pengel Premier Baka]
na ini Sranang," the latter sung to a Miriam Makeba melody.

In 1967, accompanied by a sextet, Vrolijke Jeugd made their first album in
the Netherlands for the Dutch Dureco label. During its existence, the group
made eighteen LPs and four singles with Dureco and Negram, including
recordings for Radio Apintie.

After settling in the Netherlands in 1972, Waal returned to Suriname a
few times with De Vrolijke Jeugd. The group had several hits in Suriname,
including "Lamba Lamba" (as a result of their first trip to the Netherlands),
"Sidon," and "Tangi fu bun na kodja."

De Vrolijke Jeugd still performs in the Netherlands. Waal's grandchildren
are all members of the group, and in the meantime, former members play
together in the kaseko group Nature, led by Marlène.

Sekete

Around the time of independence in 1975, *marrons-kaseko* or *sekete* style kaseko came into being. Old love songs and laments from the interior, made by communities that were once runaway slaves (maroons), were put to a different beat. The music consists of a blend of sekete entertainment music and kaseko. Dancing is not that easy due to its fast rhythm. The drumbeats and lyrics have a hypnotic effect and cause people to go into a trance to be able to communicate with Winti-spirits. European music has very little influence on maroon songs in terms of melody and harmony. That is why the sekete style provide the clearest examples of the sounds of the African continent. Maroon groups make use of old slave songs that retain a great many African characteristics. And that accounts for why, in rhythmic and tonal terms, they sound especially African. Just as in Africa, they make use of pentatonic scales.

The rise of the maroon group Cosmo Stars was an out-and-out sensation. In 1977 the Cosmo Stars came to the Netherlands. A few members of the group stayed behind and founded a new band called the Ex-Cosmo Stars and later Exmo Stars. This was the most renowned and best maroon group. The group had a competent arranger and melodious saxophone player among its ranks in the person of Carlo Jones; by giving structure to the choruses, Jones raised the level of Exmo Stars above the other groups.

Once more and more groups started playing sekete style, the music got sidelined. When someone in the Funmasters, for instance, yelled out "sekete style," Winti beats could be heard on the drums. What was actually worse was the fact that the lyrics began getting more and more obscene overtones, however unintentionally, because singers from non-maroon groups often placed all sorts of wrong accents. In fact, sekete style kaseko did not add anything to the development of Surinamese music, no matter how fresh it originally sounded.

REBIRTH OF THE SKRATYI

Surinamers began a quest to seek their own national identity after independence in 1975. In music, too, people went looking for their roots. Musicians increasingly sought inspiration from national music itself. Salsa and calypso gradually disappeared from Surinamese dance music.

With the rediscovery of Surinamese music, its prominent symbol came back: the bass drum on the trestle, or the skratyi-dron. Once again, it began to dominate both the spectacle and sound of Surinamese music—especially kaseko, because of its central position on stage. The Vijent combo made the first record in 1976 on which the skratyi could be heard: "Jajo liebie." Meanwhile, the cultural and kawina group NAKS had never gotten rid of the skratyi with their Winti-poku music. And in the Netherlands, skratyi also gave the motjo poku of the Boontjie Stars its Surinamese cachet. The skratyi never really disappeared, although it receded into the background when it came to the modern form of kaseko.

Fransje Gomes

A woman who had become famous at the outset of the 1970s also played the skratyi: Francis (Fransje) Johanna Margreta Gomes, who had been born in 1921. For quite some time, she had already been playing unadulterated bigi poku and Winti-poku, devoid of influences from other styles. However, Fransje seldom played on the "respectable"; circuit, she performed mainly in the "mati"-world, i.e., the lesbian scene. Male homosexuality is much less acceptable to most Surinamers than it is in the Netherlands (gay men used to be stoned in Suriname). However, Surinamers have traditionally been passed much less severe judgment on lesbians; it was practically a tradition for women to seek each other's company when the men were gone from home for long periods of time.

Fransje Gomes is one of the big names in Surinamese music. She is one of those portrayed in the book *Vrouwen van Suriname* (Woman of Suriname) by Vincent Soekra and John Hewitt. The music organization Poku Masra accorded her a certificate of appreciation. She determined the success of the groups she played the skratyi and is the living proof that a woman could lay down the law to the men in the macho world of Suriname music. During her career she played a variety of styles (a great deal of Winti-music, but also laku, lobisingi, and kawina) as well as a number of different groups: always behind the skratyi, and wearing trousers, which in Suriname is much less usual than in the Netherlands.

On the two records where she can be heard—other recordings were all destroyed in a fire—she left an indelible mark on Winti-music, especially that of *kopro'tu* (brass playing Winti music).

Fransje Gomes came from a family with a strong Winti tradition: she says that she heard a great many of her songs in a dream, which she wrote down after waking up. She learned to play skratyi at a young age by looking and listening to other players. A certain Roemer, who played the *sedri* (snare drum), was so impressed by her playing that he asked her to play with him.

Later, she began playing at parties with Baas Jones' Anita Band. She quickly switched to other bands, such as Blue Rhythm (she also played skratyi in the Netherlands). Via such other bands as Karifa van Cederboom, she ended up playing with the Zorg brothers, with whom she played her last licks on skratyi.

Gomes not only played Winti on the drum, she sang, too. She learned to do that as a child from the likes of Joosje Leeflang, Tante Mapira, and Jana Krap van der Kus, in the famous working-class neighborhood Van Dijk in Paramaribo. As a young woman she hung around with famous folk singers as Alex de Drie and Nelly Slagtand. On the way to Winti-séances female singer Kasnika Jaja explained to the differences between the Winti spirits. Gomes also mastered the indji-Wintis from the Cottica region, the Saramacca region, and the area of the Suriname River. In the days when Gomes was learning to play and sing, Wintis were taken quite seriously; nowadays, according to her, it is often just "Spielerei" (fooling around), but names such as Baas Adriaan and Poku Frans still stand as specialists in Winti-poku. Fransje Gomes still possesses quite a few authentic, but unknown or forgotten Winti songs. However, she does not want to give them away, because she feels they have been taken from their religious context and therefore have become obscene. In her view, the Wintis have all been mixed up by incompetent amateurs who have spoiled the culture as a result.

She herself calls the Winti music she plays on the skratyi indji-Winti. She mostly plays them with brass players (kopro'tu). The few kinds of Winti she cannot play are the Obia and Busi-indji. They don't take pleasure in the slow skratyi, since they have to be played fast. These two forms of Winti should be played on the dron (the traditional drum) and not on the modern-day drum set. In her long career she often experienced that certain Aisa-Wintis refused to dance to the brass music of the bigi poku and demanded the dron.

Owing to the low tone of its voice, for Gomes the tuba was the ideal replacement for the *agida* in the Winti. In her opinion, the modern-day brass instrument, the trombone, is incapable of carrying the music; the songs would be played much too short and with too much improvisation. And bass guitar from kaseko could not replace the tuba, the low panting/gasping of this brass wind instrument belongs to the music. And naturally for her too, the tuba is as indispensable as the skratyi itself. That is why she prefers to hear kaseko as motjo poku and indji as her form of Winti-poku. Tuba and skratyi form the heart and soul of both styles of music.

Gomes led the kawina group Opo Jeje for a time. She sang in it, but if necessary, she played the kot'-kawina (the improvising kawina drum). The lineup was made up of conga, two kot'-kawinas, kwakwa-bangi, and guitar (often exchanged for the banjo or four-stringed kwatro). The kwatro-player Frepina (Alex Nimmermeer) began his career in Gomes's band. In Opo Jeje, Gomes introduced electric instruments into kawina music. She got her first amplifier from the creole NPS party during elections in the 1960s. At that time, she was Paramaribo's greatest music star. Other groups followed her lead and introduced the electric guitar into their own groups.

Gomes regards present-day kaseko to be a form of kawina, played on the skratyi with vulgar lyrics. There are not many good drummers who play kaseko, someone like Bandoela who played for the Kaseko Masters. According to Gomes, Vijent is also a good drummer. The only good brass player in her estimation was Jopie Vrieze, who knew all the Wintis and knew how he had to blow.

All her life Fransje Gomes was a musical jack-of-all-trades, but she was versatile not only in the area of music. She built her own house herself, and from 4:00 a.m. she can still be found selling newspapers and lottery tickets in Maagdenstraat (Virgin Street) in Paramaribo. Besides that, she sells Winti-attire and lays out bodies.

She has received several lucrative offers to play again in a band but has rejected them. She no longer feels like getting behind a drum and hearing some long lanky boy yell out *Fransje Gomes naki a sani* (Fransje Gomes, beat the drum). Gomes can both still improvise well (koti) as well as cuss (kosi). And a guy like that would get chewed out, even if they would have to stop playing the music: kosi instead of koti!

Breaks

Instruments like congas can be exchanged for bongos. However, the big bass drum cannot be replaced by any other instrument. In modern-day Surinamese music it has the function of the "master drum "in traditional African ensembles. To stay in the world of Surinamese music, the skratyi again has the role of the kot'-kawina, the improvising drums in kawina music. In Winti music the skratyi fulfills the role of the two- to three-meter *agida*, the classic drum made from a single tree trunk. The bass drum is currently capable of accenting the breaks. Congas in Surinamese music have almost always had an accompanying role and were only allowed to improvise occasionally. In contrast the skratyi is constantly busy playing syncopations, continually interacting with the other instruments.

Since 1980 the influence of the skratyi has only increased. In kaseko the break on the skratyi has evolved even further, certainly compared to the bigi poku. Nowadays, every break is heralded by the skratyi. Moreover, those breaks have been extended from two measures into long phrases that sometimes go on for twelve measures.

That does not mean to say that this new development is always judged to be advantageous. At present, not many musicians are inspired to create new compositions; they often play new arrangements of existing traditional music. For instance, practically all kaseko groups play traditional pieces from the Winti cult. In the Netherlands only Sporkslede and Vijent master the basic beats of bigi poku. The rest of the skratyi drummers only play kawina or Winti or a mix of styles. Saxophonist Jopie Vrieze: "It used to be stratji players could strike the drum, now it's more like bashing it." And, according to Stan Lokhin, who for years had been one of those responsible for the current face of kaseko, not much is happening at the moment in Surinamese music. "After the first two measures, nothing but clichés follow. Now they use practically all the same chords in salsa, but they are being turned around. There are also key changes."

AFRO-DOMINATION

Saxophone player George Schermacher once said: "Suriname, that's Africa." The ever-present Afro-culture pervades all areas of life in Suriname, including music. That is why it is striking to see that practically nothing has come of the Amerindian sambura drum in kaseko. The static rhythm of the sambura is even absent from kawina. Nor has East Indian, or Hindustani music as it is referred to in Suriname, had much if any influence on kaseko. In Winti songs in which Amerindian and Hindustani gods are called down, the rhythm is always strictly African, without Amerindian or Hindustani characteristics. Conversely, kaseko has influenced Hindi-pop, the popular music of the Hindustani.

African culture also dominates on Trinidad, which calypso clearly demonstrates. It is strange that in Trinidad and Suriname, no "fusion music" has arisen, like it has for instance in Kenya with Indian film music and Swahili music.

Compared to the Netherlands Antilles, the Netherlands' influence on Suriname is much less. One reason might be the nearby presence of jungle. This has always allowed for an African component in the Surinamese community. Apart from the minimal European influence, inspiration for dance music only came from such other Afro-American genres as calypso, jazz, samba, beguine, and Cuban music. Herein kaseko does not deviate all that much from such other African music styles such as highlife from Ghana and soukous from Zaire, which in turn have been influenced by calypso, samba, and Cuban music. Within Afro-music in Africa itself and in the diaspora after slavery there has been intensive interaction of styles and ideas in which influences outside the realm of Afro-communities have not played a significant role.

7

SURINAMESE JAZZ IN THE NETHERLANDS

- Marcel Weltak -

Surinamese jazz musicians began playing jazz in the Netherlands earlier than they did in Suriname, and jazz has different backgrounds in both countries as well. This chapter deals with the rise of Surinamese jazz musicians in the Netherlands, followed by the origin of jazz in Suriname itself, and finally contemporary jazz by Surinamese musicians.

In 1933 both Duke Ellington and Louis Armstrong came to perform concerts in the Netherlands, followed by Cab Calloway a year later. "It cannot be a coincidence," wrote Herman "Doctor Jazz" Openneer later on, "that Surinamese jazz began in The Netherlands in 1935." The fee that people like Armstrong commanded for a performance—three thousand guilders—was much too high for many promoters in those days. Soon afterward, someone came up with the idea to offer Surinamers contracts and give them American names. From then on Theodoor Kantoor was known as Teddy Cotton, and Arthur Parisius became Kid Dynamite. The Dutch believed that all Blacks who played jazz were American. Rumor has it that there was a notice sent to Suriname: "Guys, come to Holland and bring your guitar and two drumsticks with you."

Before World War II, Surinamese musicians played pieces by Armstrong and Ellington, among others. Surinamese culture was virtually unknown in the Netherlands, but Surinamese musicians did not feel called upon to change the situation. As a matter of fact, most of them came to the Netherlands not to gain recognition as musicians; they were looking for a better way of life and landed as sailors or came as stowaways. Most of them got jobs as bouncers or waiters. When the gap in the music market opened up, they easily filled it.

Frits (Freddy) Blijd signed on January 3, 1928, to the steam ocean liner *Cottica* in Amsterdam harbor. He had not come on board in the same official, legal way. Three weeks earlier he had hidden himself as a stowaway among the crates of potatoes in the *Cottica*'s hold. In the Dutch daily newspaper *NRC Handelsbad* of January 7, 1989, Blijd recalls what happened: "I spent four days and nights squatting on my haunches, without food or anything to drink and was scared to death to leave my hiding place. Suddenly, I heard a voice in the dark: 'You're a stowaway and so are dying for a piece of bread and butter.' I was scared shitless. It quickly turned out whose voice it was, there were two other stowaways a couple of yards from me." Looking for food, the three of them were discovered and set to work scrubbing the deck. In one piece but considerably weakened, Blijd arrived in Amsterdam. Once there he immediately got involved in show business. "At the unemployment office they filled in my profession as 'colored,'" the then eighty-year-old Blijd tells. He gave himself the stage names Freddy Blijd and Rico Fernando and began a busy life as a drummer and tap dancer in nightclubs. "Work always just fell into my lap. One day I was standing in front of one of joints on the Reeperbahn in Hamburg when the owner comes storming outside. "Mensch, wir brauchen genau solch einen Neger wie du' [Man, we could really use a Negro like you]. I never had to audition."

One of the other stowaways was the then sixteen-year-old Arthur Parisius, later Kid Dynamite. He wanted to learn to become a professional baker in the Netherlands, but he too rolled into show business. He took music lessons and became a tenor sax player of world renown. His stage name Kid Dynamite was a guarantee for full houses, especially after war; he even played for a short while with his hero and master Coleman Hawkins. There is now a street named after him in Rotterdam.

1935 saw the formation of the first Surinamese jazz bands. In Nijmegen was "the Negro band led by Teddy Cotton," according to the Dutch magazine *Jazz Wereld* (Jazz World) in November 1935: "The playing was hot but rough here and there and the audience got goose bumps." These Negro bands also traveled abroad. Around the same time, another Surinamese orchestra led by Mike Hidalgo made recordings for Radio Sotens in Switzerland. Other members of the band were Lucien Hidalgo, Arthur Parisius, Gustaaf Kantoor, Arthur Pay, and Nic Rayer. Unfortunately, nothing has been saved from that broadcast.

THE FIRST SURINAMESE MUSICIANS IN THE NETHERLANDS

"It swung like hell," wrote the Dutch newspapers after his concerts. Before World War II, Lex van Spall was the most important Surinamese musician in the Netherlands. The jazz world considered him "a grandiose and great guitar player; one of the pioneers of Dutch jazz, maybe even the most important." The Dutch regarded Van Spall as one of their own and not Surinamese. Herman "Doctor Jazz" Openneer even called him "one of the fathers of Dutch jazz."

During his first radio recording in 1924, Van Spall could only be heard on guitar; the saxophone came later. The prewar critics clearly heard the influence of Ellington's alto saxophonist Johnny Hodges in his saxophone playing. Shortly after his first radio broadcast, he joined traveling American bands. In 1930 Van Spall played in Germany with the legendary New Orleans soprano saxophonist Sidney Bechet. Van Spall can be seen in Bechet's band in the 1934 movie *Einbrecher*. Whereas Coleman Hawkins was the father of the tenor sax, Sidney Bechet was more or less that of the soprano sax. It is interesting to note that Van Spall played soprano at the beginning of his career but switched to alto.

Jazz Wereld in January 1935 reviewed recordings Van Spall made with the American pianist Freddy Johnson: "Van Spall's swinging guitar playing can be heard in the rhythmic accompaniment. The other side of the record opens with two of the most beautiful solos we have ever heard: Lex van Spall opens the number with an alto solo, which gives a perfect picture of what this artist could do. He combines a gorgeous tone and tremendous sound volume with playing that marks the summit of expressivity and swing. This alone makes the records a precious possession."

Renowned Dutch jazz musicians such as Rita Reys, drummer Wessel Ilcken, and trumpeter Ado Broodboom got their start with Van Spall. He led his own jazz band for years. In November 1933 *Jazz Wereld* reviewed a performance by that "mysterious band" of sax player Lex van Spall, the Chocolate Kiddies. The band had a wide-ranging repertoire that included tangos and French Antillean beguines. A certain B.S. in *Jazz Wereld* advised the readers to listen to the Chocolate Kiddies, casually remarking on the resentment some people felt toward Black musicians: "From a musical point of view, the whiter or completely white elements in this ensemble will in the long run gain the most favor."

The Dutch police at the time were just as unfriendly toward Surinamese musicians. A 1936 report issued by the Amsterdam police commissioner Versteeg stated: "the performance of the band leader placed the audience in Artis Zoo. People are more able to appreciate the antic of the apes in such a palace for the animals. The performance of the anthropoid ape [gorilla, chimp] in the Negro Cat Club is a disgusting sight. Weaklings and young girls buckle under to these apes. The music they produce, if one can actually speak of music, is only fit to test the how much the eardrum can withstand."

At the time, Germany was forbidden territory for Blacks, and national socialist sentiments were also on the increase in the Netherlands. Nevertheless,
several clubs were opened in the 1930s where Black musicians could blow
their instruments. One of the first was the Negro Palace, which opened in
1936. The design and layout of the Negro Palace and other Black clubs was a
copy of American models; they exuded the atmosphere of clubs in New York,
New Orleans, or Chicago. There was also a swinging Black doorman who
showed customers to their seats. He had to tap dance and play guitar in the
breaks. Surinamers were regarded as Black Americans and were not allowed
to go out of character. Incidentally, most of the drummers retained their Surinamese last names, presumably because they did not play in the front line.
They nonetheless attracted attention, such as described in the March 1936
Jazz Wereld: "I already praised the drummer/guitarist Lou Holtuin last year."
    The Surinamese musician was a guitar player besides being a drummer.
Their playing was just as good—or bad—as the average Dutch player. The
Netherlands had only recently been exposed to jazz, as well as the "Surinamese Americans" who came to play. If Surinamers also played rumba, they
won hands down over every Dutch orchestra. Newspaper *Het Vaderland*
(The Fatherland) wrote in June 1937: "It is a pleasure to dance to the tones
produced by this good Negro band." That was written in response to a performance by trumpeter Teddy Cotton and his band in the Negro Melody
Club. In between Mike Hidalgo's "Negro dances," the audience could enjoy
the "Negro Service, Negro atmosphere and Negro Drinks, and dance to the
rhythm of the famous Negro orchestra."
    Surinamers did not always show solidarity toward one another. According
to Openneer, it is striking that in Dutch jazz, for example, there are not many
Surinamers of Javanese or East Indian descent who played any significant
role. The sole prominent musician from Suriname with an Asian background
was the drummer Arthur Pay. However, Pay had come from then British Guiana to Suriname. Before World War II, according to Openneer, Surinamers in
the Netherlands were almost always Portuguese or Jewish. "These mulattos
if they could help it, did not play with their colored fellow countrymen."
    Blacks had a hard time during the war. According to Bep Overweg, who
later married Kid Dynamite: "Blacks did not get ration books. Because of that
they always suffered from great hunger. Germans often rounded up Blacks
and mistreated them." Unlike the American musicians, the Surinamers were
not interned or sent to camps. They were, after all, Dutch citizens, with Dutch
passports and in many instances a Dutch name. Because of that, Surinamers
could go on blowing. Unfortunately, the NSB (National Socialist Movement
in the Netherlands) gradually got wind of the fact that, for instance, Gustaaf

Kantoor was a Dutch name on a Dutch passport but that its owner was Black and made music. Not that Black musicians were not allowed to make music according to their ordinances, just not Black, *entartete* (degenerate) music, which was exactly what Kantoor was playing.

The Kultuurkamer was the institution that determined which books, music, paintings, and the like were allowed to be made, showed, and sold, and by whom. In contrast to the Jews, Surinamers at first were able to become members. However, in 1943 the decision was taken that only Aryans were allowed, and the law was amended. "They are a great danger to public health, for women and for girls," according to the Dutch National Socialist Party (NSB) leader Anton Mussert, who personally had a hand in this matter. Even though he made a distinction between "good" and "bad" Surinamers, Mussert despised jazz—although his snitch, Mike Hidalgo, and his band were allowed by the Germans to keep playing on Nieuwendijk in Amsterdam. After the war Hidalgo made his way to the United States via Curaçao and Argentina. Someone who remained in the Kultuurkamer after 1943 was Max Woiski Sr., alias the musician José Barretto. He wanted to pass for white and to that end refused Blacks entry to his business La Cabana, in the Vijzelstraat in Amsterdam. This probably also led to Woiski's downfall. A Surinamer who no doubt had been refused entry wrote anonymously to the Kultuurkamer that Woiski "had renounced his race, consorts with Jews and caters to them, is a pimp and beats his wife." The story goes that, shortly after liberation and V-Day, Woiski was beat up by a group of Surinamers. After the war Max Woiski continued to play the cheerful sounds of Latin jazz in his club La Cabana. This is what the Dutch preferred hearing the most. It was not very interesting, with such lyrics as "So the chicken follow the hen, so the women follow the men." His big hit was *B.B. met R., dat is bruine bonen met rijst* (B.B. with R, that's brown beans with rice). But he did make the genre considerably more popular. In the 1960s he ran his own night club on Mallorca, where he surrounded himself with excellent musicians.

In 1937 a record of guitar solos was recorded; the musician's name was Lex Vervuurt. He had arrived three years earlier in the Netherlands to get his secondary school teaching certificate in drawing. Vervuurt had already taken classical guitar lessons in Suriname. Once people in the Netherlands discovered his talents, precious little time was left for his studies: the engagements poured in. After a short while he started playing with the Plantation Orchestra of the Surinamese trumpeter Walter Rens in the anti-fascist stage play *De Beul* (The Executioner).

Vervuurt's playing clearly was influenced by the Belgian gypsy guitarist Django Reinhardt and the American Eddy Lang. The Dutch press steadily became better acquainted with him. Theo Konijn in *Jazz Wereld* wrote of Vervuurt: "Rhythm like an oiled chronometer. Vibrations like Hawkins and the mastery of a Van Den Negus. Trumpet playing on the guitar. Piano, harp, drums, string bass on guitar . . . keep an eye on this young man, or rather an ear."

Vervuurt got a gig in the Smit brothers' accordion trio, who at the time accompanied Dutch singer Rita Corita (Endrika Sturm), among others. With them Vervuurt played popular Dutch tunes. The Smit Trio brought Vervuurt to VARA radio.

He then got a steady job with the radio broadcasting orchestra and subsequently worked freelance for practically all the radio ensembles. Before the war he had a stint with Lex van Spall's orchestra. He also made various recordings with the Jewish group Secco's Gitanos and the German American singer Greta Keller. The leader of Secco's Gitanos sought him out after reading an article in *Jazz Wereld* referring to him as a strong soloist. The group fell apart during the war because of the persecution of Jews. According to Vervuurt, he was able to work throughout the war because he was a mulatto. After the war he formed a band in Suriname with Anton Budel (saxophone), Richard Gaddum (trumpet), and Chalut (violin), a Frenchman who had fled from Cayenne, French Guiana. A year later he was gigging again in Hilversum. With the Promenade Orchestra, Vervuurt even played opera in Germany and Belgium.

In the 1950s the Dutch Wereldomroep (World Service) wanted to begin broadcasting Surinamese and Netherlands Antilles programs. (Suriname and the Netherlands Antilles had become Rijksdeel overseas territories.) They hired Eddy Vervuurt for the music. He and his group played such Surinamese folksongs as "16 April." Except for Eddie Buth on bongos, the rest of the musicians were Dutch. Yet Vervuurt did not have a high opinion of Dutch musicians: "Dutch people have no idea about the genre [Latin and jazz] and they will never learn it." So why didn't Vervuurt use Surinamese musicians? "They couldn't read music and I couldn't primitively rehearse." Later on, Vervuurt led the Zapakaras with Johnny de Miranda as vocalist. He played for NCRV radio with this band, while Woiski played pieces by Vervuurt with Van Spall for AVRO radio. After that Vervuurt played with the AVRO orchestra, accompanying Josephine Baker and Maurice Chevalier. Playing trumpet with Vervuurt at the time was René van der Lande, who had big bands in both Paris and Brussels.

Vervuurt preferred not to work with jazz groups because "playing jazz meant starving." One of the many people who played with Vervuurt was not bothered by that: Kid Dynamite.

KID DYNAMITE

Many people regarded Arthur Lodewijk Parisius, alias Kid Dynamite, to have been born a jazz musician. According to Vervuurt, "he never knew anything else." Trumpet player Nedley Elstak called Kid Dynamite a world-class tenor sax player. "It was incredible to hear Kid play the terribly difficult chords of Coleman Hawkins's *Body and Soul*," says Elstak. Kid Dynamite appealed to Dutch taste at the time because of his beautiful tone and the way he blew his tenor sax like Coleman Hawkins. He was serious, he also played Dutch music, he studied, and especially did not play "ape music," which the Dutch often called the explorations of Surinamese jazz musicians at the time.

Arthur Parisius arrived in Amsterdam in 1928 as a sixteen-year-old stow-away. Even though he wanted to become a baker, he took music lessons, which was not a bad move because of the demand for Black musicians at the time. Yet at first Parisius worked as a fire-eater and dancer for a Dutch circus and took the stage name Kid Dynamite. He was also a tap dancer for a while later, together with Freddy Blijd and bandleader Teddy Cotton, in a revue in Rotterdam. During his stint in the circus he got a flute from Kantoor, but shortly afterward he bought a clarinet to play on it while he was dancing.

Parisius had little difficulty learning to play new instruments. Fellow stow-away Freddy Blijd tells this tale: "One night, Teddy Cotton found a C-clarinet in a closet in some fleabag hotel. The one who gets to keep it is the one who can first get a sound out of the instrument. The clarinet ended up with Kid."

It was not until 1935 that his name circulated in music circles. That year he formed a quartet with Arthur Pay (drums), Jules Zegelaar (bass), and Max Pohla (piano), which he debuted in the Astoria Theater in Groningen. *Jazz Wereld* first mentioned him in 1936.

When tenor saxophonist Coleman Hawkins came to the Netherlands in 1935, Kid was hugely impressed. He switched from alto sax and clarinet to tenor sax, the instrument that would make him famous. In a literal sense, Hawkins was practically his musical father. They practiced together and played together in Negro Palace on Amsterdam's Rembrandtplein. Years later Kid would again create a furor with another famous American, Freddy Johnson. Once when a trembling Kid was sitting next to Hawkins on stage and was too scared to play, Hawkins said: "Come on, you've got what it takes." At the time Hawkins called Kid "an excellent saxophone player, really great." In 1937 Kid played dance music with Mike Hidalgo and Jules Zegelaar at Hirsch's on Amsterdam's Leidseplein: three pieces with his band, after which a white ensemble also played three pieces. Later, Kid made arrangements for Freddy Blijd's band. Blijd came up with the ideas and told Kid how he wanted the piece. Kid then worked it out and got the copyright to it. In 1938 Kid joined Lou van Ree's dance band the Collegians. It included Lucien Hidalgo on trumpet and Gustaaf "Eddy Cotton" Kantoor on bass. Another Surinamese band member was Ann Kony, who would later play in Kid's own Dynamite Band. The Collegian's pianist was Charley Nederpelt, who was to become VARA radio's "Mister VARA dance orchestra." Thanks to the arrival of Kid, who was quickly becoming a fixture in the Dutch jazz world, the band's musical prowess improved tremendously.

Just before the war Kid recorded the "Paramaribo Blues" and "Honolulu Blues," together with the Saramacca Band of Teddy Cotton, Arthur, and Walter Rens. The war meant a forced interruption. At first he tried to keep playing jazz in the Amsterdam club the Wagenwiel (Wagon Wheel), and was even able to play in a band with the accordion player Johnny Meyer on the Nieuwendijk. Whenever the Germans showed up, the band switched to German music and Kid disappeared into the crowd. Despite the war, he could not sit still; when he could no longer play, he studied clarinet at the conservatory. Kid was probably the only one of the prewar generation of Surinamese musicians who regularly took refresher courses and practiced. That enabled him to resume playing immediately after the war ended. He was offered a teaching job but he did not feel like it, and began playing Latin jazz and bebop; his playing always remained contemporary and modern. Until that point, he had scarcely had any invitations from Dutch bands, but after the war he could join Boy Edgar's Grasshoppers. In 1946 he went on a yearlong tour with the Grasshoppers through Spain and Switzerland. In this band he played alongside such Surinamese musicians as Ado Broodboom and Lou Holtuin. After his stint with the Grasshoppers, he set up the first Kid Dynamite Band, which included Teddy Cotton on trumpet and Freddy Blijd on drums. He began playing more Surinamese music, with Surinamese musicians. Clarinetist Edgar Gaddum was especially responsible for the development of Surinamese music in the band. Gaddum was also a musician when he left Suriname; besides clarinet he also played piano and soprano and tenor sax. Kid himself also composed and arranged several Surinamese songs. Partly due to the growing popularity in Germany of the "der schwarze" Kid and his band, several numbers appeared on records. Even the old Woiski began singing songs by Kid Dynamite. According to Stan Lokhin, this heralded the breakthrough of the Surinamese song. Kid also contributed in other ways to the dissemination of Surinamese music. At one competition in the 1950s he won first, second, and third prizes and an honorable mention. The tune submitted would become the signature tune for AVRO radio in Suriname.

The 1960s brought television appearances for Kid. He made the singles "Mij duik met mijn hoofd in mijn vaatje met rum" (I Dive Headfirst into My Barrel of Rum) and "Marian." It is not clear when he wrote such Surinamese numbers as "Jerusalem" and "Winti Boto."

Kid Dynamite was taken very seriously in the small jazz world. Herman Openneer: "There were no innuendos to him being Black or Surinamese, and therefore stupid." But not everyone loved his style. There were discussions about it in *Jazz Wereld* by 1937. Opinions differed outside that magazine as well. Fred van Westerborg: "a great tone, but extremely vulgar style, laying down one riff after another. . . ." Trombonist Charles Gelauff, on the other hand, called him "the best Surinamese musician I ever knew. The same kind of deep tone his example Hawkins had." Theo Konijn wrote that "his way of shifting accents even in a straight opening chorus and of creating a dreamy atmosphere in a sun tone-chorus for clarinet, without getting sentimental, attests to personality and sound musical taste." The later Bird winner Benny Carter, who Kid had taken lessons from, said: "I like that guy. What's more, I like his way of playing, he's getting better every day." From the mouth of Coleman Hawkins himself: "Tell the guys, this boy's all right." Trumpet player Nedley Elstak regarded Parisius to mean just as much in his day and age as John Coltrane did in his: "Kid's improvisations were peerless, top notch. In those days there were not many people who got what they were hearing." In Elstak's view Parisius was the premier Latin jazz sax player, "and not Sonny Rollins."

There are naturally many stories about such a legendary musician, for instance, about Kid's mouthpiece, which he himself trimmed with the help of a bench vice. He also worked on his reed while playing to get a fuller sound. The story goes that tenor saxophonist Stan Getz was playing in the Netherlands in the Scheherazade. One night Getz went to the Casablanca nightclub, where Parisius was playing to full houses. The American wanted to play Kid's instrument no matter what. But because of Kid's sharpening, the blowing opening in the reed had become quite large; and as such it took quite a lot of air to get the reed to vibrate. Stan Getz could not get a sound out of it!

Another anecdote is about Kid's popularity in Germany. While playing there in Carol Pagini's orchestra, he proudly displayed the first *Faribige* (colored guy) in Germany who could read music. Parisius could read *vom Blatt* (from sheet music) and not just play by ear (*nur vom Kopf*), which the Germans claimed Blacks always did.

At the beginning of the 1960s people stood in long lines at the Casablanca to see him play. However, jazz could not be played all night in the Casablanca; half of the time it was jazz, the other Latin. If the jazz went on too long, the owner Suykerbuyck stomped on the floor: "Dance music, if you please!"

Among other things, Kid played such standards as "Laura," "Stardust," and "I Can't Get Started." The band's lineup varied greatly but usually had a female vocalist. Annie Sterman, Ann Kony, and Millie Scott were people who sang with Kid. All kinds of bandleaders wanted to play with Parisius as well. The Kid Dynamite Band had such names in its ranks as Eugene and Mike Hidalgo, Jules Zegelaar, Teddy Cotton, Freddy Blijd, Lou Drent, and Boy Edgar. Parisius preferred playing with friends, even if they didn't have much talent. And Kid did not have a high opinion of many musicians. Hidalgo had learned to play trumpet from the Americans and Kid allowed him to play trombone for him. He also admired clarinet player Eddie Gaddum and bassist Jules Zegelaar. The latter's notes may not have always been correct, but his playing and swing must have been excellent.

The thing Kid was looking for in the last years of his life was Surinamese music with a jazz underpinning: he had clear ideas about the way in which jazz and Latin ought to be played. The mix of jazz and Surinamese music Kid Dynamite sought is nowadays called Paramaribop. He did not live to see the day: he died in 1963. He was on his way to a gig with Freddy Blijd in Germany when their car was involved in an accident. Kid died in a hospital in Hamburg.

KID'S ORCHESTRA AND OTHER POSTWAR MUSICIANS

Kid's regular drummer was Lou "Kabouya" Holtuin. He also played in various Dutch bands and in a supporting act before the Dizzy Gillespie concert in Amsterdam's Concertgebouw. Holtuin, "the Dutch Negro," as he was referred to in *Jazz Wereld*, "had a solid rhythm and gorgeous breaks." Holtuin's name came up quite often; based on the standards of the day, Holtuin was a maestro. According to another former member of Kid's quintet, trumpeter Ado "Moreno' Broodboom, Holtuin was not such a great drummer, "but there weren't many good drummers." It was hard, in Broodboom's view, to work together with the introverted great man Kid.

Kid's band included another prominent member, Freddy Blijd, who at the start of this chapter was Kid's fellow stowaway. "Whereas Holtuin was the band's technical expert, as it were, Blijd was the most creative at selling the music," according to Elstak. In Germany Kid Dynamite was known as *der Musiker* (the musician), but Blijd *machte Kasse* (made money) for the venue owner. Blijd was a successful bandleader who always lived up to his agreements, even if he had to charter an airplane. Partly because of that, Blijd was known as a bandleader from Scandinavia to Turkey. He played bongos in the Copenhagen Symphony Orchestra. Freddy Blijd's band accompanied

Eartha Kitt in Istanbul. On the way to Teheran and Baghdad, the orchestra disbanded. Blijd traveled to Beirut and Alexandria and sang in hotels. Beside his musical activities, in 1945 he became a journalist for the magazine *Nieuw Suriname*; later he was accredited by the League of Nations and subsequently United Nations in Paris, but in 1950 he left journalism and worked for a time with the old Max Woiski. His playing days with Kid ended abruptly in 1963 when Kid died in a car accident, which Blijd survived. He stopped playing two years later.

Blijd had always maintained that but Johnny Gerold was the best Surinamese drummer, not Lou Holtuin; but Gerold worked most of the time in Germany and Switzerland. Another drummer whose name regularly appears is Johnny Stoffels. However, Stoffels soon moved to Brussels, where he found sufficient work with his brother Eddie and opened a jazz club.

Another legendary band member was Teddy Cotton. Elstak, himself a creditable trumpet player, had never heard anyone with a volume as great as Cotton: "When he played on Nieuwmarkt you could even hear him all the way from Central Station. His playing had something of Armstrong in it, but more modern. Cotton had a beautiful tone; his notes sounded full in the upper register." Trumpeter, journalist, and choir conductor Stan Lokhin also heard Cotton's full sound: "No one else in Holland could play as purely in the upper register as Teddy Cotton." Cotton, real name Theodoor Kantoor, was a flamboyant personality. He had his own band but like many bandleaders played in Kid Dynamite's band. Cotton often played the introduction himself to his own vocals. Most of his own pieces were blues or had a rhythmic progression, but he did not shirk from ballads. Cotton could not read music and that is why he did not play in Dutch groups, which was often desired.

Ado Broodboom considered Cotton to be a showman first and foremost. Whenever he played a high C, the show around it made it seem like it was played an octave higher than it really was. Musicians who played with him supposedly went home in tears because Cotton always stole the show. Teddy Cotton especially imitated Louis Armstrong. There's a story that says that after his show in Berlin, Armstrong went to a jazz club where Cotton was playing. He stopped dead in his tracks: for a second, the great trumpeter thought it was he himself who was standing there playing.

One of the few Surinamese musicians to make recordings in the 1950s was Ado "Moreno" Broodboom, who was born in the Netherlands. In those days, the average pressing of a jazz record was three hundred units, which took about a week of work in the studio. Seeing as how you made fifteen guilders for that, and could make as much as two hundred for a playing a live gig in Hamburg at the time, musicians like Kid Dynamite were not too keen to do studio work even if they were offered it. That is the reason that precious little has been saved of the music made by a whole generation of Surinamese musicians from the 1940s and 1950s.

Following Broodboom's conservatory studies with Marius Jonst, the war broke out. In contrast to Kid, Broodboom tried his fortune outside the capital, where there were fewer Germans. Later on in Casablanca, Kid and Broodboom had such a feel for playing together they often began by improvising in what would now be called free jazz. In Casablanca, Broodboom played trumpet, bugle, and sometimes French horn, because that sounded great with the saxophone in the Latin pieces the owner demanded be played as dance music alongside jazz.

The arrangements in Casablanca consisted of short themes, on which everyone improvised. Later on Broodboom played in Hilversum with Steve Boston and Raul Burnett; he immediately heard they were better than what he was used to in the Netherlands. Broodboom also played with Dizzy Gillespie. Dizzy was no doubt better technically, but just like Miles Davis, Broodboom could play the blue notes (between half and whole notes) more beautifully. When work in the Netherlands slackened, he formed a group with American saxophonist Sandy Mosse and Dutch drummer Herman Schoonderwalt that toured through Sweden.

Broodboom won the Dutch Rhythm Poll, and the prize money and fame enabled him to release some singles. He also recorded an LP with flute player Herbie Mann and Lex Vervuurt on guitar. He became a studio musician for radio and television. He had three live broadcasts a week with well-known Dutch group the Ramblers and later with VARA's dance orchestra. Broodboom knew enough about music theory to become a star soloist in the Ramblers.

Together with Nedley Elstak, Broodboom also played with Boy Edgar. Elstak (who died in 1989) was searching for his own style at the outset of the 1950s. He had a quite refined way of playing. The then twenty-year-old Kid Dynamite stimulated Elstak enormously. "Take me with you," was Kid's favorite turn of phrase whenever Elstak was playing. Another source of inspiration was Dutch saxophonist Toon van Vliet, who was just as crazy about Coltrane as Kid was.

Elstak started playing bebop right after the war. One of the first pieces he played was Dizzy Gillespie's "A Night in Tunisia." During the radio broadcast—from which Elstak learned to play the piece—the middle section was lost due to a technical difficulty. Elstak then wrote a new middle section himself.

Nedley Elstak is a multifaceted musician. He studied violin for eight years, taught others to become pianists, and in so doing was one himself. As a

composer he was deeply impressed by the twelve-tone system; his compositions were always deeply personal, and he felt that he did not have to listen to
Surinamese music to find themes for new compositions. In Elstak's view, his
music was already Surinamese by virtue of his origin: "Maybe that's why my
music can never be placed in Holland." With a couple of other Surinamers,
Elstak started a club on Amsterdam's Thorbeckeplein called the Palace. Latin
was played there six days a week; on the seventh Elstak played jazz. On
the day that the Palace went bankrupt in 1955, Perez Prado had a hit in the
Netherlands; it was only after that that Latin jazz became really popular. After
closing his club, Elstak again began working regularly with Kid Dynamite,
with whom he had already done some sessions. He also played briefly with
saxophonist John Byas. In 1983 Nedley Elstak was awarded the Boy Edgar
Prize (for best Dutch jazz musician).

In Paris, René van der Lande led the first Surinamese big band in Europe.
In the 1960s he switched from playing jazz to kaseko. He played in a brass
band on Curaçao and later in Aruba in Speen's band. Speen, aka Humphry
Linscheer, led a band of five saxophones, four trumpets, two trombones, bass,
guitar, and drums. According to Van der Lande, Speen's Band had the same
qualities as the Ramblers and the Skymasters.

Stan Lokhin regarded Van der Lande to be a virtuoso trumpet player, better than Broodboom: "He improvised smoothly and played the high noted
impeccably." Moreover, Van der Lande was an excellent arranger who was
just as good at playing bass, piano, and guitar. He played pieces by Harry
James with his big bands in Paris and Brussels all the way to the Middle East.

CRISIS IN DUTCH JAZZ

The lack of theoretical background, which Vervuurt had pointed out, began
to become a disadvantage for Surinamese musicians in the 1950s: they started
losing their places in jazz. Just like the Dutch, they had to start learning
chords to play ballads. There was another chord in every beat of a ballad; a
good sense of rhythm would not do one much good here. You could play
kaseko with two chords, but not Charlie Parker. But then practically the
entire Dutch jazz world itself collapsed in the 1960s. That was due mainly
to the advent of rock and roll—the Beatles and the Rolling Stones. Lou
van Rees's concert series in the Concertgebouw ceased to exist. Many jazz
clubs disappeared, which affected Dutch and Surinamese musicians alike. It
was not until 1974 that the Bimhuis (Union for Improvising Musicians) was
founded and festivals started springing into life.

8

JAZZ IN SURINAME

- Marcel Weltak -

Surinamers made good jazz not only in the Netherlands. There was an enormous influx of jazz in Suriname itself, especially in the decades after World War II. Jazz and swing got their niche alongside other, more traditional native music and European classical and light entertainment music. Many Surinamers were inspired by jazz from the United States. A few of them founded their own jazz bands. Jazz records came into the country via the American soldiers who were stationed in Suriname "to protect the bauxite industry." Musicians in Paramaribo first heard and saw the North American orchestras in the movie houses. For instance, seeing a moving picture with Perez Prado and his band turned Surinamese percussionist Steve Boston into a fervent timbales player. At the time, the timbales were still called "kettle-drums." The leader of the Surinamese dance band Swingmasters—himself a member of the military—lent Boston a couple of military kettles, which he put drumheads on himself. To spread American culture, the US embassy in Suriname in the 1960s organized a series of concerts in Paramaribo. A wide variety of artists such as Elvin Jones, Charlie Byrd, and big bands from the University of Michigan and Ohio State University added Suriname to their touring dates. These performances were partly responsible for a brief flourishing of jazz in Suriname.

THE BIG NAMES: SCHERMACHER AND BAAS ADRIAAN

One of the most important names in the Surinamese jazz world was undoubtedly George Schermacher, a man we already came across in the chapter on bigi poku. At the time of this writing, this tenor saxophonist is in his eighties, and people still misspell his name "Scheermaker" and other variations. Yet few people confuse his music with that of others. The slight, quavering sound full of ornamentation singles him out among many and is readily recognizable.

Schermacher began playing on a small tin flute. Later he made his own flute out of a bicycle pump by sawing off the upper and low ends and drilling holes in it. A few years later a German living in Suriname bought this Surinamer of German descent a transverse flute made out of walnut, with six valves. This was how Schermacher progressed. After a while he got himself a clarinet, and still later he discovered the now rare C-melody: a saxophone in between tenor and alto. After mastering this instrument, he switched to the tenor saxophone. "I've become as conversant with it as the daily bread I eat," according to Schermacher. He is the man responsible for making tenor sax gain notoriety in Suriname. Together with Eddy Snijder's father he founded the O.K. Orkest, with Richard Gaddum on trumpet. That was the first jazz orchestra in Suriname (in those days Surinamers called any music with a modern drum kit jazz). O.K.'s other members were Sporkslede (drums) and Maasdammer (bass). Ten years later, together with clarinetist George Budel, he started the Red Star band. Red Star was filled out with Topijn on drums, Layo "MacIntosh" Gilles on bass, and Akathon on banjo. Together they played Cab Calloway and Stan Kenton arrangements, alongside Surinamese music and rock and roll. Without Red Star, but accompanied by Rudolf Adamson on piano, Budel played jazz on Bronsplein in Paramaribo, swing and ragtime.

Schermacher, like so many others, began with real jazz after seeing American music movies. He saw his favorites on the silver screen: Johnny Hodges, Cab Calloway, Coleman Hawkins, and Ben Webster. Schermacher played the first records of Sonny Rollins by ear. He also listened to records in the store, to then play them at home. At first he notated the music with the help of chord diagrams, then reconstructed it at home from memory. He then gave his musicians instructions on how to accompany his lush vibrato. It was not until 1981 that he learned to read music in the Netherlands.

He recorded his first record in Suriname and had it pressed in the United States. After a rumor that the record had become a hit there, plans were drawn up for a tour, but the trip fell through at the last minute.

Schermacher also played in other bands, such as that of trumpeter Baas Adriaan. He substituted improvisations for an extra portion of swing. "People want to dance to bigi poku. You shouldn't bother them with your ideas," in Schermacher's view. Nevertheless, he preferred jazz harmonies to Surinamese music: they gave him more room to improvise. Schermacher is still not modest, even after his arrival in the Netherlands. "Dynamite was no match for me," he says. "Kid had to blow much too hard to produce a good tone, since he trimmed his reeds so thickly. That is not what I call blowing the saxophone. The reeds have to already make a sound in your mouth and Kid could not vibrate in the throat. But there are not many who can do that," says Schermacher. "Most of them start swinging with their saxes or try it with their fingers. Teddy Cotton on trumpet was nice but compared to me jazz was in bad shape in the Netherlands."

One of the other pioneers of improvised music in Suriname was Baas Adriaan. He has already been dealt with as an important bigi poku musician, but he and his group played all sorts of new styles that had blown over from New Orleans. Seeing as how no recordings were made in Suriname in the 1930s, we do not know how his Dixieland and swing pieces sounded. Baas Adriaan is still shrouded in an aura of mystery. But what he played must have made an impression, since at the time not many Surinamers had ever heard such music.

ORCHESTRAS AND SOLOISTS

One band we know more about is the Bios Suriname Boys, founded by trumpeter Eddy Snijders. This big band was made up for the most part by musicians from the Militaire Kapel (Military Brass Band), which Snijders conducted for quite some time. Over the course of time the band had quite a few members, including the likes of Waldy Zuiverloon, Oldenstam and John Gietel on trumpet, John Hewitt on piano, Johnny de Miranda, Eddie de Koning, Bommel, Richard Gaddum, Carlo Jones, and MacDonald on saxophone, Capadose on guitar, and Layo Gilles (from Red Star) on bass. The Bios Suriname Boys only gave three concerts in 1951 and 1952. They mainly played stock arrangements from well-known orchestras and jazz musicians from the United States, such as Duke Ellington.

Another renowned jazz troupe were the Swingmasters, who played swing, Latin, and well-arranged calypsos. At first the arrangements were made from transcriptions from records. Only later were they able to get written scores from the United States. Leader/saxophonist Leo Knoppel was, like practically all the other musicians in Swingmasters, in military service.

Besides a few excellent jazz orchestras there were also a couple of piano players in Suriname who did not shy away from improvising. The first one was Loeti (Ludwig) Meye, a celebrated jazz pianist in the 1940s and first part of the 1950s in the Caribbean region and later in Europe. Meye was an all-around musician who mastered piano, saxophone, and guitar. He performed mainly in former British Guiana. Meye also played dance music.

His successor was John Hewitt, the best jazz pianist Suriname had known (according to stories). That which made Hewitt's playing distinct was his "Surinamese feeling" when performing jazz. He also played bigi poku in jazzy arrangements with lovely chord progressions. Jazz percussionist Steve Boston on John Hewitt: "You could hear traces of Nat King Cole, Errol Garner, and Ahmad Jamal in his playing. If Hewitt had gone on further, he would have rivalled Tommy Flanagan." Jazz critic Rudy Jong Loy did not discern any Garner influences in his playing. In Jong Loy's view, Hewitt had a turbulent character and therefore there were many unpredictable turns in his dynamic style of performance. The best Surinamese wind players, except George Schermacher, hailed from the western district of Nickerie, close to the border with Guyana: Tjen A Tak, Thompson, McBean. Mario Vasconcellos was the third important pianist in the turbulent 1950s. He gained that status because he was able to surround himself with good musicians. Layo "MacIntosh" Gilles from the renowned family of bass players was responsible for the "walking bass" lines in Vasconcellos's band, while Fatty Liew A Joe sang. Both musicians moved later to the Swingmasters and ended up in Hewitt's quartet. Another name in Vasconcellos's band was saxophonist Johnny de Miranda, who went on to play bass with Alberto Gemerts and in Woiski Sr.'s band was responsible for playing congas, small percussion, piano, and singing. Miranda also sang vocals in the Netherlands for the Zapakaras.

Another prominent pianist in Suriname was Felix Roach, originally from Trinidad. Roach played in the famous Torarica Hotel in Paramaribo in the 1960s. He also played regularly in the big band of Hein Duisker.

August Meye, according to both Jong Loy and Boston, was perhaps the best drummer and bongo player in the 1940s and 1950s. Meye played in all renowned bands in Suriname, including Swingmasters and later the one led by Mario Vasconcellos's (not to be confused with Lieve Hugo's) Happy Boys at a later date. According to Jong Loy, Meye was a real swing drummer.

Steve Boston, who we will deal with in the following chapter on contemporary jazz, was percussionist for Vasconcellos, among others. Already at a young age he played for the Piccadilly Boys on the Surinamese radio stations RAPAR and AVROS. He did that together with, Wim "Pancho" Chin A Loi, among others, who at the time was already an excellent Latin singer and who now lives in Sweden. According to Boston, he was one of the first professional musicians in Suriname. For most other musicians, playing in a band was work on the side in addition to their jobs in the army and Military Brass Band. Together with Hewitt, like Chano Pozo and Dizzy Gillespie in the United States, Boston tried to combine Latin with jazz. In 1962 Boston left Suriname for the Netherlands.

Another equally renowned percussionist was Franklin "Copy" Ardin, whose nickname was due to the fact that he was regarded as a copy of his great example, Art Blakey. His first band was Casino, and he subsequently went to swing with the Swingmasters. Ardin also formed a trio with Venlo on bass and Acampo on guitar, in which they played bebop at the beginning of the 1960s.

Suriname has never known any real full-time jazz groups. There have been good improvisers, but they didn't always play genuine jazz. An example of genuine jazz players were bassist Eddy Weltevreden and trumpeter Jo Dompig. Jazz critic Jong Loy considers them the stars of the nineteen fifties and sixties, because their playing went further than the musical conventions of the forties. For quite a few other players they gave the music new content.

Like other modern improvisers Haakon Nicasie—who played horn among other things—and pianist John Hewitt, Dompig and Weltevreden followed developments in New York. They played bop while others stayed behind playing swing. Jong Loy: "In terms of technique, no one could be compared to Weltevreden. Certainly, when his biggest rival, Layo 'MacIntosh' Gilles, had left the country in the 1960s."

According to Jong Loy, Dompig, who had come from the dance orchestra Don Pedro in the border town (with French Guiana) of Moengo, had something of Clifford Brown in his improvisations: "He blew the most difficult chords with the greatest ease."

Saxophonist and clarinetist Eddie de Koning (Swingmasters) could play well from sheet music but was not very good at improvising. Leo Knoppel was a good bandleader and a virtuoso sax player, but certainly no jazz musician. The multifaceted Eddy Snijders was also an excellent bandleader and trumpet player, as well as an inspiring teacher, but not in jazz. In contrast, such a man like Coutinho improvised easily on his own self-built four-string tenor guitar in the Swingmasters.

Jong Loy did not consider any of the Surinamese sax players to have been real jazz musicians. He considered Mac Donald from Orchestra Popular to be the best jazz saxophonist. The most gifted tuba player he no doubt considered to be McBean.

THE MOST RECENT DECADES

To celebrate the fifteenth anniversary of the Cultureel Centrum Suriname (CCS) (Suriname Cultural Center) at the beginning of the 1960s, Jong Loy organized the first jazz festival in Suriname. The festival had a beneficial effect on the jazz scene in Suriname. All sorts of groups started concentrating on jazz to prepare for this festival. Hein Duiker, former trumpet player in the Speens Band on Aruba, formed the Jazz Club Paramaribo together with the help of bassist Dick de Keizer, French horn player Haakon Nicasie, Humphrey Linscheer (aka Speen), and pianist John Hewitt. Duisker, with his tremulous tone, an epigone of Roy Eldridge, was as a rule, a man with good ideas who did not work them out very well. The big band has a jam session every Sunday afternoon at one of the member's homes, for a select audience. The orchestra disappeared with Hein Duisker's death in the early 1970s.

In the 1960s, jazz ran into considerable problems in Suriname. The main causes were a lack of money to form bands and a dire shortage of good teachers. Several musicians were given music lessons by Christian monks but not exactly in jazz.

Other teachers were bandmasters by profession, such as Eddy Snijders. And the CCS, set up for artistic education, did not win over many musicians to play jazz. As a requiem, in 1983 the Surinamese ministry of culture released a record on which old jazz musicians could be heard.

Nevertheless, several new incentives came to pass. That had to do with only schooled musicians, who were often looking for their own style of playing jazz in a Surinamese jacket, as it were. For instance, Herman Snijders (a relative to Eddy) set up a big band in 1987, which was supposed to breathe new life into the jazz scene. Snijders was able to make a link between North American music of the last three decades and Surinamese swing. In the Snijders Big Band, Surinamese melodies are given a new jazz form, while at the same time jazz in Suriname is provided with fresh new accents.

Another phenomenon of the 1980s was the sextet TMT, The Music Translators, founded in 1987 by the young trumpet player Iwan Van Hetten and saxophonist Kenneth Muringen. They experimented with a synthesis of Surinamese music and modern jazz. That was what Arthur "Kid Dynamite" Parisius was looking for, until his death in 1963. We will subsequently go more deeply into this Paramaribop, as it has become known in the Netherlands.

9

CONTEMPORARY SURINAMESE JAZZ

- Marcel Weltak -

In 1973, ten years after the death of Kid Dynamite, social worker and bass guitarist Vincent Henar began organizing jazz concerts in the club Kwakoe-Bijlmermeer. By Surinamese standards quite avant-garde music resounded among the tall blocks of apartment buildings. Surinamese jazz musicians had discovered the music of Charlie Parker and Miles Davis. And now ten years on, two groups, Surinam Music Ensemble (SME) and Fra Fra Sound, took over the torch from Kid Dynamite. They developed a new music form in which Afro-Surinamese, Caribbean, and Afro-American traditions all flowed together. These were the most important steps toward the creation of Paramaribop.

BETWEEN DYNAMITE AND PARAMARIBOP

There were many other Surinamese musicians in between Kid Dynamite and the Surinam Music Ensemble who committed themselves to making Surinamese jazz in the Netherlands. Nedley Elstak has already been mentioned. Another person was Zapata Jaw—stage name of Nelson Renfrum—who from 1958 had played jazz and Latin in several bands, at first on congas, but later also on drums. At the time of this writing he is accompanying the Surinamese poet Vernie February on Surinamese drums and Mandingo balafon.

Extremely important contributions were made percussionist Raul Burnett and Steve Boston. The latter had come to the Netherlands in 1962 and got several engagements with Max Woiski Sr. Boston and vocalist Chin "Pancho" A Loi, who he had also played with in Suriname, recorded an album in the Netherlands called *Different Cooking*, together with the legendary bassist Chapottin and a band led by Bebo Valdez. On that LP Valdez and Boston were looking points of contact between Surinamese and Cuban music. Later on Boston and Chin A Loi came in contact with the Cuban band Latinos, with whom they traveled to Scandinavia. Things went so well there he could have stayed for the rest of his life. But, yearning for his Surinamese friends, he returned to the Netherlands and started Combo Latino with Chin A Loi, Raul Burnett (congas), Johan Oostwold (guitar), and Alwin Coutinho (piano). The band played in the Casablanca club, Kid Dynamite's old haunt. Burnett and Boston then switched to Max Woiski Jr.'s band. Chin A Loi returned to Scandinavia and lives in Sweden. After business problems with Woiski Jr., Boston, Burnett, Groenberg, Jacobs, and Albert left his band at the end of the 1960s and founded Ritmo Natural.

Steve Boston traveled throughout Europe, giving concerts as far afield as Italy and Spain. Boston played with both older musicians in Suriname and the Netherlands, such as pianist Eddie Renata and the multitalented René van der Lande, as well as the new generation in the Netherlands. In so doing, he formed a natural transition to modern Surinamese jazz. For Boston, Kid Dynamite's regular drummer, Lou "Kabouya" Holtuin was both a gorgeous showman and a gifted drummer. Together with Alberto Gemerts and George Schermacher, Boston worked for the Dutch world service radio for years.

Boston played jazz with group Sut Eye in Germany. He also performed in an all-star band the Clark Terry Big Band, at the Montreux Jazz Festival. Nevertheless, Boston is not really a jazz musician. Jazz was part of his musical education, but he predominately played Latin. In Boston's opinion, after the death of Kid Dynamite jazz did not amount to much in the Netherlands at the outset of the 1970s. He found Kid so special because he had successfully adapted Surinamese music to European styles. "In harmonic terms Surinamers in the Netherlands in the 1950s and 1960s were further than the Surinamers at home," according to Boston. Accordingly, he never played Surinamese music. For him the only thing that existed were Cuban-style arrangements, and he stuck to them. "Percussionist don't have to be good note readers. They must be able to count measures and make the music swing," is one of Boston's most famous quotes.

Another important figure was guitarist Max Woiski Jr., who in the 1960s was successfully able to avoid being overshadowed by his father. He moved his Amsterdam club La Tropicana from the Utrechtsestraat to the Leidsedwarsstraat. Two veteran percussionists were already playing in his band, Burnett on congas and Boston on timbales. Other musicians in his band were the white Dutchmen Jan Jacobs (bass) and Ronald Langestraaten (piano) and the Surinamese singer/percussionist Johan "Groentjie" Groenberg. The latter was originally a trumpet player and began playing percussion for the first time at La Tropicana. Around 1970 Woiski could be heard every week on radio and television. His band played Dominican merengues, Colombian cumbias, and Brazilian music, but "never Surinamese music," according to band member Jan Jacobs. This Dutch bassist had only heard Surinamese musicians in the mid-1970s at jam sessions held by drummer Eddy Veldman. According to Jacob, Woiski Jr.'s music was harmonically simple but rhythmically rather complex. "There was always Surinamese rhythm after all, even when we played Cuban genres." But Cuban music has a rhythm altogether different from Woiski Jr.'s hits "Rijst met kouseband" (Rice with Long Beans) and "Je bent nog niet gelukkig met een mooie vrouw" (You're Still Not Happy with a Beautiful Wife). Just like many Surinamese songs, Cuban guarachas contain lots of triplets, but the syncopations occur at different places. The Surinamers in Woiski's band instinctively felt it, but for Dutchmen like Jacobs it was a question of understanding it.

Woiski Jr. played practically everything as merengue, two notes to every measure. When Boston, Burnett, and Groenberg played with him, the band also played Cuban guaguancos and guarachas. Groenberg took over singing from Woiski Jr. Burnett sang the Brazilian pieces. All in all, Woiski Jr.'s music, not always played to perfection, was great to dance to. That was the most important difference with a band such as Lex Vervuurt's Zapakara. Vervuurt availed himself of schooled musicians who were unable to give their music a South American flavor.

In general, Surinamese bands played a great deal of Latin until the end of the 1970s. Until then, Latin was synonymous with Surinamese music to many Dutch people; after all, it all came from the same continent, South America. But what Surinamese musicians (and Max Woiski Jr.) were busy with was a fusion of jazz, Latin, and traditional Surinamese styles. With that they hoped to reach a new, original style of music. A couple of years later, funk and avant-garde jazz were added to the mix. The music of such bands as those of Woiski Jr. is now known as fusion music: an attempt to fuse more contemporary styles with traditional Afro-music. Groups often employed both modern as well as traditional Surinamese instruments and interpreted the music from a Surinamese angle. Singer Humphrey Campbell on kaseko and fusion music: "Theoretically the fusion between kaseko with jazz, for instance, is easy: kaseko rhythms and melodies with jazz harmonies. Jazz progressions, five note chords with lots of alterations and regular solos turned the music into jazz."

HANS DULFER AND THE PERIKELS

Ritmo Natural, Max Woiski Jr.'s former rhythm section (including Steve Boston), offered their services to Dutch saxophonist Hans Dulfer after their conflict with Woiski. With him the group made a number of LPs: *Morning After, Candy Clouds,* and *El Saxofon.* Under Dulfer's leadership, at the Paradiso in Amsterdam the band accompanied such American jazz musicians as Don Byas, Ben Webster, and Philly Joe Jones. Ritmo Natural were the accompanying band who during concerts always played ruthlessly. No soloist in the Netherlands could get around them.

In the 1960s Hans Dulfer was one of the first Dutchmen to engage Surinamers. The concerts he organized at the Paradiso were important both to the Surinamese and Dutch jazz worlds. Some Surinamese musicians feel that Dulfer used others, but it was Dulfer who introduced Surinamese musicians to the modern jazz scene. Without this saxophonist, presumably little would have come of the new generation of Surinamese musicians.

Dulfer quickly renamed Ritmo Natural the Perikels (Perils). He later dubbed the funk band Solat with the same name. Because of Dulfer's participation, quite a few Dutch people were willing to go and see the Perikels gigs. The musicians had such energy and originality they often amazed the audience with their music, but the Dutch clearly regarded the Perikels as a party band.

There was frequent variation in the Perikels lineup. Sometimes the drummer was Han Bennink. Steel drummer Mr. Slim Sinister and tenor saxophonist George Schermacher also played with the Perikels every so often when the occasion called for it. Dulfer on Schermacher: "When I first heard him I was reminded of Kid; that same wavering sound." Dulfer regarded Groenberg to be the best and most technically proficient percussionist. In the Perikels, Raul Burnett was an all-arounder who liked jazz and rock more. In the 1970s Dulfer's interest shifted from Latin to Surinamese, and that explains his interest in the funk band Solat with its Surinamese sound. Solat came into being in 1972 after the disbandment of the Latin funk band Reality (which also included Raul Burnett). Solat had plenty of work and had excellent musicians, but was poorly organized, not on the commercial circuit, and (too) far ahead of their time. At first the band played Afro-funk, but with the arrival of guitarist Wilfred Kempenaar—mad about Wes Montgomery—there was more jazz in their music. From 1973 onward the group was led by Frankie Douglas, and its members included Billy Jones (ex–Twinkle Stars), Frankie's sister Mildred Douglas (later Maitai), and Lilian Jackson (later Spargo). There were also some American horn players in Solat, such as trumpeter Frank Grasso and saxophonist Harvey Weinappel.

Solat too turned into the Perikels, and the musicians more often to playing soul and jazz rock.

OTHERS

There were various Surinamers active playing jazz in the Netherlands until the mid-1970s. One of them was Wim Essed, who is a teacher at three conservatories and often played with Boston and Burnett in Hilversum (the Dutch television and radio station center). He came to the Netherlands in 1947 and began playing clarinet and tenor sax in a big band. However, the beautiful playing of the first tenor saxophonist Ferdinand Povel discouraged him so much he threw in the towel. Essed switched to double bass and studied with the excellent double bassist Maarten van Altena. He played this instrument in the Nederlands Jeugdorkest, in the student orchestra ASKO, and in various radio orchestras. He also played in Loek Dikker's Waterland Ensemble, but in the 1980s he could practically only be heard in Hilversum. He played for a long time on the TROS radio program *Sesjun* (Session); after that in the VARA radio dance orchestra with Surinamese trumpet player Ado Broodboom; and was also the bass player for quite a while in flautist Ronald Snijder's band. He accompanied vocalist Sophie van Lier with a trio consisting of trumpeter Nedley Elstak and vibraphonist/pianist Glenn van Windt. Essed also wrote arrangements, such as for the children's song by Astrid Roemer "Wat heet anders?" (What Is Called Different?).

Essed also worked for some time with his cousin, the female vocalist and bassist Henny Vonk, born in Paramaribo (pseudonym of Tjon A Yong). This gifted mezzo-soprano took a conservatory degree and came in third place at the Loosdrecht Jazz Concourse in 1965 in the modern category. However, from "a vocalist who wrote poetry every so often, a year later, Henny Vonk turned into a poet who also sang jazz songs." She won the Herman van Kuilenborg poetry prize a year later. On the LP *Vonk's First* she interprets pop songs by Lennon and McCartney, among others. For *Rerootin' Henny Vonk* the poet sang her own texts to music by Miles Davis, Ornette Coleman, and others.

Another award winner, this time the press prize at the Laren Jazz Festival, was flautist Ronald Snijders. He first began playing in the quartet Suite 4. Then he played in the Theo Loevendie Consort and the Willem Breuker Kollektief. At Raul Burnett's insistence, Snijders and Breuker played in the band Sight. Together with several Sight band members he founded his first band, Black Straight Music. Snijders has made several beautiful solo records, such as the 1977 *Natural Sources*. He led his own band in the 1980s called the Ronald Snijders Band.

Opinions about Snijders have not always been favorable. Dulfer, who has played with him: "By letting the rhythm section stop playing and then doing percussive solos, Snijders grabbed the audience's attention. They thought it was great. For the rest he was always one step behind: playing funk when no one does that anymore."

Another remarkable Surinamese group is Sheseba: Fred Kimmel and Wilfred Kempenaar. Sheseba makes a kind of Surinamese chamber music; the duo themselves lay it on a little too thick by calling it Paramari-Bach. The way they play Bach pieces do indeed sound Surinamese, just like the pieces by this German composer sound when guitarist Laurindo Almeida gives them a Brazilian feel. The phrasing employed by Sheseba is typically Surinamese and hails directly from kaseko, as in the traditional "Sukrufinga."

PARAMARIBOP: SME AND FRA FRA SOUND

Until 1975 most Surinamese musicians played in Dutch groups. There was hardly any Surinamese musician being played alongside jazz, funk, and pop; and outside kaseko, not much was happening. However, in the second half of the 1970s a discussion broke loose by various Surinamese bands: are we going to continue to play kaseko-dance music, or are we going to experiment with more modern, "serious" music? One of them was the Pablo Nahar Quartet. Bassist Pablo Nahar had entered the jazz arena through the student orchestra Octopedians. In his first group Farawe was the cellist Tristan Honsinger from Canada; Kees Smit played sax and the Senegalese Djibrill N'Doye conga. Farawe made "free-music" in the style of Anthony Braxton: after the statement of a theme, all the members started improvising. The pieces had such titles as *A = C2 is Indiaan met roodgeverfd gezicht* (A=C2 is Indian with a Face Painted Red); during Farawe concerts Nahar always played the record by the Surinaamse Militaire Kapel.

His Pablo Nahar Quartet, however, went down different roads. Besides Nahar the quartet consisted of Dennis Breidel (drums), Wilfred Kempenaar (former Solat, later Sheseba, on guitar), and Robert Sordam (ex-Milestones), vocals. In the mid-1970s the quartet played such jazz classics as Charlie Parker's "Scrapple from the Apple" and "Ornithology"; Sordam provided them with his own lyrics. For Nahar and Sordam the quartet's concerts were essentially learning sessions, but Kempenaar thought there was definitely a future in it. Kempenaar introduced a kind of romanticism into Surinamese music. Sordam: "He's even more romantic than his great example, Wes Montgomery. He has a very quiet way of soloing; it seems like certain notes are missing during his solo, but they are there nevertheless." There was always a kaseko swing to Kempenaar's playing, which is the reason he is considered to belong to the unadulterated Paramariboppers. And yet he did not consciously lay Surinamese phrasing into jazz; it was a completely intuitive matter. Because of his jazzy approach to kaseko—or vice versa—he was a great inspirer for younger musicians.

When the Pablo Nahar Quartet turned into the present-day Surinam Music Ensemble (SME), Kempenaar was the first guitarist in the group. But that caused problems because his playing (according to a few band members) was limited to playing one style. When Kempenaar went to visit Suriname, he was replaced by the American John Thomas. He in turn was replaced by the Curaçaoan Franky Douglas, who dared to take risks and would stimulate the music with fresh impulses—and because all around him all kinds of young Surinamese musicians were looking for new ways to compose outside the conventional frameworks.

Trumpeter Miles Davis (especially his LP *Nefertiti*), and to a lesser degree saxophonist John Coltrane, had been beacons for SME, which over the course of time evolved more toward hard bop. All the standard jazz conventions were thrown overboard. They want to make the "chord structures as intricate as possible." Even the harmonies that bop had evolved were razed to the ground once again.

In the latter half of the 1970s the blues was no longer the guideline of composition. For quite a few Surinamers the words of Duke Ellington: "Follow the melody" became an adage. Ellington's alter ego, Billy Strayhorn, became one of the most popular composers among Surinamese musicians. His *Lush Life* is still on the repertoire of both SME and Fra Fra Sound. The number is in the *Jazz Real Book*, a book full of American jazz standards that is an important source for many Surinamese jazz musicians but that soon, however, become more of an inspiration than example to follow. In bassist and bandleader Vincent Henar's view, it soon did not have to do with the *Real Book* with a possible kaseko roll of the drum, but of kaseko being approached from the *Real Book*.

Paramaribop, the integration of Afro-Surinamese, Caribbean, and jazz traditions, is now "officially" considered one of the latest variations of bop. The reason it is not called kaseko jazz or Suri jazz is because its first and foremost adherents hailed from Paramaribo and had experimented with bop.

In the mid-1970s this jazz with a Surinamese rhythm could be heard especially in Birdland (in the town of Alkmaar) and Showboat (Zaandijk). The rhythmic duo Eddy Veldman (drums) and Pablo Nahar (bass) are practically synonymous with Paramaribop. First together in Solat-Perikels and later in SME, the two of them invariably climbed on stage whenever there were jam sessions. That was not always a success. Veldman: "Whenever we got on stage, the white musicians left. They kept losing count of the beat: they either didn't hear it or couldn't come to grips with it. Through the syncopations from the bass drum, it didn't seem like 4/4 or 6/8 anymore, even though usually it was. For most white musicians, a clearly defined rhythm is essential." The principle driving force behind their experiments was to make Surinamese jazz, with the two-chord structure, prevalent in popular Surinamese music. What people like Nahar and Veldman wanted to hear were the complex melodies and harmonies from Black North American music integrated into Surinamese jazz. They wanted to retain the strong aspect of Surinamese music: the rhythm and the rhythmic phrasing of melody of the kaseko, for instance, without letting the music end up as mere entertainment. Veldman had a thorough education in kaseko and kawina in the working-class neighborhood Frimangron in Paramaribo. Beginning from the soul group Needles, he came via Solat to SME. Nonetheless, the rules and lineups of kaseko and jazz strongly differ. To play jazz, Veldman uses the entire modern drum kit, tom-toms, snare, cymbals, and bass drum; but in kaseko only snare and bass drum are used, and there is another bass drum, the skratyi. However, the skratyi is superfluous for such a sophisticated drummer as Veldman, because he can play the syncopations and quarter notes at the same time. In the meantime, he also plays the clave on hi-hat, the key rhythm to kaseko. He uses the cymbals to imitate the various maracas and place accents. The snare drum plays the various *kwakwa-bangi* patterns. The main patterns of the hari drum can be heard on the bass drum, the drum that keeps the beat. Since the bass drum functions as a metronome, most of the beats on the *kot'-dron* (the improvising drum) are left out.

In jazz there are certain standard figures for drumming. For the Surinamese jazz drummer, the clave offers a possibility to break up the 8/8 pattern of jazz rhythm. Veldman is instantly recognizable for his kawina syncopations on the hi-hat. Singer Humphrey Campbell says of Veldman: "You recognize him through his attitude, groove and touch, his snare drum and tasty cymbal sound. His beat is both smooth and powerful at the same time; his complete mastery lets you hear how good he is."

Veldman no longer only plays the obligatory beat. Surinamese and other Caribbean rhythms slip into his playing more and more often. In the meantime, he is so closely knit with his two drumsticks that a free-jazz concert with Idriss Ackamore is just as easy for him to play as a performance with the funk-jazz group Future Shock. He gives such a well-known piece as Miles Davis's "Donna Lee" his inimitable brand of treatment: he weaves a wickerwork of kaseko rolls around it, and the versions by Art Blakey and Tony Williams, his favorite drummers, are a thing of the past. Besides playing four-four time on the bass drum, he also plays syncopations, with the hi-hat taking over the clave. The roll on the snare drum in "Donna Lee" is the same one as in kaseko. The bass lines in this Paramaribop are the same as in kaseko to keep the swing going. Besides the difference in instrumentation, there is another big difference from "regular" jazz: kaseko's two-chord structure. In this form of Surinamese dance music, broken chords are played and one note can last twice as long as another. In jazz, each note is given the same accent, is counted out equally. This makes the phrasing entirely different: when Surinamers played jazz chords with kaseko phrasing, Paramaribop on the bass drum was born.

The LP *Dynamite Cotton Legacy* is SME's homage to the two pioneers of Surinamese jazz: tenor player Kid Dynamite and trumpeter Teddy Cotton. The record is a harbinger of later SME concerts: from authentic kawina via kaseko to avant-gardist work, the real Paramaribop. But SME's brand of kaseko is real listening music, which also can be danced to. For such kaseko bands as the Funmasters, it is only dance music.

According to Robert Sordam, the piece "Trampoline" by Hessel de Vries is an example of genuine SME music: "a mix of jazz and Caribbean music played with a kaseko-swing." Be that as it may, after two albums with such lovely music, at the time of this writing SME has still not gained wide acceptance, according to its members" "Our music is only music if it were played by Hollanders: after all, we don't have any culture," says Veldman cynically.

Another significant group is Fra Fra Sound. "Swinging, fresh music that tastes like more," Frans van Leeuwen once wrote about this band in the Dutch daily *NRC Handelsblad* (adding that things were looking dim for the band if it didn't quickly improve its financial situation). Under the leadership of bass player Vincent Henar, Fra Fra Sound began modernizing kaseko, but its members soon were completely obsessed by jazz. Henar would select a theme, on which the member could then improvise. Paramaribop is only one element of their music. Fra Fra Sound is more into making Black improvised music, with influences from kawina, bebop, and bigi poku. The group is also inspired by free jazz, Winti, and funk. Humphrey Campbell used to sing for Fra Fra Sound. He got his start in Suriname with Black Earth and was invited to come to the Netherlands by the Twinkle Stars. Campbell performed such classics as "Lush Life," "A Night in Tunisia," and "Moody's Mood for Love" with SME and Fra Fra Sound. The warm and agile timbre of his voice became known all over Europe. In 1986 he appeared on West German and Dutch television with the Dutch Jazz Orchestra. He toured West Germany, Belgium, and the Netherlands with the WDR orchestra, giving a final concert in Amsterdam's Concertgebouw. In Cologne he gave an evening-long performance of all Nat King Cole songs, a genre that suits him well. Besides jazz, Campbell also sings pieces by Al Jarreau, disco, Latin, and Indian music. He himself prefers singing tunes by Herbie Hancock, Weather Report, and his own pieces with a quartet accompaniment. Bert Vuisje wrote in Dutch daily *de Volkskrant* in a review of his performance at the Heerlen Big Band Festival: "An exceptional attraction."

THE POSITION OF SURINAMESE JAZZ MUSICIANS IN THE NETHERLANDS

Surinamese jazz musicians became reasonably accepted in the Dutch jazz world of the 1980s. That came to pass largely due to a discussion held in Amsterdam's Bimhuis venue in December 1982. The immediate cause was a rather facetious concert review by Eddy Determeyer, which caused a great stir in the Surinamese and Dutch Antillean community, in which he referred to a white woman trumpeter playing with a Surinamese band as ". . . a white Goddess amid a bunch of sweaty, black musicians, slaving away at making music. . . ." Regardless of whether or not what they were playing was any good, the way it was characterized (according to the Surinam Music Association) attested to boundless self-aggrandizement and contempt for Black music, which was something many Black musicians did not exactly experience as something new.

The monthly magazine *Jazz Nu* (Jazz Now) organized a debate because of this review, led by the *Volkskrant* music editor Bert Vuisje. Items discussed included the amount and quality of press coverage, the socioeconomic position of Surinamese and Dutch Antillean musicians, and what they experienced because of policies of Dutch music venues. Henar feels that, ever since this discussion, the press has taken Black music seriously, while venue owners finally negotiated equitable fees. This resulted not only in Surinamese jazz growing in depth during the 1980s but also in a broadening of the range of groups and musicians on offer. Alongside SME, Fra Fra Sound, and Sheseba there were now Sunchild, the Ronald Snijders Band, and the Patrick Sedoc Quartet. Surinamese musicians were now sought-after by Dutch bands.

Percussionist Franklin Ardin performs with Loos and Spellbound, drummer Marius Tjon plays with the Sun Ra Orchestra. Drummer Jan Baghwandin has played in all sorts of bands, while practically all the SME members are sought-after studio musicians.

In the margin of the jazz world operated such percussionists as Robbie "Yogi" Gilles with Taharga and Ponda O'Bryan with Sosoba. Taharga and Sosoba are both percussion groups with a great deal of room for improvisation. O'Bryan distinguishes himself from other percussionists through his knowledge of Winti, Mandingo, and Cuban music.

There are not many good Surinamese horn players. This is probably due to the premature death of Kid Dynamite; a figure had ceased to be on whom the young could model themselves. Fra Fra Sound's sax player Eddie Braaf has been one such figure for quite some time. Orlando Dost, Fra Fra Sound's former alto player, with his gorgeous tone has the capacity to become the Surinamese sax player of the 1990s.

Most Surinamese musicians these days have either or partial or complete conservatory education behind them. Surinamese jazz resembles more the music of individuals. All the musicians regularly break out of the straitjacket of existing groups, forming bands for special occasions, and to form new ideas that would otherwise not come to the fore in their regular work with their respective bands. For example, during the October Meeting held in the Netherlands in 1987 (mainly in the Bimhuis), Eddy Veldman together with American bassist Gerald Veasly and cellist Ernst Reyseger were the core of the group Cruise Button, especially formed for the occasion. Eric van de Berg (*Volkskrant*, October 10, 1987) characterized Veldman's playing in this unique band as "full of fat funky licks and with an inexhaustible groove." Veldman was also involved together with pianist Glenn Gaddum and guitarist Frankie Douglas in the Yuang Ling Lu project conducted by the American saxophonist John Zorn. Douglas was later invited to play with the orchestra of pianist Cecil Taylor in the Amsterdam Concertgebouw.

These musicians, bands, and concerts have meant that Surinamese jazz is now a going concern. Whether Paramaribop will prove to be the ultimate form remains to be seen. But financing is needed to guarantee the growth of serious Surinamese music: money for organization, education, instruments, and the like. Is financial promotion of Surinamese music a question of tackling unemployment, granting care to a minority or art? Vincent Henar, spokesman of the Surinam Music Association, would prefer to receive any government grants through the art channels. "It would then be recognition for our music."

10

POP

That which applies to Surinamese music in general also applies to Surinamese pop music: it is a conglomeration of styles in which the cultural and ethnic backgrounds of the various communities that inhabit Suriname play important roles. To put it another way: not just Afro-Surinamers have pop music; the Hindustani and Javanese Surinamers do, too.

HINDI-POP
- Dr. J. Ketwaru -

The rise of Surinamese-Hindustani popular music began in the 1940s thanks to Indian film music, which flourished enormously at the time. In terms of culture, a great many Surinamese of East Indian origin were dependent on film music. But because India had been under British rule for so long, the films made increasing use of Western music arrangements, which were sometimes integrated into Indian forms of music. The lineup of instruments, too, was usually Western: violin, guitar, saxophone, and drum kit, and it was not uncommon for there to be Hindi versions of songs by Paul Anka, the Beatles, and the Platters.

Gradually, Surinamese East Indians were inspired by Western sounds, and at the end of the 1940s there were three prominent Surinamese-Hindustani film music orchestras: Shah Noer Sabah, conducted by Effendi Ketwaru (at the time of writing director of the Surinamese Volksmuziekschool); the Indian Orchestra, conducted by Herman Dijo; and the Wina Orchestra. These groups tried to copy Indian film and popular music as exactly as possible. Surinamese singers identified with such Indian pop singers as Mukesh, Mohammed Rafi, and Talat Mahmood. An example of the idolatry of Indian pop music is Suki Akkal, the most prominent Surinamese Hindi-pop musician of the day. When Rafi died, Akkal recorded an LP entitled *Surinam Remembers Mohammed Rafi*, on which he played all the instruments.

At first, the instruments used in Hindi-pop were scarce and expensive. Only the guitar, mandolin, violin, harmonium, and dholak were relatively affordable, so these were the ones heard most. The chief aim of the imitators of Indian pop and film music was to make radio broadcasts. That took place every Sunday afternoon on radio station AVROS.

Until around 1970, Surinamese-Hindustani musicians kept imitating their Westernized Indian examples. After that, interest grew in music forms of the various communities indigenous to Suriname and for South American music in general. And thanks to a general increase in economic prosperity, musicians were able to afford expensive instruments, such as saxophones, electric guitars, complete drum kits, and keyboards. Electronic public address systems also came within reach. Partly due to these developments, Hindi-pop took on its own special sound. The compositions are now, in metrical terms, strongly influenced by Surinamese-Creole kaseko. Based on this, Surinamese-Hindustani make arrangements of their compositions, which in turn are largely derived from Indian film music. Moreover, most groups also have North and South American styles on their repertoires.

The band Pandero (still with George Schermacher on saxophone) provided the first important impulses. Starting from imitating the widespread pop music of Oscar Harris and the Twinkle Stars, with or without mixing their own indigenous sounds, such bands as Naya Roshni, Juniors, Indian Diamonds, and Pandero itself began playing calypso, merengue, disco, and reggae. Droeh Nankoe in the Netherlands and Michel Lachmon in Suriname are regarded as the greatest performers of Hindustani pop songs.

POP-JAWA
- Herman Dijo -

In the 1960s Surinamese-Javanese music was also heavily influenced by foreign forms of popular music, not just from North America but also from the country of origin, that is, Java. Javanese pop music became all the rage in no time, and the name pop-jawa was soon born. Kroncong orchestras changed into pop groups. String sections were replaced by electronic gear, synthesizers, and electric guitars. Bass guitar and drum sets took the place of traditional drums. More and more concerts were given by Indonesian pop artists, modern Javanese film experienced a heyday, and there was a large audience for radio programs broadcast in Javanese. The cultural society Tri Djokko Muljo capitalized on this in 1972, organizing the first annual pop-jawa festival. Well-known pop-jawa groups of the day were T-Group and Astaria Combo.

There are annual Surinamese-Javanese song festivals in the Netherlands as well, but because of the high costs and the relatively small target audience, few producers take risks to finance new pop-jawa records. For that reason, these groups mostly perform at celebrations and parties. A couple of more or less popular groups are the Surbrothers, Melati, and Rupia.

SURIPOP
- Marcel Weltak -

Important aspects in the transition from traditional Afro-Surinamese music to modern pop music have been discussed earlier in this book, especially the chapter dealing with kaseko. But it is not easy to pinpoint when Suripop began; there is even debate about the date of the first real hit. Judging by the number of times it was played on Dutch radio and television and the style of the song, "Akoeba" by the Happy Boys was the first one. At the beginning of the 1970s "Akoeba" sounded modern, even though it still stayed within the traditional kaseko patterns. However, its producer (and that of many other modern Surinamese bands) Stan Lokhin considers his own "Oen egi pasi" (Our Own Way) to be the first Suripop song to have sold well. He co-wrote it with Rudy Bedacht to commemorate Surinamese independence in 1975.

The Clan's 1978 hit "Sing sing tap joe koto" was certainly one of the first contemporary Suripop numbers. Its balanced blend of Surinamese styles with North American music came up with a fresh-sounding product. That had been the work of Ronny and Lucien Gorré, together with Stan Lokhin, who wrote the arrangements and produced the horn section. The song also had beautiful lyrics that made it both a hit in Suriname and Surinamese community in the Netherlands. Dutch radio refused to give it airplay, so "Sing sing" did not break through to a Dutch audience. But this did happen with "Nelis Joe Lat Atding," recorded in Suriname by Suzie Poeder. Sales shot up after a few spins on Dutch radio.

A few years later, the Blue Seven Band was formed from the core of The Clan. This band scored a hit with the Surinamese traditional song "Rorac," though also only within their own Surinamese community.

The three LPs that Max Nijman made for the Dutch label Dureco also fall under Suripop. These records with ballads were produced by Stan Lokhin. Dureco sold approximately 50,000 units of the first LP, *Katibo*, released in 1974. Thanks to these records Nijman was able to give concerts in the United States and Israel. The songs on *Katibo* were written by Nijman and Lokhin. On *Katibo*, Max Nijman was musically backed by the Twinkle Stars, without a doubt the most famous Surinamese band in the Netherlands in the 1960s and 1970s. Founded in 1965, this group initially played for students. They covered popular Beatles songs and a few Latin numbers. Twinkle Stars had several hits in the Netherlands such as "Try a Little Love," "T.O.P.," "Clap Hands for You," "Soldier's Prayer," "We Want Peace," and "Love Is Gonna Rain on You." The group was chosen a few years running as the best band in the Netherlands. And yet the music of the Twinkle Stars was not very popular among a Dutch audience. Even at the beginning of the 1970s they still associated Surinamese music with Max Woiski Sr. and his songs such as "B.B. met R, dat is bruine bonen met rijst" (B.B. with R, that's brown beans with rice). To many Dutch, the music of Twinkles Stars did not sound authentic. The vocals in the band were very smooth and the music pretty slick for Surinamese standards. A few well-known musicians have played with Twinkle Stars. Billy Jones, who at the time was based in Germany, travelled together with Archie Bell and the Drells in 1969 to Amsterdam to sing with the Twinkle Stars. In 1975 singer Humphrey Campbell joined the band, who had two previous vocalists, Jones and Oscar Harris. Stan Lokhin, and later on pianist Frank Smit, did their horn arrangements. In 1978 the group morphed into Thunderstorm; Oscar Harris began doing radio work with the Metropole Orchestra and playback performances on the Dutch circuit.

There were other groups who set themselves to making modern pop music with Surinamese lyrics. The first professional group of Surinamese musicians to play soul were the Needles. The group mainly played Jerry Butler numbers. However, the band found more work in Italy than they did in the Netherlands.

A band that came afterward was Sonora Paramarera. However, this band played not modern pop but Latin and refined calypsos by the Merrymen, in a Cuban conjunto lineup. They mainly played for Dutch audiences.

Exception, not to be confused with the white band that came later, were already playing soul numbers in 1966 such as "Let's Go Baby Where the Action Is." Members of Exception included guitarist Frankie Douglas and singer "Ray Brooks" van der Kust. They had a 1967 hit with "Somebody Got to Do It." in 1969 Douglas started Reality, a Surinamese-Dutch Antillean band with Santana-esque music. The vocalist was Tony Sherman, and the other musicians were Eddy Veltman and pianist Glenn Gaddum. After two LPs, one hit ("War"), and a six-month South American tour, the group disbanded in 1972. In 1973 Frankie Douglas again popped up, this time as leader of the funk band Solat.

Trafassi

In the summer of 1985, a cryptic set of lyrics blared over the canals and bars in the Netherlands: "Kleine wasjes, grote wasjes, stop ze in de wasmasjien. Laat maar lekker draaien, wassen, spelen, wringen" (Little loads of laundry, big ones, put them in the washing machine. Let them turn, wash, play, be wrung). This was the hit "Wasmasjine" (Washing Machine) by the Surinamese pop group Trafassi. They arranged the popular salsa-antiyana (Dutch Antillean salsa variation) song, originally written and released by the Curaçaoan musician Macario Prudencia, and made it into a smash hit.

Surinamese hits in the Netherlands are few and far between. And often the Surinamese themselves do not want to identity with them, because Hilversum (the Dutch town where public and commercial radio and TV are concentrated, just east of Amsterdam) almost always selects the most flippant and superficial numbers to then tout them as "the latest Surinamese summer hit." Surinamers who want to make money give the Dutch what they want and make disposable consumer music.

"Strijkplank" (Ironing Board), the follow-up to "Wasmasjien," flopped with the DJs in Hilversum because they had had enough; Surinamers should not have two big radio hits in a row. But the Surinamese and Dutch Antilleans themselves, the natural supporters of Trafassi, no longer accepted pandering after a white audience. Besides, Trafassi is capable of much more than that, and had proved it in the past. No wonder, with such musicians as Harold Biervliet (guitar), Lesley Leeflang (bass guitar), Ricardo Tjon A Kon (piano, flute, and synthesizer), and singer Edgar "Boegroe" Burgos. They had all paid their dues in such Surinamese beat groups as Cosmo Beat and in such kaseko groups as Happy Boys. Biervliet is probably the best guitar player in Surinamese entertainment music up until now.

Just how virtuoso Trafassi can be is evidenced by their concerts and LPs. The group is a melting pot of influences: Surinamese, Caribbean, North American, African, and Indian. For example, the group starts playing a song with a Hindustani beat, then smoothly segues to disco before ending in kaseko. There are not many groups in the Netherlands who can match that.

Despite their musical potential, Trafassi continues to concentrate on a mass audience. The band members themselves feel they are busy making a new breed of Caribbean music. But if Trafassi want to make a living out of it, they have to make so many concessions that precious little is left of the new style. Edgar Burgos puts into his own words: "If the music is too complex, nobody listens anymore. A song has to be lighthearted, nice to sing along to and no hassles. Musical boundaries can still be shifted." He views Trafassi

as a spokesperson for Surinamers: "Other people don't want or dare to do
the things we do; we give people something to talk about." Tjon A Kon says
it this way: "We make arrangements of song for a large orchestra, for a five-
man band. We do not consciously make concessions by simplifying style or
rhythm. But Trafassi's first aim is to entertain its audience."

Trafassi began in 1981, when the Dutch occasional band Stars on 45 were
enjoying their heyday with a potpourri of hit medleys. Later on, they played
during the West Indian carnival in London and for the Commonwealth
Institute in Paris. Trafassi's first 12-inch single, "Brombere," was even banned
in Suriname, because it insulted Desi Bouterse (the army sergeant who led
the country after a coup). The band members were not welcome in Suriname
for a while, but a potpourri of old Surinamese ditties in 1985 garnered them
compliments from the Surinamese government. They found the medley to be
"stimulating" for Surinamers. But Trafassi is not out to play Surinamese music
only; they leave it to other bands to do that, even though they consistently
present themselves as Surinamese. The Trafassi members see themselves as
trailblazers for other non-Dutch artists. They have learned to live with the
fact that many people consider "Wasmajien," "Brombere," and "De meisjes
van de Huishoudschool" (The Girls from Home Ed School) to be vulgar. To
them it is more important that the Dutch bought the LP *Asema*, with all
these songs on it, in great numbers.

P. I. Man and Odongo

"The difference is their hair," according to a musician who has worked for
both P.I. Man and Odongo. Indeed, Imro Belliot, alias P.I. Man, wears his hair
in Jamaican dreadlocks, while Stanley Angel—Odongo—has his hair braided.
Of course, there are other differences, but this understatement makes clear
the styles both these musicians master. P.I. Man and Odongo are Surinamese
musicians of the 1980s who appeal most to the imagination. They both came
from the same band—the Milestones—and now play music from two different continents. Odongo seeks his inspiration in African music, while P.I.
Man is strongly swayed by music from the Caribbean region.

P.I. Man is the Anglicized version of the Amerindian *pyjaiman*, the shaman, medicine man, and cultural-religious leader who in the practice of
his profession is also a gifted composer and lyricist. P.I. Man often refers
to his Amerindian ancestry and calls his music Afro-Caribbean rock. His
preferences include kaseko, soca, and calypso. On his two LPs *Tukusy* and
Masannah, you mainly hear an underlying reggae influence, even in other
numbers carried by a different beat.

Braiding of the hair is an African custom, and Odongo's braids are a reference to his having descended from African slaves. For him, the basis of Surinamese music lies in traditional religious Winti music, which is a mix of African and Amerindian religion. The influence from Winti is abundantly clear on his album *Look Your Winti*. Odongo is an obiahman, a spiritual medium, who makes Winti-poku with electric instruments that nevertheless exude a strong African influence. His greatest example is the Nigerian saxophonist/singer Fela Kuti, who now after years of political incarceration is packing halls in Africa and Europe.

Both these performers learned the fundamental principles of Afro-Surinamese music from the female vocal group Abaisa. But the drummers Ba Erwin Groenhardt, Ba Gompel, and Ban Henk Lamsburg from the percussion group Akrema also left their marks on them, and their singing was influenced by kawina singers Johan Zebeda and Big Jones and by kaseko singer Lieve Hugo. After taking lessons from Abaisa and Akrema, Odongo and P.I. Man founded Milestones, which also included Dennis Echteld, Guilly Koster, and Robert Sordam. It later became the Winti group Krah, turning finally into Milestones Emancipation before disbanding.

The Milestones were a versatile group, that once produced and performed the musical *Fajasition* by the poet Jules Niemel. The piece portrayed a group of Surinamese youth and after quite a few shows in the Netherlands was also performed in Suriname. For both singers music became a way of life. After Milestones Emancipation disbanded at the end of the 1970s Odongo surrounded himself with his backing band, the Spirits, and in 1980 P.I. Man founded his current backing band, Memre Buku.

Contrary to their common musical background, their approach to Surinamese pop music differs greatly. Odongo strives to create professionally created chaos and goes for overproduction; a performance with thirty people on a small stage is no exception. Nevertheless, there is structure in his chaotic music, in which the (continually alternating) musicians have plenty of space to improvise. What at first appears to be the absence of a regularly occurring pattern is in reality a stripped-down version that is continually filled in by the constant alternation of musicians. This makes every performance different. Odongo is perhaps more of a performer than singer. His live appearances are often just as important as his records, if not more so. One of his performances is not something easily forgotten. He made his entrance on stage at Amsterdam's Paradiso venue nailed to an illuminated cross. He has from time to time been accused of being unmusical because he does not adhere to the norms of a tonal system. His reply is that he lives "within the totality of the universe," with all its sounds but without binding rules.

When it comes to arranging his compositions, P.I. Man thinks in standard structures that may then be continually rearranged. His greatest concern is with sound: his Afro-Caribbean sound, which also contains African elements—Afro-beat, highlife, juju. His work is transparent and relatively easy to follow, even for listeners who are not familiar with Afro music. Still, he is concerned with more than just sound. Reggae is important to him, for instance, because of its lyrics about Black consciousness. This second aspect reveals his second goal: to give encouragement to people who suffer or fail. Both Odongo and P.I. Man refer in their lyrics to the past and future of the Black man. In that connection Odongo thinks big. In "Are You Wondering" he sings about "Africa for the Africans" and "We Want Our Country Back." Conversely, P.I. Man sings in "Ritual Bath" on the album *Masannah* about the individual who can only regain his identity through taking a cleansing bath. In "Foto libi" he talks of one who chooses the countryside over the hectic city.

Regardless of all this, neither of these musicians can be easily labelled. Odongo makes Winti-poku but with snippets of kaseko, free jazz, Afro-Cuban genres, Afro-beat, and even rock and roll à la Frank Zappa. P.I. Man's Afro-Caribbean rock, soca-calypso, or roots music is both dreamy and earthy at the same stroke, with an attitude of optimism. Each of them, once united in the same band, is now searching for that which unites them: Surinamese music.

REGGAE
- Guilly Koster -

What gospel is to Christians in the United States, reggae is to Rastafarianism. This Jamaican music style, with its heavy bass tones and monotone guitar "chops," remind the Rastafari of his mystic being. The heartbeat, on which the reggae beat is based, can be heard on the drum set and other percussion.

Its religiously tinged, often political lyrics, but above all the personality of Bob Marley, ensured that reggae became a global success. The lifestyle, hairstyle, and colors (red, gold, and green) of such musicians as Bob Marley, Peter Tosh, and Bunny Wailer were adopted everywhere. That was also the case with Surinamers.

Suriname and Jamaica have a great deal in common. Almost all the slaves that were brought to these two countries came from West Africa (Ghana, Congo, Ivory Coast, Nigeria), and both countries have their freedom fighters. So, it came as no surprise that Surinamese bands in the Netherlands began playing reggae.

In kaseko, bass and drums play as import a role as they do in reggae, but the tempo of reggae is much slower. The most significant reason for this presumably lies in the connection between reggae and soul in the 1960s. Moreover, reggae did not undergo the influence of other Latin American streams of music such as calypso, soca, and samba, which did influence kaseko. Another factor is that the religious Winti songs were generally played at a faster tempo than most other religious music. The style of Surinamese music that most closely resembles reggae is *badji*.

The development of reggae was closely watched in Suriname in the 1960s and 1970s. At first it was called blue beat and later Jamaica ska, and finally reggae. These styles were introduced into Suriname by such artists as Byron Lee, Max Romeo, and Johnny Nash. In this way many young Surinamers became acquainted with the rasta style.

In the Netherlands (where incidentally a white group such as Doe Maar was responsible for the popularity of this music), reggae took on the function of icebreaker for Surinamese bands: because of reggae they were able to gain access to the pop music circuit, but not with kaseko. Reggae began to thrive after Bob Marley's first concert in Amsterdam's Jaap Edenhal (1976). The Milestones, from which sprang such groups as P.I. Man and Memre Buku, Odongo and the Spirits, and Conga Willi, were one of the first to go deeply into the Rastafari movement. In search of this new style, they met personally with Bob Marley and in the 1970s traveled to Birmingham, London, and Manchester, where reggae was reigning supreme.

The roots cult grew faster in Rotterdam than elsewhere in the Netherlands. Reggae trips to England were organized, predominately from this port city. All sorts of Rotterdamers brought reggae to a higher level. Easy, Communication, and Mighty 5 and the Rebels performed as support acts for such famous foreign groups as Steel Pulse, Culture, and Inner Circle. Musicians from several of these Rotterdam groups finally formed Revelation Time, at the end of the 1980s the most popular reggae band in the Netherlands. Partly due to the dreadlocks of soccer star Ruud Gullit, the band was able to release the single "Captain Dread." The group Revanche (Revenge) is especially well known for the three corpulent brothers who steal the show. And finally, the mixed band the Equals offer women an equal place in reggae. Excellent Surinamese reggae albums include *Right Time* by Inity, *Tranga Jesi* by Blakka Roetoe, and of course the records by Revelation Time. Little by little, a Surinamese "toasters" guild also came into being. Toasting is the rhythmic and often rhymed talking along with reggae music; Sranan Tongo is an excellent vehicle for this. As usual in reggae, Surinamese toaster also gave themselves names derived from the Rasta monarchy, such as Prince Judah, Rootsman, Ras-I, Super Dan, and Hi-Fi Levi.

Now that more and more cultures are starting to make inroads into Dutch music culture, Surinamese reggae has become more well known. But the question is if it isn't too late, since in general reggae is not exactly undergoing a revival. Maybe the task of doing just that might even fall to Surinamese bands.

HIP-HOP
- Guilly Koster -

Despite all the efforts, Suripop in the Netherlands has still not been accepted. The Twinkle Stars, Max Nijman, and Happy Boys are names that sold well abroad, especially in Africa, England, and Scandinavia. The story of Solat, Odongo, P.I. Man, the Needles, and all those Surinamese bands who cover American pop music or produce original work and sought a place in the Dutch music world, is still not over.

A hit parade in the October 17, 1987, issue of Dutch music magazine *Oor* (Ear), with the telling title "Het zwarte gat" (The Black Hole), shows that Dutch pop journalists prefer to concentrate on rock and roll and other white music styles. Even during the wave of soul that crashed over the Netherlands in 1987 it turned out that even the best Dutch pop journalists had trouble with Black music, even if it came from the USA.

Pop journalist Marcel Wouter wrote in that same *Oor* issue that hip hop was undergoing the same problems that other forms of Black street music faced in the past. The "white press" was presumably not taking hip hop seriously, because it was music being made by young Black people.

At the beginning of hip hop, all the raps were in English. But there soon appeared Surinamese crews who wanted to highlight their roots. That is why the crew What If from Venray (in the southern Dutch province of Limburg) entered the Grote Prijs van 1987 (The Great Competition of 1987) with raps in Sranan Tongo, based on kawina and salsa. In The Hague a female crew rapped in Sranan Tongo, as did a boys' crew in Rotterdam.

Suripop, as performed by hip hoppers rapping to kawina accompaniment, has a bright future. The word "rap" in the Surinamese variant of Dutch is already synonymous with "talk." Nevertheless, in the Netherlands this expression of Black youth culture with the heavy kick drum sound that has blown in from the USA has remained a subcultural phenomenon. It can only be hoped that Surinamese hip hoppers do not become discouraged.

"A lot of young musicians pride themselves on their Surinamese origin, but do not display much Surinamese influence in their music. Rappers such as Tony Scott and Urban Dance Squad's Root Boy have enjoyed great success in both the Netherlands and abroad. DJ Juan Elmzoon works as All Star Fresh in the group Kingbee and makes Western-oriented dance hits such as "Back by Dope Demand.""

11

SURINAMESE WOMEN IN MUSIC

- Marcel Weltak -

The main roles in Surinamese music have almost always been played by men. Important genres such as kaseko had their origin in the night life of Paramaribo—not exactly the place for women to come into their own. There is also a traditional lack of an urge to make political statements in Surinamese music, which in twentieth-century European music is explicitly present, and which European women have utilized. Nevertheless, women certainly have left their mark on Surinamese music. We have already met the most famous and legendary of them all: Fransje Gomez.

Surinamese women were also active in the Netherlands. In the 1930s Alma Braaf (stage name Lolita Mojica) performed in Dutch venues with the then young Max Woiski Sr. She mostly sang Cuban songs. She was followed by Ann Kony, who sang jazz numbers in the Collegians and later did the same in Kid Dynamite's band. Henny Vonk (pseudonym of Tjon A Yong) was a singer in various jazz formations in the 1960s.

Not until the 1970s did Surinamese women in the Netherlands begin singing in their own language. An example of that, though somewhat outside pop music, is actress/singer Gerda Havertong, who traveled the length and breadth of the Netherlands with a repertoire of Surinamese songs composed by Armand Baag. Havertong raised the bar of Surinamese song. Her rendition of "Aisa," the traditional song about Mother Earth, would not sound amiss among classic European songs. Her many radio and television appearances have probably made her the best-known Surinamese woman singer: she can be seen practically daily on the Dutch version of the children's program *Sesamstraat* (*Sesame Street*).

Another Surinamese woman who sings in her own national language is Annemarie Hunsel. Besides kaseko, she sings pop music, sometimes with Surinamese lyrics. Hunsel became famous in the Netherlands for her Surinamese rendition of Bob Dylan's "I Shall Be Released."

In 1982 a few Surinamese women in Amsterdam were rehearsing a song they were going to perform to add luster to a newly formed women's group. While rehearsing they discovered they could easily fill an entire evening with song, and so under the leadership of the social worker Lilian Mijnals, they formed the new kaseko group Oema Soso (Women Only). The six women in Oema Soso never really lived up to their name, because they were always accompanied by male musicians, but they did lay the basis for a new trend: the oema groups, which shot up like mushrooms but just as quickly disappeared. Two *oema* groups, Oema Prisirie (Woman Pleasure) and Oema Lobi (Woman Love), merged into the band Nature by Marlène Waal and dedicated themselves to African music, the basis of Afro-Surinamese music.

Oema Soso quickly became a household name even in white circles, and they performed for both men and women, together or separately. The strong point of all oema groups were their lyrics in Sranan Tongo; their kaseko texts were kindly disposed toward women, which quickly led Surinamese men to reproach them for their "feminism." On top of that, the group regularly performed for the gay movement, which in Surinamese culture only elicits disapproval. The name Oema Soso alone was like waving a red flag at a bull. Incidentally, the women in Oema Soso knew exactly what they wanted, and they consciously sought to be provocative with such lyrics as "Oema soso e tjari a commando" (Women only are calling the shots). Because in some Surinamese circles feminists and lesbians are tarred with the same brush, they preferred not to be labeled "feminist" and were flexible enough to adapt their lyrics. But Lilian Mijnals realized that the women in this group could not just be Surinamese women: "The mere fact that these women decide to make music makes them feminists." The existence of Oema Soso itself contributed to Surinamese women becoming actively aware. "Once they have discovered that they can do something, they will go ahead and do it." Within the space of a few years, Oema Soso had racked up more shows for Dutch audiences than many more long-lived Surinamese bands. Apparently, the Dutch were more charmed by Surinamese women in music and saw in them a more attractive cultural challenge than in traditional male kaseko. However, other groups have yet to make use of the bridge that Oema Soso has built.

A new generation of Surinamese female vocalists became active in the second half of the 1980s: Ruth Jacott, known for her leading role in the musical *Cats* in 1988, and jazz singer Denise (Jannah) Zeefuik. Both studied a couple of years at conservatories. In Germany, Lea Abullah has made something of a name for herself with English-language disco numbers. For the time being, it looks as though Surinamese women making music have tired of such national traditions as kaseko and lobisingi.

ACKNOWLEDGMENTS
(TO THE 1990 EDITION)

The makers of the book would like to take this opportunity to thank the following persons without whose contributions this book would not have been possible: Gerrie van Noord (photograph editing), photographers Tony Thijs, Rien D'Rozario and Ernest Potters, Mrs. Bep Overweg, Mrs. A. Smit, Lex Vervuurt, Stan Lokhin, Mr. E. van Spall, Hans Dulfer, Steve Boston, Robert Sordam, Vincent Henar, Marlène de Waal, Martijn Stoffer, Waldy Samson, Roderik Huizinga, Peter Bos, Hans de Wildt, Hans Vatter, Edgar Burgos, Ronnie Manojd, H. S. Siban Aliredjo, Herman Openneer, Mr. Hidalgo, the staff of the Royal Tropical Institute, Amsterdam, and the Rijkmuseum voor Volkenkunde, Leiden.

APPENDIX 1: SELECTED DISCOGRAPHY
(TO THE 1990 EDITION)

This list is not exhaustive and contains mainly LPs and a few EPs or maxi singles. Many Surinamese artists release their own (maxi) singles. Due to the large number and scant accessibility of these, they are only sporadically mentioned here. As far as could be determined are listed: name of the label on which the record was released, distribution company and order number. The records where only the order number is mentioned were released on (Dutch) label Dureco.

Artist	Title	Label, Year of Release
Akrema	Akrema	SMA 1981
Armand Baag	Kon Hesi Baka	CBS 1978
Bakadjari Band	Switi Smeri Vol. 1	Sranan
Bally Brashuis	Blaka Boeba	Kwakoe Records
Big Jones	Big Jones	Philips
Blakka Roetoe	Tranga Jesie	SMA 1982
Boogie & the Exmo Stars	Life in Ganzenhoef	Exmo Prod.
Boogie & the Exmo Stars	Telefon, mi koe mi koenoe	Exmo 1984
Contact 2000	Oeroe Ve	self-released
Cosmo Stars	Mooi Lobi	Cosmo
Djinti	Tiri fri' Jari	Dureco 1986
Droeh Nankoe	Songs for various occasions	Dureco 1988
Eddy Jankipersadsing	Dance Melodies	©1976
Exmo Stars	The Best of, Live in Wilobi	Exmo Prod.
Exmo Stars	Djaroesoe	EXP 803
Fra Fra Sound	Panja Gazz	SMA 1987
Funmasters	Volume II	Funny Records 1983
George Schermacher	Kota Dansi	FL 433.001
Happy Boys	Akoeba	Dureco 1977

Artist	Title	Label, Year of Release
Happy Boys	Switi Momo	Dureceo 1978
Harridath Jairam	Habara Katavat Lagal Der	Sunil Records 1977
Johnny de Miranda	The Sunny Sound of Surinam	CNR 1974
Johnny de Miranda	Suriname Onafhankelijk	Blue Elephant 1975
Johnny de Miranda	Faja Lobie	Blue Elephant 1975
Kaseko Masters	Pepsi	Cosmo
Kawina Band	Drompoe	LP FLP 7613
Ketwaru	Ketwaru	OM 444062
Kolebrie	Sopiang	Unice Records
Krido Soro	Gending Jara	Borobudur
Lamie & Trjondro Utomo	Lamie & Trjondro Utomo	Dsico Amigo
Lex Vervuurt en zijn Zapakaras	Groeten uit de West	Telstar
Lieve Hugo	King of Kaseko	EMI 1974
Lieve Hugo	Lieve Hugo	LP FLP 433.013
Lilian Mijnals (Oema Soso)	Famiri Man	EXP 808
Lilian & Helen Mijnals (Oema Soso)	A Moe Doe Joe	EXP 812
Maranatha Koor	Maranatha in Concert	Dureco 1979
Maranatha Koor	Kresneti in Sranang	FL 433.005
Maranatha Koor	Volksliedjes	LP FL 433018
Maranatha Koor led by W. J. F. Leerdam	Maranatha Koor led by W. J. F. Leerdam	FL 433.005
Mardie Becksowirono [gamelan orchestra]	Mardie Becksowirono	Keris
Master Blaster	Massi Dang	Cosmo
Max Nijman	Katibo	Dureco 1983
Max Nijman	Wan dei lobi	FL 433.007
Max Nijman	Ini wan dé	FL 433.017
Max Woiski & en zijn La Cubana Orkest	Flageolet Blues	
Mbanjum Wiromo [gamelan orchestra]	Mbanjum Wiromo	Keris
Mento	Para Mudo	Mento Music
Mighty Botai	Totness Coronie	©1973
Mighty Botai	Onafhankelijkheid Suriname	LP FLP 7511
Mighty Botai	Botai wang Bidji mang	LP FLP 7512
Naks	Grontapoe na asi tere	Fajalobie 1978

Artist	Title	Label, Year of Release
Naks	This Is Suriname	OM 444. 020
Naks	Soema doe boeng, na eng neng	LP FL 433.014
Naks	Kar'djebrie m'dadie	OM 444. 086
Naks	Soko Psalms	Dureco 1986
Naks	Okrobrafoenetje	KLP 740311
Odongo & the Spirits	Look Your Winti	SMA 1987
Orchestra Washboard	Washboard Spirit	Imperial
Oscar Harris & the Twinkle Stars	Oscar Harris & the Twinkle Stars	Dureco CA 26
Oscar Harris & the Twinkle Stars	Oscar Harris & the Twinkle Stars, deel 2 [part 2]	Dureco CA 156
Oscar Harris	A Day Will Come	PE 877.061
Oscar Harris	De beste van Oscar	JDL 25.013
Oscar Harris	Try a Little Love	HLT 123017
Oscar Harris	When Friends Say Goodbye	OM 444.121
Oscar Harris	Sing Your Freedom Song	PE 822011
P.I. Man & Memre Buku	Masanah	SMA 1985
Ponda O'Bryan, Afro-drum ensemble	Ndama	SMA 1987
Rhythm Masters	Sabre san je doe	Fisureco 1982
Ritmo Natural	Morning After	EMI 1970
Ritmo Natural	El Saxofon	EMI 1971
Ritmo Natural	Candy Clouds	EMI 1972
Roekom Langeng Trismo	[unknown]	Fisureco
Ronald Snijders	Quartz	BSM 1983
Ronald Snijders	Natural Sources	BSM
Ronald Snijders	A Safe Return	BSM 1980
Ronald Snijders	Black Straight Music	BSM 1981
Ronald Snijders	Funky Flute	BSM
Ronald Snijders	Zonnige Surinamers	BSM 1986
Roots Syndicate	Check It	Rock & Groove
Sabakoe	Madonna	Cosmo
Sonora Paramarera	Lobi Dee	PE 877.075
Sukru Sani	On Tour '89	Cosmo
Stan Lokhin Band	Spider Vox	Fajalobie 1978
Surinam Music Ensemble	Body Guide	SMA 1983

Artist	Title	Label, Year of Release
Surinam Music Ensemble	Dynamite Cotton Legacy	SMA 1987
Surinam Music Ensemble	No Kiddin'	Timeless 1990
Trafassi	Trafassi volume 3	TRA Records 1983
Twinkle Stars	Trintyl deel 1	PE 877034
Twinkle Stars	Trintyl deel 2	PE 877089
Twinkle Stars	Hang On Sloopy	PE 877094
Twinkle Stars	De beste van the Twinkle Stars	JDL 25.008
De Vrolijke Jeugd	Surinaamse klanken	OM 444.006
De Vrolijke Jeugd	In memorium J. A. Pengel	OM 222018
De Vrolijke Jeugd	Wie lobie wie sweeti sranang	OM 444066
De Vrolijke Jeugd	Sunny Suriname	DU 51071
De Vrolijke Jeugd	Vrolijke Surinamse Jeugd	OM 333101
Young Cosie	Iwan Esseboom & Lilian Mynals, werede	Cosmo
Young Sound	Live at de Melkweg	Dureco 1986
Zahe Jehan and his Amos Band	Amos Qawali	RCS

Various artists	Title	Label, Year of Release
v.a.	Musique Boni et Wayana de Guyane	Disque Vogue
v.a.	From Slavery to Freedom: Music of the	Lyrichord 1977
	Saramakka Maroons of Suriname	
v.a.	Javanese Music of Suriname	Lyrichord 1977
v.a.	Da Rutu fu Sranan	Dureco 1986
Secco's Gitanos et al.	Swing van Nederlandsch Fabricaat, deel 1	Panachord 1983
Secco's Gitanos et al.	Weerman	Panachord 1987
	Hoor es	Tropenmuseum 1975
	Roodkapje	TRA Records
	Sunny Live	TRA Records
	Lapu Lapu Nusantara	Killroy Kil 1982
	Caribbean Power	©1975
	Wan Pipel [soundtrack]	OM 555.050
	Muziek uit de West	CA 162 Dureco

APPENDIX 2: CONTENT OF MUSIC CASSETTE (TO THE 1990 EDITION)

Side A

1. Lieve Hugo—*Mi bèbè* (H. Uiterloo) EMI 1C056 2587, 1975. 3:55

2. P.I. Man & Memre Buku—*Bèbè bong* (Imro Belliot) SMA LP 006, 1985. 3:49

3. Max Woiski Sr. en zijn Zuidamerikaans orkets [and his South American Orchestra]—*B.B. met R.* (Max Woiski) Imperial SILW 1028, 1956. 2:56

4. Vrolijke Jeugd—*Sranang gron ton gotoe nonja* (R. Waal) Dureco 331515, 1987. 2:50

5. Ensemble Alberto Gemerts & George Schermacher—*Watra long na mie ai* (trad.) Recording W.O. Studio XI B 238.731, 1968. 2:15

6. TRIS-Kapel conducted by A.C. van Hoek (vocals: Rud Watkion)—fragment of *Poeroe foeroe* (E. Snijders) Polydor 2441.010, 1969. 1:55

7. Big Jones—*Koejakoedia* (trad.) Phillips 427.032, 1960. 2:58

8. Trafassi—*Chitra lowe* (H. Biervliet/Trafassi) TRA Records 83.003, 1983. 4:34

9. Happy Boys—*Akoeba* (trad./adapted by Lokhin/Sayamanson) Dureco 331515, 1977. 3:52

10. Oscar Harris & The Twinkle Stars—*Mina Mina* (Lokhin/Harris) Dureco Pink Elephant PE 822.004, 1973. 3:10

11. Fransje Gomez—*Na ondro watra mi dè na pokoe de kari mi* Track A1 from LP *Winti pokoe* Unice Records 081-08, 1981. 4:22

12. Surinam Music Ensemble—Gro'njan (trad./R. Gilles) SMA LP 007 B 505 675-3, 1987. 3:26

Side B

13. Terbangen Ensemble Roekom Langeng Trismo (vocal: A. Paimo)—fragment from *Wong oerip alam doonjoh* (Katidja) Karmoen Karto Product, 1982. 2:09

14. Gamelan orkest Mardie Becksowirono—*Pari Anjar*—Ventu FC30.021, 1981. 3:45

15. Eddy Jankipersading—*Oedho bhoorwa medhoer poete djaiho* (trad. wedding song) Track 12 of LP *Dance Melodies* 77011, 1976. 3:16

16. Awana (Saramaccan from Goejaba)—*Seketi ko'boeka* and *Seketi* recordings Wereldomroep (Radio Netherlands World Service) on June 8, 1978. Royal Tropical Museum, Amsterdam.

17. Caribbean Indians along the Marowijne (singers, durn and krawasi players)—*Rouwopheffingsritueel* [Ending of period of mourning ritual] Track B5 from LP *Indiaanse liederen uit Suriname/De Karaiben langs de Marowijne, recordings 1966–68*, Royal Tropical Museum, Amsterdam, 1975. 2:22

18. Maranatha choir—*Wi tata* (John Nelom) Track A1 from *Maranatha in Concert* Dureco Faja Lobie FL433.019, 1979. 2:39

19. NAKS—*Mie afo kemoto na nengre kondre* (NAKS) from LP *Soko Psalms* Dureco MS 251 A, 1986. 2:45

20. Kid Dynamite (vocal and tenor sax), Lou Hidalgo (maracas), and the Bonanza Boys led by Dick Elgg—*Wintidansi waarbij de slang wordt vereerd* [Winti Dance in honor of the snake] (trad.) Recording AVRO's Radioscoop, 1956. 3:34

21. Ronald Snijders—*Bakadjari* (R. Snijders) from LP *Quartz* BSM 0104, 1983. 4:26

22. Fra Fra Sound—*Aisa* Track 13 from *Panja Gazz*, 1987. 4:22

23. Droeh Nankoe—*Bidai* (K. Bandhu/P. Saidi) Track B4 from EP *Songs for Various Occasions* Dureco 115001, 1988. 5:44

APPENDIX 3: SELECTED DISCOGRAPHY TO THE SECOND EDITION

Note: Where dates are not listed, they are unknown.

Ai Fu Ai—*Voorzichtig* Kasakawi uit Suriname, Conga Music CD-5007

Akrema. SMA Records. SMALP001. 1981

Robby Alberga: *Different Realities*. Jair Records. 1996

Aleke Roots. Fredje Studio

Aptijt—*Boeke en andere poku's,* Top Notch. 2015 re-release compilation

Bally Brashuis & Blaka Boeba. Kwakoe Records KLP 740312. 1980

Imro Belliot (1949–2014) see P.I. Man

Botty Man: *The Best of Botty* (CD). N.p. (Paramaribo). 2007

Cry Freedom: Lobi (CD). N.p. (Paramaribo). 2007

Djinti: *Ala Firi* [All Feelings]. Tiri Records

Dropati: *Let's sing and dance with Dropati. The Grandmother of Baithak Gana.* Windsor Records, Trinidad & Tobago W006. 1968

Energy Crew and Friends: No More War (CD). Sony (Paris). 2004

Iwan Esseboom & the Funmasters—*Wittie Visie (En Andere Poku's,* Top Notch. 2016 re-release compilation

Faya Wowia: Bosikopoe, Vol. 3 (CD). N.p. (Paramaribo). 2005

Fra Fra Big Band
—*A Tan So*. Lucho 7708-2. 1993
—*Maspoti Makandra*. Pramisi Records. 1998
—*With the Spirit Of Life*. Pramisi Records. 2013

Fra Fra Sound www.frafrasound.nl
—*Third Life Stream*. 1990
—*Panja Gazz +4* [CD edition of 1982/1987 album on vinyl]. 1991
—*Kalinha's Serenade*. Lucho 7707-2. 1993
—*Worship Mother Earth*. 1994
—*Global Village Residents*. Music and Word Records MWCD 3014. 1996
—*Kaseko Revisited*. Kotabra. Pramisi Records Pra CD 97001. 1997
—*Mali Jazz. Collaboration Musique d'Afrique*. Pramisi Records CD 99003.
   1999
—*African Journey*. Sheer Sound, XPH-JRY-UEH-5. 2003
—*Kultiplex*. Pramisi Records. 2003
—*Kulembanban/Kid Dynamite Tribute*. Pramisi Records. 2004
—*Krosbé*. Pramisi Records. 2004
—*Dya So*. Pramisi Records. 2007
—*Black, Dutch and More with The Spirit Of Life* [30th anniversary album].
   Pramisi. 2010

Ghabiang: *Tanapu in de rij*. Artie Records. ARCD 210270. 1993

Robby Harman: *Harmanized*. In de Knipscheer/Ora Media Publishing, CD
+ book ISBN 978-90-6265-942-5. 2016

Oscar Harris: *Soldier's Prayer en andere poku's*. Top Notch. 2014 re-release
compilation

Annemarie Hunsel. *Alin E Fadon Ini Mi Hati & Live at Amos*. (Surinam)
Galaxy Europe Music, AH 003. 1997

Denise Jannah. *A Heart Full of Music*. Timeless CD SJP 414. 1993

Carlo Jones & the Suriname Kaseko Troubadours. Music and Words Records
MWCD 3011. 1995

Fransje Gomez (1921–2004) All of her recordings were lost in a fire except for two records.

A 12-inch vinyl record with four tracks was released on a Dutch label specializing in Surinamese music under an alternate spelling of her name:
—France Gomes: *Winti Pokoe.* Unice Records. 1981

There are two examples of her drumming work on YouTube:
—Fransje Gomes meets Oema Prisiri en Afu Sensi. https://www.you tube.com/watch?v=522hQMVrn9g
—Na tapoe sjoro w'pristi—winti poku. https://www.youtube.com/watch?v=9rswSAO3iH8

Kenny B. *Kenny B.* Top Notch. 2015 https://www.facebook.com/LikeKennyB/

Kid Dynamite. *Kulembanban (En Andere Poku's).* Top Notch. 2014 re-release compilation

Kolebrie: *Sopiang.* Unice Records 0076

Koropina meets Kaseko Loco & The Old Timers: *Sranan Kondre.* KP90207

Ewald Krolis & The Caribbean Combo: *Switie Bamaro.* Unice Records LP UR 0068. 1979

Ewald Krolis & The Caribbean Combo: *Switie Bamaro.* Fantasia 402

Lieve Hugo. *King of Kaseko. The Beauty of Surinam.* EMI 7949472. 1990

Marius Liesdek [see Big Jones]

Stan Lokhin Band: *Spider Vox.* Faja Lobie Records FL433.012. 1978

Kara Dara. Pramisi Records PRA CD 0805. 2009

P.I. Man & Memre Buku. *Tukusy.* SMA Records SMALP2. 1982

P.I. Man & Memre Buku. *Masannah.* SMALP006 Novib Series. 1985

Jeangu Macrooy
—*Brave Enough* (EP). Unexpected Records. 2016
—*High on You.* Unexpected Records. 2017
—*Horizon.* Unexpected Records. 2019
—*Birth of a New Age.* Unexpected Records. 2021

Master Blaster—*Als Je Mij Een Vingertje Wijst (En Andere Poku's).* Top Notch. 2016 re-release compilation

Johan Misiedjan: *Opo Dansi.* B&L Music 20021. 2002

NAKS Kaseko Loko plays kaskawi. *Switi Momo*

Droeh Nankoe
—*Songs for Various Occasions.* Dureco 1150101. 1988
—*Prashanti/Highest Peace. Bhjanas sung by Droeh Nankoe.* Pan Records PAN 2051. 1998
—*Baithak Gana (Songs from Bihar, Uttar Pradesh, and Surinam).* Pan Records PAN 2037 Ethnic Series. 2003

Frank Ong-Alok—*Mijn God mijn God Waarom Heb ik U Verlaten? Autobiografische levensfacetten* [My God, My God Why Did I Abandon You? Autobiographical Facets of Life]. Book and CD. In de Knipscheer, Haarlem, 2017 ISBN 978-90-6265-921-0

Kries Ramkhelawan: Daroe Tamakhoe Mehraroe

Ritmo Natural—double CD/DVD box, Zimbraz/Music & Words MWCD 3044. 2012 rerelease of old vinyl albums & DVD of live footage

La Rouge: *Ritsen.* La La Music. 2000

William Souvenir: *Na'f Mi Wang.* Music & Words MWCD 3012. 1996

William Souvenir: *A Tin Télé.* Music & Words MWCD 3010. 1994

Lamie & Tjondro Utomo. Disco Amigo DA 33023

Sranan Moksie Patoe. Compilation with Walvis, Ai Sa Si, Caribbean Combo, Kaseko Masters. SU CD 1002. 1996

Big Jones: *Wan bosu bana*. Soundtrack from *Faja Lobbie*. Philips Records

Berg & Dal Boys: *Djie Deng Oema*. Disco Amigo VR 20-994

La Caz: *Meets the Surinam Stars*. LC 06. 2001

Melody Travellers (Coronie Band): *De palmen*. Traditional Records Co-cos2000025

Melly (Meldric) and Friends: *Probleem* (CD). N.p. (Paramaribo) CDR 3930. 2009

Raj Mohan www.rajmohan.nl
—*Kantráki* [Contract Laborer]. Pan Records PAN 213. 2005
—*Main ghazal hoon*. Pan Records PAN 217. 2009
—*Daayra*. Continental Record Services. 2011
—*Dui mutthi*. EP, Pan Records PAN 223. 2013

De Nazaten (van Prins Hendrik) http://www.nazaten.nl
—*Kownu boy e dansi*. Pan Records PAN 163. 1997
—*Kachéché*. Pan Records. 2000
—*Poku Kon Na Wan*. Strotbrock Records. 2003
—*On Stage*. Pan Records. 2007

De Nazaten and James Carter. *Skratylogy*. Strotbrock. 2009

Ponda O'Bryan & Afro-Drum-Ensemble: *Ndama*. Surinam Music Association SMA011. 1987

Max Nijman: *Adjossi en andere poku's*. Top Notch. 2014 re-release compilation

Paco Sound: *Wan Uma No Habi Fadon*. Paco Sound. 2003

Papa Touwtje: *Gangster*. 1994; re-released as *Gangster en andere poku's*. Top Notch. 2014

Pawana Omano: *Kuranore*.

Pawana: *Semeria Woyuhpore'* [A Calling Card for the Descendants]

Positif Vibration: *Busi Data*. CD. N.p. (Paramaribo). 2008

Revelation Time: *Time Will Tell*. Concordia Records CON02002. 2003

Riddim Espace Sound. CD. SDRM 390706005. 2008

Shirityo-Yare: *Iepiororo*. Sirius Records

Ronald Snijders released most of his records on his own Black Straight Music (BSM) label:
—*Natural Sources*. LP. 1977
—*Funky Flute*. LP. 1985
—*Ode Aan Eddy Snijders*. 1990
—*Interfaces*. 1991
—*Portable Beach*. 1992
—*Oude en nieuwe Surinaamse kinderliedjes*. 1994
—*Kaseko Mundial! Live*. 1996
—*LP Track compilation*. 1997
—*Meet The World*. 1998
—*The Best of Ronald Snijders*. 1999
—*Kleurrijke liedjes*. 2000
—*Bijlmerjazz*. BSM0120. 2001
—*Variyento*. 2004
—*Ronald Snijders to Africa*. BSM0125. 2005
—*West by West & Soulkawina*. 2005
—*Ronald Snijders extended funk band*. 2008
—*Made for music*. 2013
—*The Nelson & Djosa Sessions*. V2 Benelux VVNL28432. 2016

South South West: *Fa Waka*. M Records SSW0297CD-DDX 058929.

Success Fighters: *Aluku Liba*. CD. Rediarta SF.AL/01-07. 2007

Sukru Sani: *Pompo Lollie (En Andere Poku's)*. Top Notch. 2016 re-release
compilation

Sukru Sani: *Presirie Kawina*. 1990

Sukru Sani: *Hoge Druk, Lage Druk*. Afro Records. 1992

Sukru Sani: *Voel Je 't?* Arti Records. 1994

Surinam Music Ensemble: *Main Topic.* SME Stemra 150493. 1993

Trafassi: *Wasmasjien en andere poku's.* Top Notch. 2014 re-release compilation

Tumak Humak: *Underwater Activity.* Tuma Records TMC004. 1991

Typhoon: http://www.mctyphoon.nl
—*Tussen Licht en Lucht.* Top Notch. 2007
—*Chocolade* [with the New Cool Collective]. EP. 2010
—*Lobi Da Basi* [Love is the Boss]. Top Notch/Universal. 2014
—*Lichthuis* [Light House]. Top Notch. 2020

Orchestra Washboard: *Washboard Spirit.* Imperial (2)—5C054-24198

Hugo Uiterloo (1932–1975) see Lieve Hugo

Wan Ton Melody: *Boun Na Soso fou Feni.* CD. Wan Ton Melody WM2797.
2007

Max Woiski Jr.:
—*Rijst met kouseband (en ander poku's).* 2 CD. Top Notch/Universal
TN1405 CD 3786656-37886657. 2014
—*At the Tropicana, Amsterdam.* CNR SKLP 4225. 1968; re-release CNR 241
344, ca. 1970 (Remastered and available on iTunes), CNR Records, 2014
—*Woiski A Go Go: Live recording at La Tropicana.* CNR ZZ 1613. 1970

Max Woiski Sr.:
—*BB met R en andere poku's.* Sranan Gowtu, Top Notch/Universal TN1316
CD 3734725. 2013
—*Bigi Brasa.* EMI Music Holland BOSPCD 252. 1998

Max Woiski Sr. & Max Woiski Jr.: *Ritmo Tropical.* DVD+2CD. Source I Media
S1M2564574. 2011

Yakki Famirie & Conjunto Latinos: *Blakamang Oeng No Njan Blakamang.*
Arti Records. 1991

Yakki Famirie: *Concentratie.* Arti Records. 1993

Yakki Famirie. *Gowtu.* World Connection WC 43006. 1999

Various Artists/Compilations

Busikondé Sama de Guyane: Musique et chants traditionnels. 2CD. Recorded and Annotated by Apollinaire Anakesa. CADEG (Centre d'Archives de Documents Ethnographiques de la Guyane) RADdO AVPL 61. 2008

Drums of Defiance: Maroon Music from the Earliest Free Black Communities of Jamaica. CD. Recorded and Annotated by Kenneth Bilby. Smithsonian Folkways SF CD 40412. 1992

Forty Years of Surinamese Music in the Netherlands. Marcel Weltak, Robin Austen, and Guilly Koster. In de Knipscheer and IKO Foundation, Haarlem. 2CD and 104-page book ISBN 978-90-6265-936-6, 2016. Includes one track each from: Pawana, Ai sa Si, Combinatie XVI, Ewald Krolis, Iwan Esseboom, La Rouge, Sukru Sani, Yakki Famiri, Dhroeh Nankoe, Dropati, Raj Mohan, De Nazaten + Sana Budaya Paramaribo, Gerda Havertong (Armand Baag), Oema Soso, Djinti, Trafassi, Stan Lok Hin, Lieve Hugo, Ondongo Angel, Surinam Music Ensemble, Andro Biswane (Kara Dara), Dave MacDonald, Iwan VanHetten, Eddy Veldman (Opo Yeye), Fra Fra Sound, Franky Douglas, P.I. Man, Norman van Geerke, Jeaninne LaRose, Powl Ameerali (Roy MacDonald), Steve Mariat, Re-Play, Harto Soemodihardjo (Manoushka Breeveld), Kenny B., Robby Harman, Pablo Nahar, Ronald Snijders, Robin van Geerke

The Kings of Baithak Gana. Baithak Explosion. Manodj Music.

Lavi Danbwa: Chants, musique, danses Aluku. CD. Recorded and Annotated by Yvan Ho You Fat. Association Lavi Danbwa STAZ 020. 2007

The Maroni River Caribs of Surinam—Royal Tropical Institute The Music Collection. Pan Records PAN 4005. 1996

Music from Aluku: Maroon Sounds of Struggle, Solace, and Survival. CD. Recorded, Compiled, and Annotated by Kenneth Bilby. Smithsonian Folkways SFW CD 50412. 2010

Musique Boni et Wayana de Guyane. LP. Recorded and Annotated by Jean Hurault. Disques Vogue/Musée de l'Homme LVLX 290. 1968

Music from Saramaka: A Dynamic Afro-American Tradition. LP. Recorded and Annotated by Richard Price and Sally Price. Ethnic Folkways FE 4225. 1977

Roots de Guyane. CD. Virgin PM 538 03098. 2003

From Slavery to Freedom: Music of the Saramaka Maroons of Suriname. LP. Recorded by Verna Gillis, with Notes by Richard Price. Lyrichord LLST 7354. 1981

Songs from Surinam 3. CD compiled by Hans Gouweloos. Dureco 11 63712. 1998

Songs from Surinam 4. Compiled by Hans Gouweloos. Dureco 11 64322. 1998

The Spirit Cries: Music from the Rainforests of South America and the Caribbean. CD. Produced by Mickey Hart. Annotated by Kenneth Bilby and James McKee. Rykodisc RCD 10250. 1993

Sranan Gowtu. Aptijt, Damaru, Iwan Esseboom & the Funmasters, Lieve Hugo, Happy Boys, Big Jones, The Mighty Botai, Oscar Harris, La Rouge, Master Blaster, Max Nijman, Max Woiski Jr., Max Woiski Sr., Papa Touwtjie, Sukru Sani, De Surinaamse Vrolijke Jeugd, Trafassi. Top Notch. 2013

Sranan Gowtu 2. Eddy Assan & Silvy Singoredjo, Bontjie Stars, Errol Burger & the Cosmo Stars, Edgar Burgos & Traffasi, Kid Dynamite, The Falling Stones, Alberto Gemerts, Kenny B and Jeffrey Spaulding, La Rouge, Scrappy W., Max Woiski Jr., Max Nijman, Max Woiski Sr., Lieve Hugo, Oscar Harris and the Twinkle Stars, Ronald Snijders, Tjatjie, Enver, Beer, Ernie Wolf, Thunderstorm, Papa Touwtjie. Top Notch. 2016

Switi: Hot! Kaseko Music. CD. Dutch Rock Music Foundation SPN 010. 1993

I Greet the New Day: Classical Songs and Music of the Ndyuka Maroons of Suriname. CD. Recorded and Annotated by André R. M. Pakosie. Stichting Sabanapeti and Radio Nederland Wereldomroep. 2002

Aiatonda and Naya Bingi Foundation: Lobi Moes Dé. CD. N.p. (Paramaribo). 2006

Tambours de la terre 1: Afrique-Amérique. CD. Annotated by Laurent Aubert. Auvidis Ethnic B 6773. 1992

Various Songs of Suriname—Sranan Poku Styling. Arti Records SUI 1000. 1994

Voudou. Compiled and annotated by Leendert van der Valk. Excelsior Recordings, Excel 96493. Includes tracks by Lieve Hugo, Oscar Harris and the Twinkle Stars, and Kid Dynamite in the Surinamese section of his compilation of voodoo-related music from the southern US, Haiti, Benin, and Togo. 2017

Wailing Roots: Original Aloukou Soldiers. CD. Déclic Communication 50364-2. 1994

Wailing Roots: Feeling & Dub. CD. Mélodie ACP CG 014. 1995

APPENDIX 4: FILMOGRAPHY/VIDEOGRAPHY/ DVDS, 1960-2021

1960 *Faja Lobbi* [Fiery Love]. Symphony of the tropics. Directed by Herman van der Horst. It was shown at film festivals in Berlin and Adelaide. The film won the Golden Bear Award for best documentary at the 1960 Berlin festival. It portrays the interior of Suriname, by filming villages along the course of the Marowijne River, and how the multicultural society of Creoles (Afro-Surinamers), Hindustani, Javanese, Chinese, Boeroes (descendants of Dutch farming immigrants), Amerindians and maroons (Bush Negroes) live cheek by jowl. *Faja Lobbi* also refers to the national flower of Suriname, *Ixora*. In 2010 *Faja Lobbi* was published as part of a 3-CD box set about Suriname by the Nederlands Instituut voor Beeld en Geluid (Dutch Institute of Sound and Images). Complete film: https:// www.youtube.com/watch?v=mgV3yPANxMU

1977 *Kon hesi baka* [Come Back Soon]. Directed by Henk Barnard. Children's series based on the book of the same name. https://www.youtube.com/ watch?v=UR-ZLY8zR84

1993 *Bewogen Koper* [Moving Brass]. Directed by Johan van der Keuken. Written by Rob Boonzajer Flaes and Johan van der Keuken. Documentary shows brass bands from Nepal, Suriname, Indonesia, and Ghana.

1997 *Aleke-Sound*, part one. VHS videotape. Directed by André R. M. Pakosie. ARMP Production.

2001 *Une voix sur le Maroni*. DVD. Directed by Hélène Lee. France Mexique Cinéma, Radio France Outre-Mer, and Centre National de la Cinématographie.

2001 *Kid Dynamite.* Directed by Hans Hylkema. Pieter van Huystee Film & TV/NPS. Complete film in Dutch: www.youtube.com/watch?v=AtJ_ UstnsSQ

2009 *Aluku Liba: Maroon Again.* DVD. Directed by Nicolas Jolliet. ArtMattan Productions.

2009 *Songe et Awasa: danses tradtionnelles Aluku.* DVD. Directed by Yvan Ho You Fat. CRDP Guyane and Association Lavi Danbwa.

2010 *Let Each One Go Where He May.* Directed by Ben Russell. Ben Russell Productions.

2012 *Iko King of Kaseko: Het Metropole Orkest speelt Lieve Hugo.* 2 DVD/CD. S1M2566448. Fifteen-minute excerpt of the concert on YouTube: https://www.youtube.com/watch?v=mFoDbae4AfI

2013 *Typhoon (Van de regen naar de zon)* [From the Rain to the Sun]. Live performance for the Dutch King Willem and Queen Maxima and the Prime Minister on the 200th anniversary of the Netherlands as a republic. Excerpt: https://www.youtube.com/watch?v=NQeOHEQo5nk

2016 *Easy Man: The Story of Ronald Snijders, His Music and the the Nelson & Djosa Sessions.* Directed by Niels Nieuborg and Jasper Cremers (aka Nelson & Djosa) and Dennis de Groot. 44 minutes. Official trailer: https://www.youtube.com/watch?v=XHnMhmXWT98

2016 *Gold,* the socially conscious song from the EP *Brave Enough* by Jeangu Macrooy. https://www.youtube.com/watch?v=sOzFc8MZ_TQ

2016 *De stilte van het ongesproken woord* [The Silence of the Unspoken Word]. DVD and book of poems by three prominent Surinamese poets, Dobru, Shrinivasi, and Trefossa set to music by Dave MacDonald and Robin van Geerke. In de Knipscheer & IKO Foundation.

2016 *Het wonderbaarlijke leven van Kenny B* [The Miraculous Life of Kenny B]. Directed by Walter Stokman. VPRO 54-minute television documentary/road movie. http://www.walterstokmanfilms.nl/

2016 *Typhoon, Blues & Blessings.* Broadcast on BNN, Dutch national television. http://www.npo.nl/3doc/27-02-2016/BNN_101378505

2018 *Typhoon in Amerika.* Broadcast on EO, Dutch national television. https://www.npo3.nl/typhoon-in-amerika/VPWON_1284051

2021 *Birth of a New Age*, eponymous title track to the album and the official Dutch entry to the 2021 Eurovision Song festival. Official Eurovision Song video: https://www.youtube.com/watch?v=p4Fag4yajxk

APPENDIX 5: SRANAN SONG LINES AND TITLES

Brombere—Septic Tank Truck

Faja Siton no bron mi so—A Surinamese children's song meaning Hot stone don't burn me so. During slavery time in Suriname there was a coffee plantation, run by a slave master named Jan (called Masra Jantjie). During the harvest, the slaves had a certain quota of coffee beans to bring in. If you were short of your quota, Masra Jantjie, would make a fire into which he would put stones. When the stones where really hot, those slaves had to stand in a circle and were then forced to pick up the stone and pass it around the other slaves. If any of them dropped the stone, they would get a severe beating!

Fransje Gomez, naki a sani—Fransje Gomez, beat the drum

Jajo liebie—A Wayward Life

Komisi de na botri—The Cook Is in the Kitchen

Konu Oloisi lassie, mi yere a bubu tekin—The King's Clock Has Gone Missing. I Heard the Ghost Swiped It.

Kwasi, da lobi fu Yaba—Kwasi, Yaba's Lover

Lele sina go—[a shout with no specific translation]

Malango—[an archaic Creole form of dance music]

Mi sjie deng jonkuman—I Have Seen the Young Men

Mini, mini I kon njang—Mini, Mini Come and Eat

Mi na kakafowra, mi kroon de na mi ede—I Am the Rooster, My Crown Is on My Head

Mis' Elena, trin tran tring, min na moni masra—Miss Elena, ding, dong, ding, I'm the Guy with the Money

Oen egi pasi—Our Own Way

Oema soso e tjari a commando—Only the Women Are Calling the Shots

Poeroe foetoe—Move Your Feet

PPB (Pengel Premier Baka na in Sranang)—Prime Minister Pengel Back in Suriname

Sing, sing tap joe koto—Beautiful Flower, Keep Your Petals Closed

Tai hori, brada, naga sisa—Come Together, My Brothers and Sisters

Tai na boeriki—Tie Up the Donkey

Te mati e kori yu, a no e lafu—If Your Buddy Is Screwing You It's No Joke

Watra en long na mi ai—Water Flows from My Eye

LIST OF ACRONYMS

Suriname

AVROS—Algemeen Vereniging Radio Omroep Suriname [General Association Radio Broadcasting Suriname]

RAPAR—Radio Paramaribo

STICUSA—Stichting voor Culturele Samenwerking [Foundation for Cultural Cooperation], founded in 1948 to foster cultural exchange between Holland, Indonesia, Suriname, and the Netherlands Antilles; disbanded in 1988

SURIPOP—originally denoting the first Suriname Popular Music Festival, Suripop went on to become a generic term to describe pop music of Surinamese origin

TRIS—Tropen Macht in Suriname [Tropical Armed Forces in Suriname]

The Netherlands

AVRO—Algemeen Vereniging Radio Omroep [General Association of Radio Broadcasting]

BIM—Bond voor Improviserende Musici [Union for Improvising Musicians]; their venue is called BIMHUIS [huis= house]

NCRV—Nederlandse Christelijke Radio Vereniging [Dutch Christian Radio Organization]

VARA—Vereniging van Arbeiders Radio Amateurs [Association of Amateur Radio Workers]

GLOSSARY OF MUSICAL INSTRUMENTS

agida—Largest Afro-Surinamese drum. It is two to three meters long and 40–50 cm across, fashioned out of the single trunk of a tree. Played with one hand and a stick; especially reserved to communicate with the deities of the earth (Loko & vodu). Before playing, the drum is cleaned with mpemba (kaolin).

anklung—Bamboo rattle of Javanese origin.

apinti—The national Afro-Surinamese drum: conical shape 50–100 cm high, diameter 30–40 cm. usually played with two hands or one hand and a stick. Used to communicate with the gods and send messages. (Ghana: Akan tribes: *apentema*; other names: *apretia, oporenten, atumpan*)

Apuku-dron—Hollowed-out tree trunk about 130 cm long, diameter 20–30 cm. It tapers down, getting narrower toward the bottom. Ghana, Saramaccaners use it to call the *Apuku*-forest deity.

bedug—Large drum in Surinamese *terbangen* (Indonesian tambourine) ensembles. (Java)

benta—In Suriname, this refers to various stringed instruments and thumb pianos. These instruments have largely fallen into disuse.

bongo—Short, cylindrical hollowed-out tree trunk about 40 cm long, diameter 20–25 cm; not related to the modern Cuban bongo.

bonko enchemrya—Sacred drum in Cuba whose shape and system of stretching the skin is related to the Surinamese bongo.

bonang—Gamelan instrument with pan-shaped sound source made of brass, which was replaced by iron. (Java)

bototutu—Iron horn for communicating between riverboats, especially on the Maroni. Nowadays largely replaced by the radio or megaphone.

dantaal—Long metallic bar on which the player indicates the beat with a small V-shaped rod. (India)

dawra (dawura)—Iron cowbell with origin from the Akan tribes in Ghana.

deindein—Saramaccan name for the pudja drum. Also the name of the pulse in Saramaccan music.

demung—Seven-bar gamelan gong set that replaced the ketuk and kenong in Surinamese gamelan ensembles. (Java)

dholak or **dhol**—South Asian two-headed hand-drum. It may have traditional cotton rope lacing, screw-turnbuckle tensioning, or both combined. Often used in *Filmi Sangeet* (Indian film music), chutney music, chutney-soca, baitak gana, *taan* singing, bhajans, and the local Indian folk music of Jamaica, Suriname, Guyana, Caribbean, South Africa, Mauritius, and Trinidad and Tobago, where it was brought by indentured immigrants.

dhapla—Large drum played deep into the night at Hindustani weddings.

djendjen—Cowbell in the shape of a clock to summon gods of Surinamese origin.

godo—Two calabashes, the larger of which is filled with water and the smaller turned upside down to float on the surface of the water. It is played with sticks. (Suriname)

golu-benta—Hollowed-out calabash gourd with strings stretched across it. In Africa such instruments are still quite popular. (Sierra Leone: *congoma*; Ghana: *primprimsua*)

grumi—Wooden washboard of Surinamese origin played with two thin sticks as a scratchboard, akin to the North American washboard.

hari dron—Term used to refer to the "basic rhythm drum" in an Afro-Surinamese drum ensemble.

harmonium—Hand-pumped keyboard created so that the instrument could be played while the player was sitting on the floor. Used in India, Pakistan, Nepal, Afghanistan, and other Asian countries as an accompanying instrument in Hindustani classical music, Sufi music, Bhajan and other devotional music, Qawwali, Natya Sangeet, and a variety of genres including accompaniment to classical Kathak dance.

jankabuari—Surinamese American tribe Arawak transverse flute.

kawinadron—Cylindrical hollowed-out tree trunk Surinamese drum, about 45 cm long and 25 cm in diameter, stretched on both sides with a system of cords. Laid across the lap and played on one end with a stick and on the other by hand.

kawtutu—End-blown cow horn used to summon the gods.

kendang—Indonesian drum in gamelan ensemble.

kempul—Type of gamelan gong.

kenong—Type of gamelan gong.

ketuk—Type of gamelan gong.

kotek-an—Rice stamper.

koti dron—Surinamese term used to refer to the "master drum" that plays improvisations in an Afro-Surinamese drum ensemble in response to the hari dron.

krawasie—Rattle with the seeds of the poisonous krawasie tree in a basket of braided warimbo palm leaves. Suriname Amerindian rattle of the Kari'na tribe.

kwakwa—Surinamese hollowed-out tree trunk with a slit drum, played with two sticks. Besides its rhythmic function, it also has a role as "talking drum," that is, to convey messages.

kwakwa-bangi—Derived from the kwakwa; a wooden bench that is played with two sticks, probably hailing from Africa. (Congo: *nkpokpo*)

kwatro (*cuatro* in Spanish-speaking countries)—Four-stringed guitar; prevalent in Venezuela and Curaçao, where it is called *kwarta*.

langadron—Alternate name in some areas for the apuku-dron.

langaudu—Alternate name in some areas for the apukudron.

maracas (or **pyja-rattles**)—Rattles with seeds of paracua plant in a calabash, supplemented with *tawono* pebbles from a riverbed. Suriname Amerindian rattle of the Kalina tribe.

man-dron (langadron or **langaudu)**—Like the agida drum, made from a hollowed-out single trunk of a tree, but shorter, about 150 cm and diameter of 25–30 cm; played with both hands.

mata—Wooden mortar of Surinamese origin, the stomping of which can create rhythmic accompaniment to work songs.

mridangam—South Asian (Indian) double-sided drum whose body is usually made using a hollowed piece of jackfruit wood about an inch thick.

naal—South Asian (Indian) wooden two-headed drum. Heads held in place and tuned by bolts. Player holds the naal horizontally and plays both heads. Commonly used in folk music and during marriage celebrations.

nagara—Indian drums played with two sticks as part of an ensemble performing Ahirwa *ke naadj*.

pakro-tutu—Surinamese horn made from a shell to summon the gods.

papai-benta—Thumb piano. (Africa: *sanza, likembe, mbira*)

penurus—Javanese seven-bar gamelan gong set that eventually replaced the saron in Surinamese gamelan ensembles.

pudja—Afro-Surinamese short, hollowed-out tree trunk drum, about 50 cm long and 25–30 cm across.

pyjai-rattles—See maracas.

sakka—Suriname Amerindian calabash gourd filled with seeds through which a stick is inserted.

sambura—Large cedarwood drum, snakeskin (boa constrictor) or deerskin head, resonating tongue of maripa palm, filled with seeds that make a hissing sound. Beaten with short thick sticks. Suriname Amerindian drum of the Kari'na tribe.

sarangi—Hindustani kind of violin.

saron—Extensive fourteen-bar gamelan gong set.

sedri—Surinamese word for snare drum.

siksak (sek-seki)—Percussion instrument made from iron tube filled with pits or seeds.

sitar—Plucked stringed instrument used mainly in Hindustani music and Indian classical music.

skratyi (skraki)—Surinamese large, round bass drum mounted on a trestle with cymbals on top.

suwu-an—Gamelan gong.

tabla—South Asian membranophone percussion instrument (similar to bongos), consisting of a pair of small drums.

terbangen—Indonesian tambourine.

tjapu—Hoe head beaten with metal stick; on Curaçao known as chapi.

tumaun—Saramaccan name for the apinti drum.

washboard—Originally an American percussion instrument, employing the ribbed metal surface of the cleaning device as a rhythm instrument. Derives from the practice of hamboning as practiced in West Africa and brought to the new world by African slaves. (see also grumi)

GLOSSARY OF MUSICAL STYLES

adonke (adunke)—Saramacca form of African-derived dance.

ahirwa ke naadj—Combination of music and dance almost always depicting religious Hindu stories. This is often done to the accompaniment of birahas.

aleke—Rootsy, drum-based music created by and for young Ndjuka maroons, descendants of runaway slaves living in the interior who moved to the coastal towns.

angguk—Fixed Islamic songs.

awasa—Virtuoso dance of the Saramacca tribe.

badji—Calypso-like bigi poku music from the western district of Suriname; influenced by neighboring Guyana.

baithak gana—Style developed by second-generation Surinamese Hindustani; means music played by people sitting on the ground, making use of simple texts and a sober musical accompaniment, which usually consists of harmonium, dholak, and dantaal. Well-known players include Eddy Jankipersading, Dropati.

bandammba—Saramaccan type of bellydance made by women sinuously grinding their lower torsos.

bangsawan—Type of Javanese theater that was accompanied by kroncong music.

banja—The most important form of dance and music within the cycle of ancestor songs. Those present during a banja session (or pré) can be possessed by the spirit of an ancestor. Arose in the nineteenth century.

bal-masque (masked ball)—For quite a long time bal-masque was the only form of celebration in which European instruments were played. For some Afro-Surinamers, this ball had significance within the rites to venerate their ancestors. On some Caribbean islands there still exist related styles that use masks, such as John Canoe in Jamaica and *diabolitos* in Cuba.

bazuinkoor (choir of trumpets)—Instrumental music played especially at birthday celebrations, based on German chorales and English hymns that through the church are familiar to many Surinamers.

bhadjan—Religious songs of Surinamese Hindus.

bigi poku—Probably a corruption of English "big" and Dutch *pauk*: music of the big kettledrum or timpani. The big drum in the bigi poku is the *skratyi-dron* (skratyi drum) or bass drum. This drum owes its name to the trestle that supports it while playing it on stage. During marches and processions, however, the skratyi is hung from a strap on the belly of the player. Renowned players are Baas Adriaan and George Schermacher.

biraha—Lament and funeral music, sung after the loss of a loved one.

bungu bungu—Predecessor to bigi poku; onomatopoetic name for music originally played at fairgrounds that echoes the sound of the carousel (merry-go-round). Most famous exponents the brothers "Noso ka" and "Flenflen" Gilhuis.

chautaals—Sung especially by Hindus in connection with Holi-Phagwa, a Hindu celebration to mark the transformation of nature in spring.

gamelan—Traditional ensemble music of Java and Bali in Indonesia, and Suriname made up predominately of percussive instruments. The most common instruments used are metallophones played by mallets and a set of hand-played drums called *kendhang* that register the beat.

gending-gending—Javanese songs.

ghazals—Romantic songs of a nonreligious nature, usually sung in Urdu. Artists include Raj Mohan, Droeh Nankoe.

indji-tuka—Intermediate Amerindian beat.

Indji-Winti—There is hardly anything left of once-flourishing Amerindian music. Its influence can still be heard most clearly in the so-called Indji-Wintis, because the Winti cult is a mixture of African and Amerindian religions. Indji-Wintis remind the listener of the manifold spirits and their power in daily life. The dances of people in trance refer to Amerindian dances.

jarankepang—Surinamese Javanese trance inducing horse dancing.

kanga—Collective term for all sorts of children's games, most of which are of African origin.

kaseko—Afro-Surinamese popular urban dance-music style featuring electric instrumentation, brass parts, and a prominent rolling snare drum.

kaskawi—Style of kawina music developed in the 1990s, to which electric instruments and elements of kasesko have been added.

kawina (kawna, kauna)—foremost drum-based dance music of coastal Suriname's Creole people. Traditionally vocal and drum only music. Kawina is played in 4/4 meter, with the fourth beat getting the accent through the heaving rhythm of the *timbal*, the old name for the conga in Suriname. A well-known kawina singer is Big Jones, who can be seen in the movie *Faja Lobbi*.

ketopak—Javanese Arabic-tinged plays.

krawasie—Krawasie songs are played when a person dies, at funerals, and the lifting of the period of mourning.

kroncong—Indo-European creole music. Name of a ukulele-like instrument and an Indonesian musical style that typically makes use of the kroncong (the sound *chrong-chrong-chrong* comes from this instrument, so the music is called *keronchong*). Surinamese kroncong ensembles mostly use three or more acoustic guitars, a ukulele (sometimes a banjo), a double bass (or bass guitar), and a cello. However, cellists are scarce, which means the *gedugan* (kendang-like playing) is usually taken over by a guitar. Best known Surinamese kroncong group is the band Mata Hari.

kursow—Both in Sranan Tongo and Papiamentu, *kursow* is the word for Curaçao. The kursow was a dance only performed by Curaçaoan male railroad workers in Suriname and their Surinamese or Curaçaoan wives. The culture of Curaçao is traditionally oriented toward Spanish America, and that is the reason it never had a prominent place in Afro-Surinamese music. As far as can be ascertained, it has disappeared altogether.

laku—Surinamese dance spectacle in drama form.

lobisingi—Afro-Surinamese form of comic opera. Herskovits in his 1936 book *Surinamese Folklore* typified the lobisingi as "an established form of social criticism by ridicule bearing particularly on the reprehensible conduct of women." The lobisingi as an art form was almost always performed only by women.

ludruk—Javanese farces.

menor—Form of religious Javanese theater.

motjo poku—Sprang from a "civilized" music style, the lobisingi, but the character and structure of motjo poku is much rougher. The lyrics often are about sex and in general are quite obscene and coarse. In this regard, motjo poku resembles calypso, which later on would strongly influence kaseko.

nadjams (nazaams)—Religious Islamic songs in which texts from the Quran are sung.

opegooie—another name for bigi poku.

Paramaribop—This integration of Afro-Surinamese, Caribbean, and jazz traditions is now "officially" considered one of the latest variations of bebop.

paturia ke naadj (ganika)—Dance ensemble hired to play at weddings. Minimum of four artists: sarangi (Hindustani violin) or harmonium player, dholak player, singer, and dancer.

prisiri-kawina—There are two kinds of kawina. Prisiri-kawina is the oldest: not religious like the Winti kawina, but a kind of social music people could relax to, played on a sakka, two kawina drums, and a reson or kwatro (four-stringed guitar). Over the course of time, each plantation developed its own style.

qawwali—Muslim devotional songs sung in Urdu.

sambura—Kalinasambura songs' first and foremost priority are to convey messages from tribe to tribe, not between individuals.

sekete (marrons-kaseko)—Old love songs and laments from the interior, made by communities that were once runaway slaves (maroons). Cosmo Stars were popular players of sekete.

set-dansi—Idiosyncratic Surinamese combination of music and dance, descended from slave ensembles that played English and French court dances at parties of the plantation owners.

sohars—Romantic songs at weddings. All kinds of comic texts that poke fun at the bridal couple and their respective parents. Well-known artist Dropati.

sokkos or **sokko songs** (also **sokko psalms**)—Sung in an African language during worship of ancestors, sokkos are almost impossible to translate into Sranan Tongo. There is no instrumental accompaniment; the songs consist solely of introductory hymn and chorus. Sokkos usually initiate the ceremonies, even if there is a switch to other styles. Sokkos probably originate from Ivory Coast (from a tribe by the name of Sokko) or Guinea, where the Sosu or Susu tribe live. These are also referred to in Suriname by the name Sokko.

songé—Virtuoso dance of the Saramacca people.

steel-gamelan—Gamelan in Suriname also came under the influence of nearby Caribbean music, especially steel bands from Trinidad.

susa—Play in dance form, mainly performed by men.

terbangen—Ensembles based on the so-called "solo-tutti" concept: a single cantor or precentor begins and the rest follow. Texts come chiefly from the Quran, the Islamic holy scriptures, and are intended to honor the prophet Mohammed.

terbangen-cilik (terbangen-kencring)—Consists of kinds of tambourines and a bedug, which resembles a large Turkish drum.

terbangen-gede (terbangan-maulad nabi)—Typical Surinamese formation in which many hand drums and a kendang are the main elements.

tuka—Religious Islamic theater.

wayang-kulit (wayang-lulang)—Indonesian shadow puppet plays.

wayangwong (Ramayana)—Shadow plays with actors who perform the Ramaya

Winti—Afro-Surinamese traditional religion that originated in South America and developed in the Dutch Empire; this resulted in the syncretization of religious beliefs and practices of Akan, Fon, and Loango slaves with indigenous American beliefs. Has its own repertoire of sacred drumming and dance styles, mostly in 12/8 meter.

Winti kaseko—kaseko music mixed with Winti texts.

Winti-kawina—Winti songs, mostly in 12/8 meter, transposed to 4/4 meter. Due to their religious content, the Wintikawina was played at a faster tempo. The solo drum must perform more variations to be able to communicate with the various Winti spirits.

SOURCES AND BIBLIOGRAPHY

Adekoya-van Geelen, Simone. *Marroncultuur in een modern jasje: een studie naar Surinaamse Marronjongeren in Nederland en hun verbintenis met Surinaamse Marronmuziek en-cultuur* (Maroon Culture in a Modern Outfit: A Study of Young Maroons in the Netherlands and Their Connection to Maroon Culture). M.A. thesis, Radboud Universiteit, 2007.

Agerkop, Terry, Kenneth Bilby, and Peter Manuel. "Suriname." In Stanley Sadie, ed., *The New Grove Dictionary of Music and Musicians*, new revised edition, Volume 24, 721–25. London: Macmillan, 2001.

Agerkop, Terry. Seke'ti: *Poetic and musical eloquence among the Saramaka Maroons from Suriname*. Dissertation, University of Brasilia, 2000.

Agerkop, Terry, and Saamaka Doon. *Introduction to the drumming tradition of the Saramaka Marrons*. University van Amsterdam, 1991.

Bebey, Francis. *African Music: A People's Art*, translated from French by Josephine Bennet. Chicago: Lawrence Hill Books, 1975 (reprinted 1992). Original edition *Musique de L'Afrique*, 1969.

Bilby, Kenneth. "La musique aluku: un héritage africain." In Marie-Paule Jean-Louis and Gérard Collomb, eds., *Musiques en Guyane*, 49–72. Cayenne: Bureau du Patrimoine Ethnologique, 1989.

Bilby, Kenneth. *The Remaking of the Aluku: Culture, Politics, and Maroon Ethnicity in French South America*. Dissertation, Johns Hopkins University, 1990.

Bilby, Kenneth. "War, Peace, and Music: The Guianas." *Hemisphere* 1(3) (1990): 10–12.

Bilby, Kenneth. "The New Music of French Guiana: Maroons and Reggae." *The Beat* 10(4) (1991): 34–38.

Bilby, Kenneth. ""Roots Explosion': Indigenization and Cosmopolitanism in Contemporary Surinamese Popular Music." *Ethnomusicology* 43(2) (1999): 256–96. University of Illinois Press on behalf of Society for Ethnomusicology. http://www.jstor.org/stable/852735

Bilby, Kenneth. "Maroons and Contemporary Popular Music in Suriname." In Ralph Premdas, ed., *Identity, Ethnicity and Culture in the Caribbean*, 143–54. St. Augustine, Trinidad and Tobago: University of the West Indies, 1999.

Bilby, Kenneth. "Aleke: nieuwe muziek en nieuwe identiteiten." *OSO* 19(1) (2000): 49–58.

Bilby, Kenneth. "Making Modernity in the Hinterlands: New Maroon Musics in the Black Atlantic." *Popular Music* 19(3) (2000): 265–92.

Bilby, Kenneth. "Aleke: New Music and New Identities in the Guianas." *Latin American Music Review* 22(1) (2001): 31–47.

Bilby, Kenneth, and Diana Baird N'Diaye. "Creativity and Resistance: Maroon Culture in the Americas." In Peter Seitel, ed., *1992 Festival of American Folklife*, 54–61. Washington, DC: Smithsonian Institution, 1992.

Bilby, Kenneth, and Rivke Jaffe. "Marronmuziek: tussen traditie en mondialisering." In Alex van Stipriaan and Thomas A. Polimé, eds., *Kunst van Overleven: Marroncultuur uit Suriname*, 166–75. Amsterdam: KIT Publishers, 2009.

Binnendijk, Chandra van, and Faber Paul, eds. *Sranan. Cultuur in Suriname*. Koninklijk Instituut voor de Tropen, Amsterdam/Museum voor Volkenkunde, Rotterdam/Vaco, Paramaribo 1992.

Boonzajer Flaes, Rob. *Bewogen koper. Van koloniale kapel tot wereld blaasorkest*. De Balie\Novib, 1993.

Boots, Alice, and Rob Woortman. *Cotton Club: De bewogen geschiedenis van een café* (The Moving History of a Café). Amsterdam: Atlas Contact, 2014.

Bouquet, B. *Kaseko-muziek in Nederland*. Masters thesis, Amsterdam, 1985.

Bruin, H. de, and B. Scholtens. "Aleke-Festival, performances by Kifoko, Labbi Boys en Lamora Sound." *De Ware Tijd*, March 11, 1988.

Campbell, Corinna. *Personalizing Tradition: Surinamese Maroon Music and Dance in Contemporary Urban Practice*. Dissertation, Harvard University, 2012.

Carlin, Eithine B., and Goethem van Diederik. *The Amerindians of Suriname*. Amsterdam: KIT Publishers [date unknown].

Comvalius, Th. A. C. *Krioro, een bijdrage tot de kennis van het lied, de dans en de folkore van Suriname, Paramaribo* (Krioro, a contribution to the knowledge of the song, dance and folklore of Suriname) [publisher and date unknown].

Crossover concert Magazine. Media Productions & IKO Foundation. 2008.

Daniel, Yvonne. *Caribbean and Atlantic Diaspora Dance: Igniting Citizenship*. Urbana: University of Illinois Press, 2011.

Drie, Aleks De. *Sye! Arki Tori!* Compiled by Trudi Guda. Afdeling Cultuur Studies van het Ministerie van Onderwijs, Wetenschappen en Cultuur (Department of Cultural Studies of the Ministry of Education, Science and Culture), 1985.

Drien, Aleks De. *Wan tori fu mi eygi srefi*. Compiled by Trudi Guda. Afdeling Cultuur Studies van het Ministerie van Onderwijs, Wetenschappen en Cultuur (Department of Cultural Studies of the Ministry of Education, Science and Culture), 1984.

Gooswit, Sylvia M. *Van Tembang tot Jaran Képang. Traditonele Javaanse zang, muziek en dans in Suriname*. Paramaribo: Afdeling Cultuurstudies van het Ministerie van Onderwijs en Volksontwikkeling, 2010.

Groot, Silvia M. de. *Surinaamse granmans in Afrika: vier groot opperhoofden bezoeken het land van hun voorouders*. Utrecht: Het Spectrum, 1974. (Aula paperback, 28.)

Groot, Silvia M. de. *Surinam Maroon chiefs in Africa in search of their country of origin*. Amsterdam: self-published, 2003. (Abridged English translation of *Surinaamse granmans*.)

Gooswit, Sylvia M., and Wonny M. Karijopawiro. *Tayup en janggrung in Suriname, een Javaanse dansvorm*. Paramaribo: Academie voor Hoger Kunst-en Cultuuronderwijs te Paramaribo, 1997.

Hanenberg, Hans van den. *Bruine bonen en kouseband: een biografie van Max Woiski senior en junior.* Amsterdam: Top Notch/Nigh & Van Ditmer, 2016.

Helman, A. *Cultureel Mozaïek van Suriname.* Zutphen: De Walburg Pers, 1978.

Herskovits, M. J. *The Myth of the Negro Past.* New York: Harper & Brothers, 1941.

Herskovits, Melville, and Frances Herskovits. *Suriname Folklore.* 1936; reprint, New York, AMS Press, 1972.

Herskovits, M. J., and F. S. Herskovits. *Rebel Destiny: Among the Bush Negroes of Dutch Guiana.* New York: Columbia University Press, 1934.

Hoogbergen, Wim. *The Boni Maroon Wars in Suriname.* Leiden: Brill, 1990.

Hoop, Carlo. "De magische vetheid van het geluid." *OSO* 19(1) (2000): 117–21.

Hurault, Jean. *Les Noirs Réfugiés Boni de la Guyane française.* Dakar: IFAN, 1961.

Hurault, Jean. *Africains de Guyane.* The Hague: Mouton, 1970.

Jaffe, Rivke, and Jolien Sanderse. "Surinamese Maroons as Reggae Artistes: Music, Marginality and Urban Space." *Ethnic and Racial Studies* 33(9) (2010): 1561–79.

Kagie, Rudie. *De eerste neger* (The First Negro). Het Wereldvenster (Unieboek), 1989. 2nd enlarged revised edition, Schilt Publishing BV, 2006.

Ketwaru, E. N. K. "Naks Kawina Week." *VMS Noot, orgaan van de Stichting Volksmuziekschool* 2(10) (1982).

Ketwaru, E. R. "De ontwikkeling van de Sarnami muziek van 1873 tot heden. *Kala, Tijdschrift voor de Academie voor Hogere Kunst en Cultuur* 4(1–2) (1992).

Kiban, J. *Muziek, zang en dans van de Karaïben in Suriname* (Music, Song and Dance of the Carib Indians in Suriname). Paramaribo: N.V. Varekampen, 1966.

Kloos, Peter. "Indiaanse muziek en Caraïbische liederen. Hoofdstuk VI Esthetische cultuur" (Amerindian Music and Carib Songs Chapter VI Aesthetic Culture), 349–59. In Helman, Albert, ed., *Cultureel mozaïek van Suriname.* Zutphen: Walburg Pers, 1977.

Leefmans, John. "Klassieke componisten uit Suriname" (Classical Composers from Suriname). *OSO* 1(19) (May 2000): Themanummer Surinaamse Noten. http://www .osojournal.nl.

Manuel, Peter, with Kenneth Bilby and Michael Largey. *Caribbean Currents: Caribbean Music from Rumba to Reggae.* Philadelphia: Temple University Press, 1995.

Mosis, A. *Inleiding tot de traditionele Aukaanse muziek en dans* (Introduction to traditional Aukan Music and Dance). Manuscript, Paramaribo, 1988.

New Grove Dictionary of Music and Musicians, new revised edition, Volume 24, 721–25. London: Macmillan, 2001.

Openneer, Herman. *Kid Dynamite: De legende leeft* (The Legend Lives On). Amsterdam: Schilt Publishing, 1995.

Otter, den Elisabeth. *Rhythm, a Dance in Time.* Amsterdam: Royal Tropical Institute, 2001.

Pakosie, André R. M. "Onstaan en ontwikkeling van de aleke: de popmuziek van de Marronstam der Ndyuka" (Origin and Development of aleke: the pop music of the Ndyuka Maroon tribe). *Siboga* 9(1) (1999): 2–24.

Price, Richard. *The Guiana Maroons: A Historical and Bibliographical Introduction.* Baltimore: Johns Hopkins University Press, 1976.

Price, Richard. "Maroons in Suriname and Guyane: How Many and Where." *New West Indian Guide* 76(1/2) (2002): 81–88.

Price, Richard. *Rainforest Warriors: Human Rights on Trial.* Philadelphia: University of Pennsylvania Press, 2011.

Price, Richard. *Peuple Saramaka contre État du Suriname: Combat pour la forêt et les droits de l'homme.* Paris: Karthala, 2012.

Price, Richard, and Sally Price. *Two Evenings in Saramaka.* Chicago: University of Chicago Press, 1991.

Price, Richard, and Sally Price. *Les Marrons.* La Roque d'Anthérons: Vents d'ailleurs, 2003.

Price, Sally, and Richard Price. *Maroon Arts: Cultural Vitality in the African Diaspora.* Boston: Beacon Press, 1999.

Price, Sally, and Richard Price. *L'Art des Marrons.* Châtaeuneuf-le-Rouge: Vents d'ailleurs, 2005.

Reijerman, Meike. "Sranankondre a no paradijs: de constructie van localiteit in de populaire muziek van de Saramaka" (Suriname Is No Paradise: the Construction of Locality in Popular Music of the Saramacca Region). *OSO* 19(1) (2000): 59–82.

René, Antoin. *Kaseko Workshop: Basic kaseko patterns for keyboard.* Staer Music, 2007.

Rijven, Stan. "'The World Is My Home': A Portrait of Ronald Snijders." *Songlines* 122 (November 2016): 46–47.

Samwel, Diederik. *Sranan Gowtu: Iconen uit de Surinaamse muziek* (Suriname Gold: Icons of Surinamese Music). Amsterdam: Top Notch series, Nijgh & Van Ditmar, 2015.

Sanderse, Jolien. *Jonge Marrons als wereldburgers: de invloed van (mondiale) muziek op de identificatie en culturele representatie van jonge Marrons in Paramaribo* (Young Maroons as Global Citizens: The Influence of [World] Music on the Identification and Cultural Representation of Young Maroons in Paramaribo). M.A. thesis, University of Utrecht, 2006.

Sanderse, Jolien, and Rivke Jaffe. "Jonge Marronmuzikanten: muziek en marginaliteit in Paramaribo" (Young Maroon Musicians: Music and Life on the Edge in Paramaribo). *OSO* 26(1) (2007): 43–60. http://www.osojournal.nl.

Sansone, Livio. "The Making of Suriland: The Binational Development of a Black Community between the Tropics and the North Sea." In Margarita Cervantes-Rodríguez, Ramón Grosfoguel, and Eric Mielands, eds., *Caribbean Migration to Western Europe and the United States*, 169–88. Philadelphia: Temple University Press, 2009.

Sedoc, N. O. *Aisa Winti.* Paramaribo, 1979.

Snijders, R. *Surinaamse kaseko muziek, een onderzoek naar haar geschiedenis, concept, betekenis en repertoire* (Surinamese Kaseko Music, a study of its history, significance and repertoire). M.A. thesis, University of Amsterdam, 1991.

Snijders, Ronald. *Surinaams van de straat—Sranantongo fu strati* (Surinamese Street Language). Amsterdam: Prometheus, 2000.

Snijders, Ronald. *De man met de piccolo* (The Man with the Piccolo). Groet, Netherlands: Conserve, 1998.

Stedman, John Gabriel. *Narrative of a Five Years Expedition against the Revolted Negroes of Surinam.* Complete Critical Edition Edited and with an Introduction and Notes by Richard Price and Sally Price. Baltimore: Johns Hopkins University Press, 1988; iUniverse, 2010 (orig. 1796).

Stipriaan, Alex van. "Muzikale creolisering: de ontwikkeling van Afro-Surinaamse muziek tijdens de slavernij" (Musical Creolization: the development of Afro-Surinamese music during slavery). *OSO* 19(1) (2000): 8–37. http://www.osojournal.nl.

Stipriaan, Alex van, and Thomas Polime. *Kunst van overleven. Marroncultuur uit Suriname.* Amsterdam: KIT Publishers, 2009.

Thoden van Velzen, H. U. E., and W. W. Van Wetering *The Great Father and the Danger: Religious Cults, Material Forces, and Collective Fantasies in the World of the Surinamese Maroons.* Koninklijk Instituut voor Taal-, Land- en Volkenkunde, Leiden. Dordrecht: Foris Publications, 1988.

Valk, Leendert van der. *Voudou, Van New Orleans naar Cotonou op het ritme van de Goden* (Voudou, From New Orleans to the Rhythm of the Gods). Amsterdam: Atlas Contact, 2017. [Section 4, "Winti Soul," deals with the music of the African Surinamese music of the interior.]

Van Kempen, Michiel. "Liederen, dansen, spelen" (Songs, dances, games). In Michiel van Kempen, *Een geschiedenis van Surinaamse literatuur* (A History of Surinamese Literature), vol. 2, 251–69. Breda: De Geus Publishers, 2003.

Van Renselaar, Herman C. "Tongoni 2." *Vox Guyanae* 3(6) (1959).

Voorhoeve, Jan, and Ursy M. Lichtveld, with English translations by Vernie A. February. *Creole Drum: An Anthology of Creole Literature in Surinam.* New Haven: Yale University Press, 1975.

Vuisjie, Bert. *Ado Broodboom, trompet.* Haarlem: In de Knipscheer, 2017.

Weltak, Marcel. "Afrikaans Surinaamse muziek." *OSO* 19(1) (2000): 38–48. http://www .osojournal.nl.

Weltak, Marcel, ed. *Surinaamse Muziek in Nederland en Suriname* (Surinamese Music in the Netherlands and Suriname). Utrecht: Kosmos Publishers and Surinam Music Association, 1990.

Weltak, Marcel. "Van doden en vrouwen in de Surinaamse muziek." In Maaike Meijer, ed., *Cultuur en migratie in Nederland. Kunsten in beweging 1980–2000,* 77–95. Amsterdam: University of Amsterdam Press, 2004.

Weltak, Marcel, Robin Austen, and Guilly Koster, eds. *Veertig jaar Surinaamse muziek in Nederland: De muzikale fakkeldragers.* Haarlem: In de Knipscheer and IKO Foundation, 2016. [Includes double CD of music from 1975–2015.]

Weltak, Marcel, Robin Austen, and Guilly Koster, eds. *Forty Years of Surinamese Music in the Netherlands: The Musical Torchbearers.* Translated from the Dutch by Scott Rollins. Haarlem: In de Knipscheer and IKON Foundation, 2016. [Includes double CD of music from 1975–2015.]

Wermuth, Mir. "Ritme en rijm in de diaspora: Surinaamse jongeren en popmuziek" (Rhythm and Rhyme in the diaspora: Surinamese Youth and Pop Music). *OSO* 19(1) (2000): 122–36.

Wooding, C. J. *Winti, een Afro-Surinaamse godsdienst in Suriname* (Winti, an Afro-Surinamese Religion in Suriname). Meppel, Krips Repro., 1972. Reprint, Rotterdam: Uitgeverij Dubois, 2013.

Yzermans, J. "Ontstaan en ontwikkeling van de creoolse populaire muziek in Suriname, 1800–1940" (The Rise and Development of Creole Popular Music in Suriname). *OSO* 6(1) (1987).

CONTRIBUTOR BIOGRAPHIES

Marcel Weltak (b. 1948) studied economics and philosophy in Groningen and Amsterdam. In Suriname he was staff member of the S.W.I. (Stichting Wetenschappelijke Informatie, Foundation for Scholarly Information) and of the daily newspapers *De West* and *De Ware Tijd*. He was also editor of the Surinamese-Dutch monthly magazine *Adek* and arts correspondent for the Dutch daily newspapers *De Waarheid* and *De Volkskrant*. Besides publishing the first edition of *Surinaamse muziek in Nederland en Suriname* in 1990, he has written articles in various music and cultural magazines as *Jazz Nu, OOR, Vinyl*, and *Onze Wereld*, as well as a chapter on women in Surinamese music in Maaike Meijer, *Cultuur en migratie in Nederland. Kunsten in beweging 1980–2000*, University of Amsterdam Press, 2004; *Oor's Eerste Nederlandse Popencyclopedie* (Oor's First Dutch Pop Encyclopedia); *Jazzjaarboek* (Jazz Yearbook); and *De beste Reisverhalen* (Best Travel Stories).

Dr. Lou Lichtveld (pen name Albert Helman, 1903–1996), the "grand old man" and most productive author of Dutch West Indian writing, was born Lou Lichtveld of Arawak descent in the capital city of Paramaribo. His writing career began in the 1920s and spanned over seven decades until his death. A veritable Renaissance man, he was also a talented composer of modern classical music in his own right under his own name. Among his most celebrated books are his first full-length novel *De stille plantage* (The Silent Plantation) (1931), which portrayed the conflict between an idealistic protagonist and the slave traders and owners of colonial plantations in a historical eighteenth-century setting. It has become a classic in Dutch literature and is still in print in its twenty-third edition and was published in French and German translations. After retirement, he travelled extensively throughout the Third World doing anthropological and ethnographic research. This provided the material for a number of works of historical, sociological, and ethnographic interest alongside his literary fiction and poetry. He spent the last years of his life in the Netherlands. A definitive authorized biography of his remarkable life by Dutch Caribbean literary historian and novelist Michiel van Kempen entitled *Rusteloos en Overal* (Restless and Everywhere) appeared in 2016 from In de Knipscheer.

Herman Dijo was leader of the Indian Orchestra in Suriname. This orchestra played flawless renditions of the still immensely popular music from Bollywood films. Dijo's day job was as policeman and musical director of the police band. He was promoted and subsequently asked to conduct the Surinamese military band. Like most musicians who played in the police and military bands, Dijo moonlighted in groups performing dance music from Cuba, Trinidad, and Haiti. These varieties of music were later combined with kawina music, out of which kaseko arose. Herman Dijo was one of the musicians at the forefront of kaseko. He later left for the Netherlands in 1975 to study at the conservatory.

Ponda O'Bryan (Orlando O'Bryan, aka Ponda), born in Amsterdam, was a sought-after percussionist. O'Bryan is a master of the Mandingo *djembe* drum and the Surinamese *apinti* drum. He toured with the renowned Dutch flutist Chris Hinze and various African bands. But his heart lay with Surinamese jazz. He played with both The Surinam Music Ensemble and Fra Fra Sound. He was also a member of Akrema, an ensemble that performed Winti music from the coastal strip of Suriname. In recent years he has chiefly been occupied with teaching at the Amsterdam Music School and in West Africa.

Guilly Koster was born in Suriname and came to the Netherlands as a child. He grew up in the Bijlmermeer, the district now referred to as Amsterdam Southeast that developed into the heart of the Surinamese music scene in the Netherlands. It was where Lieve Hugo Uiterloo, the star of kaseko also resided. Koster was part of the Surinamese group the Milestones, then took up playing electric bass and formed his own band, Rubadub, which made successful tours in Germany and Austria. Koster also became a television producer and presenter, co-hosting with Ivette Forster the first Black talk show on the Dutch National Public television channel VPRO in the late 1980s, called *Bij Lobith* and later, at the end of the 1990s, *Massiv*.

Dr. Jainul Ketwaru is a tabla player and music teacher who played on several albums by Ronald Snijders and released the album *Ketwaru* in 1974 together with his late brother Effendi Ketwaru (sitar, bamboo flute, xylophone, mandolin), Evert Derks (violin), and Nadia Ketwaru (tanpura).

INDEX

Abaisa, xxv, 18, 109
Abdullah, Lea, 115
Abeni, 23
Aboikani, Gaaman, xviii
abolition of slavery (1863), xxxviii, 12, 18, 21
aboma snake (boa constrictor), 5
Acampo, 90
a cappella, 14, 17, 20
Ackamore, Idriss, 100
Adamson, Rudolf, 37–38, 87
"Adjossi," xxvii
adonke, xviii
Adriaan, Bas, 59, 69, 86–88, 148
Aflaw (the woman who faints), 18, 20
Afrankeri, 18, 20
African Creoles, 27
Africans, xxxiii, xxxvii
African slaves, xxvii–xxviii, 10, 18, 109, 146
African Surinamese music, 23
afrobeat, xxvii, 110
Afro-Surinamers, 10, 12, 22, 103
Afro-Surinamese culture, 23
Afro-Surinamese music, 21–24
Afu Sensi, 23
Agerkop, Terry, viii, 153
Aghori (ballet), xvi
agida (drum), xxxviii, 13, 16, 22, 69, 70
agogo (cowbell), 57
ahirwa ke naadj (Indian combination of
    music and dance), 28
Aisa (mother earth), xxv, xxxii, 17, 114
Aisa-banja, 18
Aisa-Wintis, 69

Ai Sranang, xxvii
Akan (Ghanaian tribe), 12–13
Akathon, 87
Akbar the Great, 26
"Akoeba," 105
Akrema, xxiv, 23, 109
Akuriyo (Amerindian tribe), 3
alaap, 26
Alberga, Robby, xxviii, 126
aleke, xviii, xx–xxi, 126, 136, 147, 153–55
Alexandria, Egypt, 83
Alfonso, Hebert, xxix
Alkmaar, the Netherlands, 99
Allah, 27
All Star Fresh (DJ Juan Elmzoon), 113
Almeido, Laurindo, 97
Altena, Maarten van, 96
althorn, 41
altiplano, 8
Aluku, xi–xiii, xviii, xxxiii, 11, 131, 133, 137,
    153
Aluman, Nardu, 6–8
Amatstam, Ragmad (1953–2011), xvii
Ambonese (Moluccans), 33
American Civil War, xxxviii
American Songbook, xxxi
Amerindians, ix, xxii, xxxiv, xxvii, xxx,
    xxxiii, xxxiv, xxxviii, 3–4, 8–9, 12, 14, 16,
    63, 71, 108–9, 144–46, 149, 155
Amsterdam, vii–ix, xii, xxiv–xxv, xxvii,
    xxix, xxx, 9, 21, 23, 37, 40, 48–49, 63,
    73–75, 77, 79–80, 93, 95, 102, 106–7, 115,
    117

Amsterdam Conservatory, xxx, 40, 48
Amsterdam-Zuidoost (Amsterdam
   Southeast), xxiii, 23
Anana Keduaman Keduampo, xix, 16
Anansi-tori (Anansi spider stories), 19, 50
Andes, 8
Andriessen, Hendrik, 49
Angel, Stanley (Odongo), xxvii–xxviii, 108,
   110
angguk, 35
Anglican church, 41
Anglo Dutch War of 1672–74, x
Anikel Awagi and the Masoewa Band, xx
Anita Band, 69
anitri (Moravian Brother), 38
anitri kerkie (Moravian church), 36
Anka, Paul, 103
anklung, 35
Anna, Tante, 35
apentema, 13
apinti (drum), xiii–xx, xxxviii, 13, 16, 19,
   22, 29
Apollo Theater, xxxi
apretia, 13
apukudron, 14
Arabic, 26
Arawak (Amerindian tribe), x, 3–4, 8, 9
Archie Bell and the Drells, 106
Ardin, Franklin "Copy," 90, 102
Arens, Albert, xxi
Ariabuku (aria book), 38
Armstrong, Louis, 73, 83
Artis Zoo (Amsterdam), 75
Aruba, 85, 91
asafo, 13
Asanti Buba, 23
Ashanti, 14, 60
Ashkenazi Jews, xi
ASKO (youth jazz orchestra), 96
assimilation, xiii
Astaria Combo, 104
Astoria Theater (Groningen, Netherlands),
   79
A Tin Télé, xx
atsigo, 13

atsimevu, 13
atumpan, 13
Aucaners (Djuka), xviii, xx, 11, 15
Aukan (language), xx
Austria, xxvi, 159
avant-garde jazz, 94
avant-garde rock, xxviii
Averekete, xxiv
Avex Records (Japan), xxxi
AVRO orchestra, 78
AVRO radio, 78, 80
AVROS radio (Suriname), 89, 103
awasa, xviii, xx, 15, 17

Baag, Armand, 114
Bach, Johann Sebastian, 37, 46–47, 57, 97
badji, 55, 57, 111
Baghdad, 83
Baghwandin, Jan, 102
Bahasa Republik Indonesia, 34
Baisa, 23
baithak-gana, xiv, xv, xxxii, 27, 126, 129, 133,
   147
*Baithak Gana: Songs from Bihar, Uttar
   Pradesh and Surinam*, xv, 27
baka-fotu-banja, 18
Bakadjari (Backyard) Festival, xxiv
Bakadjari Band, xxiv
Baker, Josephine, 78
"Bakka Thalia," xvi
balafon, 92
balata-bleeders (rubber tappers), 38, 41
bal-masque (masked ball), 22
Baltimore, Maryland, xxix
bandammba, xviii, 147
Bandoela, 70
Bangsa Jawa, xvii
bangsawan (type of Javanese theater), 33
banja (style of dance), xxiv, 14, 17–23, 148
banja-pré, 17–18
banji-banja, 18
bangji-banji, 18
banjo, 33, 56, 59, 60, 70, 149
Bantu, 13, 15
Bapak Masekan, 33

Barak G, xxiii
Bareto, José (Max Woiski Sr.), 77
bari-dron, 57
Baron (maroon leader), 11
bass drum, xxv, 19, 42, 43, 56–57, 67, 70,
   99–100, 146, 148
bass guitar, 33, 69, 85, 104, 107, 150
Bätsorgel (German make of organ), 38
bauxite, xxxviii, 7, 56, 86
bazuinkoor (brass instrument ensemble),
   xxvii, xxxii, 23, 36, 41–44, 47, 55, 148
BBC, xxix
B.B. met R., dat is bruine bonen met rijst
   (B.B. with R, that's brown beans with
   rice), 77, 106
Beatles, 85, 103, 106
Bebey, Francis, 14
bebop, xxi, xxii, 80, 84, 90, 100, 150
bebuka, 33
Bechet, Sidney, 75
Bedacht, Rudy (Corly Verlooghen), 52, 105
bedug (Javanese drum), 33
Beethoven, Ludwig van, 46, 51
beguine, 56, 63, 71, 75
Beirut, 83
Belfor, Minister, 38
Belgium, xxvi, 51, 78, 101
bells, 28
Belliot, Imro (P.I. Man), xxvii, 108, 110–12
Benin, xi, xxiv, 13
Bennink, Han, 95
benta (various stringed instruments and
   thumb pianos), 13
Benton, Brook, xxvii
Berg, Eric van de, 102
Berg en Dal, Suriname, 47
Berklee College of Music, xxxiii
Berlin, Germany, 48–49, 51, 83, 136
Berlin, Irving, xxxi
Bernard-dorp, 9
Bethania, xxvi
Beurs van Berlage (Amsterdam), 50
bhadjan, xv, 27
bhatwaan, xiii
Bhojpuri, xiii, xv

Bible, 38
Biervliet, Harold, 64, 107, 123
big band, 65, 85, 88, 89, 91, 93, 96, 101, 127
Bigi Poika, 9
bigi poku, xxxviii, 43, 55–59, 61–63, 68–71,
   86–89, 100, 147–48, 150
Big Jones, 21
Bihar, xiii, xv
Bijlmermeer (Bijlmer, Amsterdam
   Southeast), viii, xxiii–xxv, 92, 159
Bilby, Kenneth, vii, xii, xxxiii, 133–34, 153–54
BIM (Bureau for Improvising Musicians),
   xxiii
Bimhuis (Amsterdam jazz venue), 85,
   101–2, 141
Bios Surinam Boys, 88
biraha (lament, funeral music), 28
Birdland (Alkmaar nightclub), 99
Birds of the Sea (LP), 65
Birmingham, England, 111
Birth of a New Age, xxx
Black Earth, 100
Black Rock Coalition, xxxiii
Black Straight Music, xxiii, 97, 121, 131
Blaka Buba, 23
Blakey, Art, 90, 100
Blakka Roetoe, 111, 119
Blaxtar (Keven de Randamie), xxix
Blijd, Frits (Freddy), xxxix, 73–74, 79–80,
   82–83
Blue Note (label), xxviii, xxxi
Blue Rhythm, 69
Bluesbusters, 64
Blue Seven Band, 105
Body and Soul, 79
Boketi (flower bouquet), 18
bolero, 61
Bollywood, xiii, 159
Bommel, 88
Bonam, Eugene, 64
bonang (gongs), xvi–xvii, 31, 143
bongo (Afro-Surinamese percussion
   instrument), 14
bongos (Cuban instrument), 61, 70, 82
Boni (maroon leader), 11

Boni (maroons aka Aluku), xi, 11
bonko enchemrya, 14
bonuman (Afro-Surinamese medicine
    man), 12
Boontjie Stars, xxvi, 68
borgu-banja, 18
bossa nova, 62
Boston, xxix
Boston, Steve, 84, 86, 89, 92–96, 117
Botoman (boatman), xviii
bototutu (iron horn used in riverboats),
    13, 143
Bottom Line (NYC music venue), xxviii
Boulanger, Nadia, 49
Bouterse, Desi, 108
Boy Edgar Prize (for Best Dutch jazz musi-
    cian), 85
Braaf, Alma (Lolita Mojica), xxx, 114
Braaf, Eddie, 102
Brabants Mannenkoor (Brabant Male
    Choir), 48
Brahma, 28
Braxton, Anthony, 97
Brazil, x, xi, 3–4, 12, 18, 62
Brecht, Bertolt, 46
Breidel, Dennis, 97
Breuker, Willem, 96
British Guiana, 56, 76, 88. *See also* Guyana
Broodboom, Ado "Moreno," 75, 80, 82–83,
    96
Bronsplein (Paramaribo), 87
Brown, Clifford, 90
Brussels, Belgium, 78, 83, 85
bubbling, xx
Budel, Anton, 37, 78
Budel, George, 87
bugle, 57, 84
bungu bungu, 55, 60
Burgos, Edgar "Boegroe," 107, 117, 134
Burnett, Raul, 84, 92–96
Bush Negroes, xi. *See also* maroons
Busi-indji, 69
Buth, Eddie, 78
Butler, Jerry, 106
Byas, Don, 95

Byas, John, 85
Byrd, Charlie, 86

Cabenda, 64
"cadence folk," 37
calabash, xxxviii, 5, 12, 27
caledonia (dance), 56
Calloway, Cab, 73, 87
calypso, xxvii, xxxviii, 58–63, 67, 71–72, 104,
    108, 110–11, 147, 150
Calypso Rose, 61
Campbell, Humphrey, 94, 99–100, 106
Canada, xiii, xxxi, 97
cantor, 33, 152
Capadose, 88
capoeira, 19
Captain (head of Amerindian community),
    4
Caracas, 49
Carib (Amerindian tribe), x, 3
Carnatic music, 25
carré (dance), 56
Carter, Benny, 81
Casablanca (Amsterdam nightclub), 81,
    83, 93
Casino (band), 90
cassava, 7, 21
Castillion, Arturo, xxiii, xxviii
Catholic Church, 4, 7, 38, 41, 50; cathedral,
    47; choirs, 41; faith, 4; liturgical music,
    43; songs, 43
Catholic Youth Group Brass Band, 50
Cats (musical), xxxi, 115
Cayenne, French Guiana, xx–xxi, 78, 153
CBS records, 49
CCS (Cultureel Centrum Suriname—
    Suriname Cultural Center), 90–91
cedar, 5
cello, 33, 41
Central Station (Amsterdam), 83
Centraal choir, 37, 39
Centrumkerk (Downtown Church in
    Paramaribo), 48
Chalut, 78
chamber music, 50–51

Chapottin, 92
chautaal, 28
Chevalier, Maurice, 78
Chicago, Illinois, 76
Chin A Loi, Wim "Pancho," 89, 93
Chinese, xxxiv, xxxvii, 19, 64, 136
Chocolate Kiddies, 75
chorales, 57, 59
church organs, 38
chutney (music style), xiv, 143
Ciconna di Chiesa (concert for orchestra
    and male choir), 48
Clan, the, 105
Clark Terry Big Band, 93
classical Indian music, 26, 29
classical Javanese dance, 32
clave, 15, 21, 57
Cole, Nat King, 89, 101
Coleman, Ornette, 96
Collegians, 80, 114
Cologne, Germany, 101
Coltrane, John, 81, 84
Combo Latino, 93
comic opera (lobisingi), 19, 20
commedia dell'arte, xxv, 20
Commewijne (district), 21, 33
Commewijne River, 11, 21
Commonwealth Institute (Paris), 108
Communication (reggae band), xxiv, 111
Concertgebouw (Amsterdam), 50, 63, 82,
    85, 101–2
Concertgebouw De Doelen (Rotterdam),
    52
congas, 21, 22, 29, 32, 56, 61, 64, 69–70, 89,
    92–93, 97
Conga Willi, 111
Congo, xi, xix, 10, 12, 19, 57, 110, 145
congoma (Sierra Leone thumb piano), 13
conjuntos, 61
Conservatory of Suriname, xxi–xxii
contract laborers (workers), xiii, xxxviii, 27
contradanza, contredanse, 56
Copenhagen Symphony Orchestra, 82
Corita, Rita (Endrika Sturm), 78
cornet, 41, 56

Coronie, 11, 14, 22, 38, 120, 130
Cosmo Beat, 107
Cosmo Stars, xx, xxii, 67, 119, 134, 151
Cottica (ship), 73
Cottica region, 69
Cottica River, 11
Cotton, Teddy (Theodoor Kantoor), xxiii,
    73, 74, 76, 79–80, 82–83, 88, 100
Coutinho, Alwin, 90, 93
Creighton University (Omaha, Nebraska),
    xvii
Creoles (Afro-Surinamers), 10, 11, 17, 19, 21,
    23, 27, 136
creolization, xxxiv, 156
Cruise Button, 102
Cruz, Celia, 60–61
Cuba, xx, 14, 22, 60–63; Cuban music, 71–72
cultural apartheid, xiii
Culture (reggae band), 111
cumbia, 94
Curaçao, xxvii, 19, 22, 50, 66, 77, 85, 98, 107,
    145–46, 150
Czechoslovakia, 46

Dadaist artists, xii
Dahlberg, Johan Victor, 48
Dahomey, xi, xix, xxiv
Dallas, Texas, xi
Damaru, xxii, 134
dancehall (Jamaican), xxxii
Daniels, Yvonne, viii
danzón, 56
Da Tipa Tojo, xx
Datra (Doctor), 18, 20
Davis, Miles, 84, 92, 96, 98, 100
dawra (iron cowbell of African origin), xix,
    12, 15, 17, 19, 58
dawura (Ghanaian Akan tribe cowbell),
    12, 57
deer(skin), 5
*De Griekse muziek in 't licht der moderne
    toonkunst* (Greek Music in Light of the
    Modern Western Music), 48
deindein (pudja), 14
De Leusden (Dutch slave ship), 52

Delft, the Netherlands, 44
De man met de piccolo (The Man with the Piccolo), 49
demung, 32
De Nazaten, xxv–xxvi, 130, 133
Denswil, Esperanza (Pink Oculus), xxxii
dessa, xvi–xvii
De Stijl, xii
Determeyer, Eddy, 101
De Trekkers brass band, 43, 50
Devali (Hindu feast), 45
dhantal, xiv
dhapla, 26
dholak, xiv, 26, 27, 28, 104
diabolitos, 22
"Di bawah sinar bulan purnama" (Under the beams of the moon), 34
Diepenbrock, Alfons, 48
Different Cooking (LP), 92
Dijkveld, 32
Dijo, Herman, 60, 103, 159
Dikker, Luuk, 96
disco, 101, 104, 115
Dixieland music, xxxviii, 62, 88
djendjen (cowbell), 12, 17
djor, 26
Djuka (Ndjuka), xi, 11, 147
Doelen Ensemble, 52
Doe Maar, 111
Do for Love, xxxi
Dominican Republic, xx, xxxviii, 14
Dompig, Jo, 90
Dom Records (UK), xxxi
Don Pedro (dance band), 90
Doric scale, 43
Dost, Orlando, 102
double bass, 33, 41, 58, 61–62, 96
Douglas, Frankie, 95, 102, 106
Douglas, Mildred (Maitai), 95
Dreigroschen Opera (The Threepenny Opera), 47
Drent, Lou, 82
Drie, Alex de, 18
Dropati, xiii–xiv, xxiv, 126, 133, 147, 151
drum kit (set), 32, 61–62, 87, 99, 103

du (Surinamese form of commedia dell'arte), xxv
Dufini, 23
du-groep or *partij*, 18, 20
Duisker, Hein, 89, 91
Dulfer, Hans, xxvi, 95, 117
Dureco (Dutch music label), 66, 105
Dutch (people), 27, 36
Dutch East Indies, 49
Dutch Edison Award, xxx–xxxi
Dutch Jazz Orchestra, 101
Dutch Moravian Brothers, 37
Dutch Reformed hymns, 38
Dutch Rhythm Poll, 84
Dutch Rhythm Steel and Showband, xxvi
Dutch West India Company (WIC), xi
Dutch West Indies, xxxix
Dutch world service radio (Radio Netherlands World Service), 93
Dylan, Bob, 114
Dynamite, Kid, xxiii, 51, 73, 76, 78, 80–85, 87, 91–93, 100, 102, 114

Easy (reggae band), xxiv, 111
EBG (Evangelische Broeder Gemeente, Moravian Church), 36, 38
Echteld, Dennis, 109
Edgar, Boy, 80, 82, 84
Edison Award, xxviii, xxx
Eerste Surinaamse rhapsodie (First Surinamese Rhapsody), 50
Einbrecher (1934 film), 75
Eldridge, Roy, 91
electric guitars, 9, 104
Ellington, Duke, 73, 75, 88, 98
"El Manicero," 63
Elmzoon, Juan (All Star Fresh), 113
Elstak, Nedley, 79, 81–85, 92, 96
EMI, 65
EMI Bovema, 64
English hymns, 39–40, 42, 47
Enschede, xxx
entartete (degenerate) music, 77
Equals, 111
Esseboom, Iwan, xxiv, 122, 126, 133, 134

Essed, Wim, 96
Essent Award, xxxi
ethnomusicology, xxxiv
euphonium, 41
European Song Festival, xxx
Eurovision Song Festival, xxxi
Evangelische Broeder Gemeente (EBG)
   (Moravian Church), 36, 38
Exception, 106
Ex-Cosmo Stars (Exmo Stars), 67

Fajasition, 109
Farawe, 97
Farsi, xv
Faverey, Robby, 52
February, Vernie A., vi, 92
Federation of Music, xxiv
Felter, Botai (Mighty Botai), 64
feminism, 115
Fernando, Rico (Freddy Blijd), xxviii, 73,
   79, 80, 82
Fischer, Nora, 52
Flanagan, Tommy, 89
Fleming, Rene, 52
Flentrop organ (Dutch make of organ), 38
flute, ix, xxii, xxxvi, 56, 87, 107, 121, 131, 144,
   159; Amerindian, xxxvii, 5, 7–8, 13, 33
folk music, xxxiv, xxxvii, 4, 49, 51, 143, 145
folk songs, 40, 50
Fon, xix
fonfonfrom, 13
forest telephone, 13
Fra Fra Big Band, xxiii
Fra Fra Sound, xxiii, xxviii, xxxiv, 92, 97–98,
   100–101, 119, 125, 127, 133, 159
France, x, xx–xxi, xxvi, 136
free jazz, xxviii, 84, 100, 110
free-music, 97
French Antilles, 56–57, 60
French Guiana, xii, xx–xxi, 3, 7, 60, 63, 78,
   90, 153
French horn, 84
Frepina (Alex Nimmermeer), 70
Frimangron (Paramaribo), 99
fugue, 47

funk, xxx, 94–95, 97, 100, 106, 131
funk-jazz, 100
funk kaseko, xxvi
Funmasters, 67, 100, 119, 126, 134
fusion (music), 71, 94
Future Shock, 100

Gaddum, Edgar, 80, 82
Gaddum, Glenn, 40, 102, 106
Gaddum, Richard, 78, 87–88
gamelan, xvi–xvii, xxxviii, 30–33, 120, 124,
   143–46, 151
ganika (aka *paturia ke naadj*), 28
ganza (Brazilian shaking instrument), 12
Garner, Erroll, 89
Garros, Roland, 49
gat, 26
gedugan, 33, 150
geet, xv
Gelauff, Charles, 81
Gemerts, Alberto, 89, 93
Gemeentemuseum (Municipal Museum)
   in The Hague, 51
gending-gending (Javanese songs), 31
Germany and Germans, xxvi, 36, 38, 40, 41,
   47, 49, 66, 75–76, 78, 80–83, 93, 101, 106,
   115, 159; chorales, 39, 41, 42, 47; music,
   38, 80
Gerold, Johnny, 83
Gershwin, George, "Summertime," 40
Getz, Stan, 81
Ghabiang, xx
Ghana, xi, xix, 10, 12–13, 15, 19, 57, 71, 110,
   136, 142–43
ghazal, xv, 27–28
Gietel, John, 63, 88
Gilbert, Wil (Dutch musciologist), xxxviii,
   xxxix
Gilhuis, "Flenflen" and "Noso ka," 60
Gilles, Layo "MacIntosh," 64, 87–88, 90
Gilles, Robbie "Yogi," 102
Gillespie, Dizzy, 82, 84, 89
God, 4, 6, 36
godo (water drum), 12, 17
Gold Coast, xi, 10

gold diggers, 21, 41, 58
golu-benta (stringed instrument), 13
Gomez, Fransje (Francis Johanna
    Margreta), 19, 68, 114
Gompel, Ba, 109
gong-set, 32
Gorré, Ronny and Lucien, 105
gospel, 110
Grasshoppers, 80
Grasso, Frank, 95
Great Britain, x
Gregorian chant, 43
Groenberg, Johan "Groentje," 93–95
Groenhardt, Ba Erwin, 109
Grote Stadskerk (Moravian Main City
    Church), 37–38
grumi, 12, 143, 146
Guadeloupe, xx
Guangdong (province of China), xvii
guaguancos, 94
guajeos (bass runs), 62
guarachas, 61, 64, 94
Guinea, 10, 17, 151
guitar, 21, 28, 33, 42, 51, 58–59, 62–66, 69–70,
    73–78, 84–85, 88, 90, 93, 97, 103–4, 107,
    110, 145, 150–51
Gullit, Ruud, 111
guru, xv, 25
Guyana, xiii, 38, 46, 50, 58, 89

habanera, 56
Hague, The, xv, xxix, 23, 51, 112, 155
Haiti, xx, 56, 62, 135, 159
Hajary, Majoie, 46, 48
Hamburg, Germany, 74, 82–83
Hancock, Herbie, 101
Handel, George Frideric, 37
Happy Boys (Lieve Hugo), 61, 64, 89, 105,
    107, 112, 119–20, 123, 134
Happy Boys (Vasconcellos), 89
hari, 15, 56, 57, 99
Harman, Robby (Robert Harman Sordam),
    xxviii, 97, 100, 109, 117, 127, 133
Harmanized, xxviii
Harmonie (church choir), 39

harmonium, 27–28, 47, 104
Harris, Oscar, 104, 106, 121, 123, 127, 134
Havertong, Gerda, 114
Hawaiian instruments, 33
Hawkins, Coleman, xxiii, 74–75, 78–80, 87
Haydn, Joseph, 46
Heerlen Big Band Festival, 101
Helman, Albert (Lou Lichtveld), viii, 39,
    46, 50
Helstone, Johannes Nicolaas, 47, 51
Hemingway, Ernest, 50
Henar, Vincent, xxii, 92, 98, 100, 102, 117
Hernhutters (Moravian church), 41
Herskovits, Frances, vii, xii, 55
Herskovits, Melville J., vii, xii, xxiv, 20, 55
Herz und Mund und Tot und Leben, 46
Het pand der goden (The Premises of the
    Gods), 47–48
Hetten, Iwan van, 91
Hewitt, John, 68, 88–91
Hidalgo, Eugene, 82
Hidalgo, Luciën (Lou), 74, 80
Hidalgo, Mike, 74, 76–77, 79, 82
Hi-Fi Levi, 112
highlife, 71, 110
Hilversum, the Netherlands, 78, 107
Hindi-pop, 71, 96, 103–4
Hinduism, 28
Hindustanis and Hindustani Surinamers,
    xiii–xv, xxxii–xxxiii, xxxiv, xxxvii, 40,
    103; gods, 71; music, 25, 26, 27, 71, 107
hip hop, ix, xxiv, xxix, xxxi–xxxiii, 112
Hirsch (nightclub), 79
Hiwat, Yannick, 52
Hodges, Johnny, 75, 87
Holband, Heloise, xxiv–xxv, 21
Holi-Phagwa (Hindi celebration), 28
Holland Festival, 63
Holtuin, Lou "Kabouya," 76, 80, 82–83, 93
homophony, homophonic music, 42
"Honolulu Blues," 80
Honsinger, Tristan, 97
Hudson, Rock, 50
Huguenots, xxix
Hunsel, Annemarie, 114
Hylkema, Hans, 137

Ibo, 13

Ilicken, Wessel, 75

indentured servants, xxxviii, 19, 30–31, 33

India and Indians, xiii, xv, xvi, xxxviii,
    25–26, 29, 103, 143, 144; classical music,
    26, 29; film music, 71, 103–4; pop music,
    104

Indian Diamonds, 104

Indian Orchestra, 103

indja-tuka, 63

indji-poku, 22

indji-winti, xxxviii, 16, 69, 149

Indo-Europeans, 33

Indonesia and Indonesians, 32–34, 49, 136,
    141–42, 148; music, 32, 149; pop artists,
    104

Ingi-banja, 18

Inner Circle, 111

Inquisition (Spanish, 1492), xi

International Colonial and Export
    Exhibition (Amsterdam, 1883), xii

Ireland, xxxi

Istanbul, 83

Italy, 46, 93, 106

Ivens, Joris, 50

Ivory Coast, 10, 17, 110, 151

Jaap Edenhal (Amsterdam), 111

Jackson, Lilian, 95

Jacobs, Jan, 93–94

Jacott, Ruth, xxviii, xxxi, 115

Jaja, Kasnika, 69

Jamaica, xiii, xx, xxxviii, 22, 110–11, 133, 143,
    148–50

Jamal, Ahamad, 89

jankabuari (Arawak transverse flute), 8, 144

Jankipersading, Eddy, 27, 124, 147

Jannah, Denise (Denise Zeefuik), xxviii,
    115, 127

Janssen, Simon C., 37

Japan, xxvi

jarankepang (horse dancing), xvi, 35, 149

Jarreau, Al, xxviii, 101

jazz, xxviii, xxx, xxxviii, 56, 60, 71, 73–76

Jazz Nu, 101

Jazz Real Book, 98

Java and Javanese, xvi–xvii, xxxiii–xxxiv,
    xxxviii, 27, 29–36, 40, 45, 76, 103–5, 122,
    136, 142–43, 145, 147, 148, 149–50; film,
    104

Javanese language, xvii, 104

Jazz Club Paramaribo, 91

Jazz Wereld (Jazz World, Dutch magazine),
    74–76, 78–80, 82

Jesu, Joy of Man's Desiring, 46

Jesus Christ, 4

Jews, xxviii, 76–78

John Canoe, 22

Johnson, Freddy, 75, 79

Joli Coeur (maroon leader), 11

Jones, Baas, 69

Jones, Big, 21

Jones, Billy, 65, 95, 106

Jones, Carlo, xxii, xxvi, 64, 88, 127

Jones, Elvin, 86

Jones, Philly Joe, 95

Jong Loy, Rudy, 59, 89–90

Jongoe Bala, xxvi

Jonst, Marius, 84

jorka-banja, 18

Juda, Arnold, 40

juju, 110

July 1, 1863 (abolition of slavery day), 21–22

Juniors, 104

kaiso, 60

Kalina (Amerindian tribe), xxx, 3–7, 9, 145

Kambell, William "Wilmo," 64

kampong-gede, 31

kanga (children's games), 17, 19

Kantoor, Gustaaf, 74, 76–77, 80

Kantoor, Theodor (Teddy Cotton), xxii, 73

Kantraki, xv, xxxiii

Karifa van Cederboom, 69

Kari'na, x

kaseko, ix, xiii, xvii, xx–xxii, xxiv–xxvi,
    xxix, xxxii, 42–43, 55, 57–71, 85, 94, 97–
    100, 104–5, 107–11, 114–15, 120, 127–29,
    131, 134, 137, 149, 150–52, 154, 156, 159

kaseko jazz, 98

Kaseko Masters, 70, 120, 129
Kaseko Orkester, xxvi
kase la corp ("break the body"), 60
Kasimex House Band, xxvii
kasir (beer brewed from cassava), 7
kaskawi, ix, 129, 149
Kassav', xxi
Katibo (LP by Max Nijman), 105
kauna. *See* kawina
kawali. *See* qawalli
kawina (kauna, kawna), xx, xxi, xxiii–xxv,
    xxvii–xxviii, xxx, xxxii, 3, 5, 8–9, 12, 14,
    19, 21–23, 38, 55–58, 60–61, 63, 65, 68–71,
    99–100, 109, 112, 120, 131, 149, 151–52,
    155, 159
kawinadron, 14
kawna. *See* kawina
kawtutu (cow horn), 13
Keizer, Dick de, 91
Keller, Greta, 78
Kempenaar, Wilfred, 95, 97, 98
Kempen, Michiel van, viii, 157, 159
kempul, 32, 144
kendang, 32–33, 144, 152
kenong, 32, 144
Kenny B. (Kenny Bron), xxii, 128, 133–34,
    137
Kensmil, Alma, 50
Kenton, Stan, 87
Kenya, 71
Kerkplein (Church Square in Paramaribo),
    48
Kern, Jerome, xxxi
ketopak (Arab-tinged theater), 32, 149
kettle drum, 56, 86
ketuk, 32
Ketwaru, Effendi, 103
Ketwaru, Dr. J., 25, 103
khyal enthumri, xv
Kid Dynamite (Arthur Parisius), xxiii, 51,
    73, 76, 78, 80–85, 87, 91–93, 100, 102, 114,
    124, 127–28, 134, 137, 155
Kid Dynamite Band, 80, 82, 83
Kifoko, xix–xx, 154
Kifoko House Band, xx

Kimmel, Fred, 97
King, Martin Luther, xxix
Kingbee, 113
Kingbotho, xix
King Fighter, 61
King Koyeba, xxi
Kitt, Eartha, 83
Knoppel, Leo, 88, 90
Koafi, 23
Kodjo's Spirit, 52
"Kodokoe" (Kromanti song title), 62
kodono (period of mourning), 6
Koele Koele, 64
"Komisi da botri" (The cook is in the
    kitchen), 44–45, 139
"kon'frijari" (fair), 61
Konijn, Theo, 78, 80
Koning, Eddie de, 88, 90
Koninginnedag (Dutch Queen's Day), 44–45
Koninklijke Zangers (Royal Singers), 48
"Konu Oloisi lassie, mi yere a bubu teki en"
    (The King's Clock Has Gone Missing, I
    Heard the Ghost Swiped It), 59, 139
Kony, Ann, 80, 82, 114
kopro 'tu (brass, string, big bass drum
    ensembles), xxv, 68
Koraalboek (Hymnal), 38, 40
kosi (cuss), 70
Koster, Guilly, xxviii, 109–12
kot dron (master drum), 15–16, 56, 58, 99
kotek-an, 35, 144
koti (improvise), 57, 70
kot'kawina, 69–70
kot poku, 56
kot'-singi, 20
Krah, 109
Krap van der Kus, Jana, 69
krawasie (Amerindian rattle), xxx, 5, 6, 8
krawasie songs, 6, 7
Krido Rini, 32
Krido Suoro, 32
krioro-dron (literally Creole drum, a ca-
    pella songs), 17
Krishna, xv, 28
Krolis, Ewald, 64, 128, 133

Kromanti, 62
Kromopawiro, Orlando, xvii
kroncong, 33–34, 104, 147, 149, 150
Kroon, Harriet, viii, ix
Kross, Tanja, xxi
Kuli (Hindu), 19
Kuli Constro (British Consul), 19
Kultuurkamer, 77
Kumanti Verekete, xix
kursow, 22, 150
Kus, Jana Krap van der, 69
Kust, "Ray Brooks" van der, 106
Kuti, Fela, 109
Kwakoe-Bijlmermeer (club), 92
Kwaku (Summer Festival), xxiii
kwakwa (tree trunk slit drum), xxviii, 12, 15
kwakwa-bangi (wooden bench played with
    sticks), 12, 17, 19, 21–22, 56–57, 69, 99, 145
kwatro (quatro), 8, 21–22, 41, 58, 65, 70,
    145, 151
Kwinti (maroons), xi, xviii, xxi, 11

La Cabana, 77
La Caz, xxvii, 129
Lachmon, Michel, 104
La Fiesta, xxvii
laku, xxiv, 17–19, 21–23, 68
laku-pré, 19
La Larme d'or (opera), 49
Lande, René van der, 64, 78, 85
Lang, Eddy, 77
langadron (drum), 14, 17, 19
langaudu (drum), 14
Lalla Rookh (ship), xiii
Lamsberg, Ba Henk, 109
lancer (French dance), 56
langadron (mandron), 14, 17
langa-singi, 20
Langestraaten, Ronald, 93
languadu (mandron), 14
lanti-banja, 18
Laparra, Ramon, xxii
La Passion selon Judas, 49
Laren Jazz Festival, 96
La Rouge, xxvii, 129, 133–34

Larsatie, Lamie, xvi
L'art du piano, 49
Las Casas, Bartolomé de, x
Latin jazz, 77, 80–81, 85
Latin kaseko, 64
La Tropicana (Amsterdam nightclub), 93
Latur (district of Paramaribo), xix
lava (bridal ceremony song). xiii
Lawa (region of Suriname), 60
Lawa River, xii, 11
League of Nations, 83
Leba, xxiv
Lee, Byron, 111
Leeflang, Josie, 69
Leeflang, Leslie, 107
Leerdam, Walter, 39–40
Leeuwen, Frans van, 100
Legba, xix, xxiv
Leidesplein (Amsterdam), 79
Leidesdwarsstraat (Amsterdam), 93
Leipzig conservatory, 47, 51
Lelydorp, Suriname, 59
Lennon, John, 96
lesbian love, 20–21, 115
Libretto, Adolf Jonathan Egbert, 37
Lichtveld, Dr. Lou (Albert Helman), viii,
    xxxvi, 39, 46, 50, 158
Lichtveld, Ursy M., vii
Liedboek der Kerken (Church Hymnal), 38
Lier, Sophie van, 96
Lieve Hugo (Hugo "Iko" Uiterloo), xxii,
    xxv–xxvi, 62–64
Liew A Joe, Fatty, 89
Liew On, Alfred, 44
likembe, 13
Linscheer, Humphry (Speen's Band), 85, 91
Living Colour, xxxiii
Lloyd Weber, Andrew, xxxi
Loange River (Congo), xi
Lobi da Basi (Love Is the Boss), xxix, xxxiii
lobisingi (love songs), xxiv, xxv, 19, 20–21,
    23, 46–47, 55, 58–59, 68, 115, 150
Loeango songs, 62–63
Loevendie, Theo, 96

Lokhin, Stan, xxxviii, 40, 64, 71, 80, 83, 85,
    105–6, 117, 121, 128
Lokono (Amerindian tribe), x, xxx, xxxiii, 3
Lolita Mojica (Alma Braaf), xxx, 114
London, xxix, 108, 111
Look Your Winti, xxvii, 109
Loos, 102
Loosdrecht Jazz Concourse, 96
Lord Kitchener, 61
Lowlands (Dutch pop festival), xxxi
ludruk (Javanese farce), 32
Lutheran church (Waterkant, Paramaribo),
    38, 47

Maagdenstraat (Paramaribo), 70
Maasdammer, 87
mabu-poku, 21
MacDonald, 90
Machito, xxxix
Macrooy, Jeangu, xxii, xxx, 129, 137–38
Madeira, xvii
"Ma Hilli" (Heloise Holband), xxiv
madjiera (Indian tambourine), 28
Mahmood, Talat, 103
Makeba, Miriam, 66
Malay, 33–34
mambo, 63
mandolin, xiv, 28, 41, 104, 159
mandron (Surinamese drum), 13–14, 17, 19
Mann, Herbie, 84
Manchester, 111
Manuel, Peter, viii, 153
manumission, 11
Mapira, Tante, 69
maracas (Cuban), 61
maracas (pyja-rattles), 5, 6
Maranatha choir, 37, 39–40
marching music, xxxviii, 45, 57, 59
Mariënburg plantation, 31, 33
Maripasoula (French Guiana), xii
Maripa palm, 5
Marley, Bob, 110–11
maroons, vii, ix, xi, xix–xx, 10, 23, 67, 133,
    137, 153, 155, 156–57
maroons-kaseko, 67

Marowijne (Maroni) River, viii, xii, 7, 11,
    13, 136
Marowijne (district), xxi, 124
masala, 26
Masekan, Bapak, 33
Masra Award, xxiv
Mass in F major, 52
master drum, 15, 70, 144
mata (wooden percussion instrument), 12
Mata Hari (Surinamese Javanese kroncong
    orchestra), 34
Matawai (maroon tribe), xi, xviii, xxi, 11, 17
Maulads (Islamic holidays), 28
Max Havelaar (Multatuli), 40
mazurka, 47, 56
mbira, 13
McBean, 58, 89–90
McCartney, Paul, 96
Melati, 105
Memphis, Tennessee, xxix
Memre Buku, xxviii, 109, 111, 121, 123, 128
Memre Buku Armory, 44–45
Menor (religious Javanese theater), 35
merengue, xx, xxx, xxxviii, 14, 94, 104
Merrymen, 106
Messas, Baas, 38
metallophone bells, 15
Methodist church, 41
Metropole Orchestra, 106
Meye, August, 89
Meye, Ludwig (Loetie), 88
Meyer, Johnny, 80
microtones (sruti), 26
Middelburg (Zeeland), xvii
Middle East, 85
middle passage, xxiv
Mighty Botai, xx, 120, 134
Mighty 5 & the Rebels, 111
Mighty Power, 63
Mijnals, Lydia, 115
Milad-U-Nabi (birthday of Mohammed),
    28
Milestones, the, xxviii, 97, 108–9, 111
Milestones Emancipation, 109

Militaire Kapel (Military Brass Band),
    xxxvii, 43–45, 49, 88, 97
Miller, Glenn, 43
Mi Lobi Sranan, xvii
"Mi na kakafowru, mi kroon da mi ede"
    (I am the rooster, my crown is on my
    head), 19
"Mini mini, kon njang" (Mini Mini, Come
    and Eat), 40, 45, 139
minor second, 26
Miranda, Johnny de, 88–89
"Mis' Elena, trin tran tring, min na moni
    masra" (Miss Elena, ding, dong, ding,
    I'm the Guy with the Money), 40, 140
Misiedjan, Johan, xx–xxi, 129
missionaries, 47, 52
Moengo, Suriname, xxi, 90
Mohammed (prophet), 27, 28, 33
Mohan, Raj, xv–xvi, 130, 133, 149
Moluccans, 33
Mondriaan, Piet, xii
Mongolian empire, 26
Montgomery, Wes, 95, 98
Montreaux Jazz Festival, 93
Moravian Brothers, 37–38
Moravians: church, 36, 37, 46; choirs, 41;
    missionaries (Herrnhutters), 52
Moroccans, xxviii
Moscow, xx
Mosse, Sandy, 84
Mother Earth (Aisa), xxiii, xxxi, 17, 114
motjo poku, 55, 58–59, 61, 63, 68, 69, 150
Mozart, Wolfgang Amadeus, *Die
    Zauberflöte*, 40, 46
mpemba (white kaolin clay), xix
mridang (Indian percussion instrument),
    27
Mukesh, 103
mulatto, 76, 78
Multatuli, 49
Multi Music Federation (MMF), xxiii
Mumbai, xv
mundedansi, xxvi
Muringen, Kenneth, 91
Musique de l'Afrique, 14

Mussert, Anton, 77
Muziekschool (textbook), 48
MW Records, xx

naadj, 28
naal, 27–28, 145
nadjam (*nazam*) (religious Islamic songs),
    28
Na'f Mi Wang, xx
nagara (Indian drums), 28
Nahar, Pablo, xxi, 97–99, 133
NAKS, 68, 120, 121, 124, 129, 155
Nankoe, Droeh, xiv–xv, 104, 119, 125, 129, 149
Na Pina Wiki (The Poor Week), 46
Nash, Johnny, 111
National Volksmuziekschool (National
    Folk Music School), 51
Nationale Partij Suriname (NPS), 66, 70
Nature (band), 115
Naya Roshini, xiv, 104
nazam (*nadjam*), 28
Nazaten, De, xxvi, xxviii, 130, 133
NCRV radio, 78
Ndjuka (Djuka), xi, xviii, xx–xxi, 11, 147
N'Doye, Djibrill, 97
Nederlandsche Handelsmaatschappij
    (sugar company), 31
Nederlands Jeugdorkest (Netherlands
    Youth Orchestra), 96
Nederlands Philharmonisch Orkest
    (Netherlands Philharmonic Orchestra),
    51
Nederpelt, Charlie ("Mister VARA dance
    orchestra"), 80
Needles, the, 99, 106, 112
Negram (record label), 66
Negro Cat Club, 75
Negro Melody Club, 76
Negro Palace, 76, 79
Nelom, Johannes Theodorus (John), 40,
    43, 45
Nelson Mandela Park, xxiii
neo soul, xxx
Netherlands, vii–ix, x, xii–xvii, xx–xxxi,
    xxxiv, xxxviii, 9, 14, 17, 18, 20–23, 36–38,

40, 43–44, 46, 48–49, 50–52, 61, 64,
66–69, 71, 73–85, 87, 89–93, 95–96, 100,
101–2, 104–7, 109–14, 157–58
Netherlands Antilles, 14, 56, 71, 78, 141
Netherlands East Indies, xvi, xxxviii
New Amsterdam, x
New Orleans, Louisiana, xxix, 62, 75–76,
88, 157
New York, New York, xiv, xxvi, xxx–xxxi,
49–50, 76, 90, 155
Nicasie, Haakon, 90–91
Nickerie, 37–38, 58, 89
Nickerie River, 11
Niemel, Jules, 109
Nieuwendijk (Amsterdam), 77, 80
Nieuwmarkt (Amsterdam), 83
Nieuw Suriname (magazine), 83
Nigeria, 10, 109, 110
Night at the Cotton Club, A, xxxi
Night in Tunisia, A, 84, 101
Nijman, Max, xxvi–xxvii, 105, 112, 120, 130,
134
Nimmermeer, Alex (Frepina), 70
nkpokpo (Congolese wooden bench instru-
ment), 12, 145
Nobel Memorial Prize in Economic
Sciences, 49
non-western music, xxxviii
Noorderstad church (Paramaribo), 38
Noordpool, Stanley, 52
North American Pentecostal Church, 41, 43
North American spirituals, 65
North Sea Jazz (festival), xxxi
nose flute, 13
notu-banja (baka-futu-banja), 18
NRC Handelsblad, 73, 100
NSB (National Socialist Movement in the
Netherlands), 76

obia, 69
obiahman, 109
obia pre, 69
O'Bryan, Ponda, 10–24, 102, 121, 131, 159
Octopedians, 97
odo (proverb), xviii

Odongo (Stanley Angel), xxvii–xxviii, 108,
110
Odongo and the Spirits, xxvii, 109, 111
Oema Lobi, 115
Oema Priserie, 115
Oema Soso, 115
"Oen egi pasi" (Our Own Way), 105
Ohio State University jazz band, 86
Ojeda, Alonso de, x
O.K. Orkest, 87
Oldenstam, 88
omangano (period of mourning), 6
Onafhankelheidsplein (Independence
Square) in Paramaribo, 45
Onkel Seedo, xxii
Onze Wereld (Our World, magazine), viii
Oor (Ear, Dutch music magazine), 112
Oost West (East West, magazine), 47
Oostwold, John, 93
opegooie, 55, 59
Opel, Jackie, 64
Openneer, Herman (Doctor Jazz), 73,
75–76, 81, 117, 155
Opo Jeje, 69–70
oporenten, 13
Oranjeplein (Paramaribo), 45
Orchestra Popular, 90
oremi (pyjai songs), 6
organ, xiv, 26, 37–39, 47–48
Os, 63
Overweg, Bep, 76

Pablo Nahar Quartet, 97–98
Pagini, Carol, 81
pakrotutu (horn), 13
Palace (Amsterdam nightclub), 85
Panama, 52
Pandero, 104
Pandit Rambaran Jaggan, xiv
Pandits, 29
pangi (loincloth), xii
papa (rhythm), xix
papai-benta, 145
Papiamentu, 22, 150
Para (district in Suriname), 32

Para (plantation Creoles), 11
Para creek, 11
Paradiso (Amsterdam concert venue), 95,
109
Paramaccan, xi, xviii; language, xix
Paramari-Bach, 97
Paramaribo, Suriname, xvi–xvii, xix–xxii,
xxiv, xxx, xxvii, 6, 11, 17, 19, 22, 37–38,
46–48, 51, 55, 59, 65, 69–70, 80, 86–87,
89, 91, 96, 98–99, 114
"Paramaribo Blues," 80
Paramaribop, xxi, xxiii, 82, 91–92, 98–100,
102
para-pas'dron, 16
"Parijs" (song by Kenny B.), xxii
Paris, xxii, 49, 78, 83, 85, 108
Parisius, Arthur Lodewijk (Kid Dynamite),
xxii, 50, 73–74
Parker, Charlie, 85, 92, 97
parlando, 6
partij (du group), 18
partij-banja, 18–20
Patrick Sedoc Quartet, 101
paturia ke naadj (Indian combination of
music and dance aka ganika), 28, 151
Pay, Arthur, 74, 76, 79
pelog (Javanese tonal system), 30
Pengel, Jopie, 66, 122, 140
pengulu (Javanese religious functionary), 33
pentatonic scale, 8, 30, 67
Pentecostal church, 41, 43
penurus, 32
Perikels, xxvi, 94, 99
Peru, 4
Phedra (Paramaribo theater), 65
Phrygian scale, 43
Picasso, Pablo, xii
Piccadilly Boys, 89
P.I. Man (Imro Belliot), xxvii–xxviii, 108,
110–12
P.I. Man and Memre Buku, xxviii, 111
Pink Oculus (Esperanza Denswil), xxxii
plantation Creoles, 10–11, 17
Plantation Orchestra, 77
plantations, 10

Plato (Surinamese trumpet player), 63
Platters, the, 103
Poeder, Suzie, 105
"Poeroe foetoe" (Move your feet), 44, 61, 140
Pohla, Max, 79
Poku, Frans, 69
Poku Masra, 68
Polanen, Minister, 38
Poles, xxviii
Politiekapel (Police Corps Brass Band),
xxvii, 43, 44, 45, 49
polka, 56
polyrhythm, 15, 57
Pop-Jawa (Javanese pop), xvii, 104–5
Porter, Cole, xxxi
Port of Spain, Trinidad, xiv
Portugal, xi
Portuguese, xvii, 33, 76
Povel, Ferdinand, 96
Pozo, Chano, 89
Prado, Perez, 85–86
Praeludium Pacis, 51
precentor, 6, 33
Price, Richard, vii, xxxiii, 134, 156
Price, Sally, vii, xxxiii, 134, 156
primprimsua (Ghanaian thumb piano), 13
Prince Judah, 112
Prince Koloni, xx
Prins Bernhard Kampement (Prince
Bernhard Barracks), 44
prisdoti (songs for the earth), 16
prisir-kawina, 21
prodo-banja, 18
Promenade Orchestra, 78
Protestant church, 7, 36, 38, 52
Prudencia, Macario, 107
Psalms, 47
pudja (drum), 14, 17, 19, 56–57
Puerto Rico, xx
pyjai, xxx
pyjaiman, xxvii, 4, 6, 12, 108
pyjai songs, 6–7

qawwali, 27–28, 144, 151
quadrille, 56

Quechua Indians, 9
Queen Maxima, xxix
Quran, 27–28, 33

Radio Apinti, 66
Radio Nederland Wereldomroep (Radio
    Netherlands World Service), 51, 78, 93
Radio Philharmonic Orchestra of Norway,
    51
Radio Sotens (Switzerland), 74
Rafi, Mohammed, 103
raga, xv, 25–26, 29
ragtime, 37, 87
Ramayana, 32, 152
Ramblers, 84–85
Ramgoelamweg (district of Paramaribo),
    xix
Ramin, "Uncle" (leader of Mata Hari kron-
    cong orchestra), 33
Ramkelawan, Kries, xxxii–xxxiii
rap, ix, xxxi, 112
RAPAR (Radio Paramaribo), 89, 141
Ras-I, 112
Rastafari and Rastafarianism, 110–11
rasta style, 111
Rayer, Nic, 74
Reality (Latin funk band), 95, 106
Red Star (band), 87–88
Ree, Lou van, 80, 85
Reeperbahn (Hamburg), 74
Reformed church (Kerkplein, Paramaribo),
    38
reggae, vi, viii, xxi, xxiii, xxx, xxxviii, 104,
    108, 110–12, 153, 155
Reinhardt, Django, 77
Rembrandtplein (Amsterdam), 79
Renata, Eddie, 51, 93
Renfrum, Nelson (Zapata Jaw), 92
Rens, Arthur, 80
Rens, Walter, 77, 80
Republic of Indonesia, 32
Requiem for Mahatma Gandhi, 49
reson (quatro), 21
Revanche, 111
Revelation Time (reggae band), 111

Reys, Rita, 75
Reyseger, Ernst, 102
rhythm and blues, xxix, xxxi
Rhythm Makers, 64
"Rijst met kouseband" (Rice with Long
    Beans), 94
Rio Funmaster, xxiv
Ritmo Natural, 93, 95, 121, 129
Roach, Felix, 89
rock and roll, 85, 87, 110, 112
Roemer, 68
Roemer, Astrid, 96
Rolling Stones, 85
Rollins, Sonny, 81, 87
Roman Catholic Church. See Catholic
    Church
Romeo, Max, 111
Ronald Snijders Band, 97, 101
Ronald Snijders Ensemble, xxviii
Root Boy, 113
Rootsman, 112
Rotterdam, the Netherlands, vii, xiv, xxiv,
    xxxii, 9, 23, 52, 74, 79, 111–12, 154, 157
Rotterdam Conservatory, vii, xiv, 52
Royal Conservatory, The Hague, xv
rubber tappers, 21, 58
Rude Boy, xxxiii
Rudeteenz, xxvii
Rupia, xvii, 105

Saävedra, Dario (Daan Samuels), 51
Sai Baba, xiv
sakka (calabash gourd shaker), 12, 15, 19
salsa, xx, 67, 71, 107, 112
salsa-antiyana, 107
Salvation Army, 64
samba, 18, 71–72, 111
sambura (drum), xxx, xxxvii, 4, 5, 71
sambura (music), xxix, 5, 9
sansa, 13
Saramacca, vii, xxi, xxxii, 11, 69
Saramacca Band, 80
Saramaccan language, xxi
Saramaccan people, vii, xviii, 15–16
sarangi, 28

Sarnami, xv

Sarnami-Hindustani music, 25, 27

saron, xvi–xvii, 31

saudade, 33

saxophone, 41, 67, 71, 75, 78–79, 84, 87–88, 103–4

Scandinavia, 82, 93, 112

Scheherazade (Amsterdam nightclub), 81

Schermacher, George, xxvi, xxxix, xxxviii, 58, 59, 71, 86–87, 89, 93, 95, 104, 119, 123, 148

Schittmeyer clavier, 38

Schoonderwalt, Herman, 84

Scott, Milly (Marion Henriette), xxx, 82

Scott, Tony (Peter van de Bosch), xxxiii, 113

Secco's Gitanos, 78

Sedoc, Patrick, 101

sedri (snare drum), 68

Seedo, Onkel, xxi

sekete (seketi), xiii, xx, 17, 67, 151

sekete-style kaseko, 67

seketi, xx

sek-seki, 57

Sephardic Jews, xi

Sesaamstraat (*Sesame Street*), 114

Sesjun (Session), 96

set-dansi, xxxviii, 56, 63

Seven Provinces of the Netherlands, x

Shah Noer Saba, 103

shaman, 4, 108

Shamanism, 4

Sherman, Tony, 106

Sheseba, 97, 101

Shleu Shleu, 62

Shiva, 28

Showboat (Dutch jazz club), 99

Sierra Leone, 13, 143

Sight (band), 97

siksak (*sek-seki*, shaking instrument), 12, 146

SIL International (formerly known as Summer Institute of Linguistics), xi

Sinester, Mr. Slim, 95

Sinfonieta, 51

singer songwriter, xxii, xxx

sitar, 26–29, 146, 159

ska, 111

skratyi (bass drum), 19, 56, 58, 61–62, 67–71, 99, 146, 148

skratyi poku, 56

Skymasters, 85

Slagtand, Nelly (Tasha's World), xxxi, 19, 69

Slave Coast (Togo, Benin, Nigeria), 10

slendro (Javanese tonal system), 30, 32

slit drum, 8, 12, 15, 144

SME (Surinam Music Ensemble), xxiii, xxxviii, 92, 98–102

SME Records, viii

Smit, Frank, 106

Smit, Jan, xxi

Smit Trio, 78

snare drum, 22, 56–58, 60, 63, 68, 99, 100, 146, 149

Snesi (Chinese), 19

Snijders, Christoffel, 51

Snijders, Herman, 91

Snijders, Richard Edgar (Eddy), 44–45, 49, 61, 87–88, 90

Snijders, Ronald, ix, xxiii, xxvi, 49, 52, 96–97, 101, 121, 125, 131, 133–34, 137, 156, 159

Snijders Big Band, 91

soca, xx, xxx, 108, 111

soca-calypso, 109

Soekra, Vincent, 68

sohar, xiii, 28

sokko songs (or psalms), 17

Solat, 95, 97, 99, 106, 112

solo tutti, 33

son, 61

songé, xiii, 15

Songs for Various Occasions (Droeh Nankoe), xv

songs of praise, 6

son montuno, xxx, 62

Sonora Matancera, 60–61

Sonora Paramarera, 106

Sordam, Robert (Robby Harman), xxvii, 97–98, 100, 109, 127, 133

Sosoba, 102

Sosu (or Susu, tribe in Guinea), 17
soukous, xx–xxi, 72
soul, xxx, xxxviii, 111
Sousa, John Philip, 43
South South West, xxvii, 131
Souvenir, William, xx
Soviet Union, 39
Spall, Lex van, 74–75, 78
Spain, 93
Spanish Civil War, 50
Spanjoru poku (Spanish music of the
    conjuntos), 61
Speen's Band (Humphrey Linscheer), 85, 91
Spellbound (band), 102
Spiral Road (American film), 50
Spirits, the (backing band), xxvii, 109, 111,
    121
Sporkslede, 71, 87
Sranan Tongo (Surinamese tongue), xii,
    xvii, xxviii, 9, 17, 21–22, 38, 47, 65, 111–12
Staatskapel (State Brass Band), 44, 49
Starke, Sabrina, xxxi–xxxii
Stars on 45, 108
Stedman, J. G., xi
steel band, 32
steel gamelan, 32
Steel Pulse, 111
Stekkel, 64
Sterman, Annie, 82
Stichting Scarabes (Scarabes Foundation),
    xxiii
Stichting voor Culturele Samenwerking
    (STICUSA) (Foundation for Cultural
    Cooperation), xxxvii, 37, 40, 141
Stichting ter promotie van popmuziek
    (SPN) (Foundation for promotion of
    pop music), xxiii
St. Matthew Passion, 46, 49
Stoffels, Johnny, 83
Strategier, Herman, 48
Strayhorn, Billy, 98
Suki Akkal, xxxviii, 103
"Sukrufinga," 97
Sunchild, xxiii, 101
Sun Ra Orchestra, 102

Super Dan, 112
Surbrothers, 105
Surinaamse Filharmonisch Orkest
    (Surinamese Philharmonic Orchestra),
    xxvii, 43, 49
Suriname: church music, 37–38; classical
    music, 45–52; East Indian music, 25;
    East Indian Muslims, 27; gamelan, 30–31
Suriname Folklore, 55
Suriname River, 11, 69
Surinamese-Hindustanis, 27; film music,
    103; language, 27; music, 25, 103. See
    also Hindustanis and Hindustani
    Surinamers
Surinamese Interior War (1986–92), xi, xix
Surinamese Javanese, 30–31; music, 104. See
    also Java and Javanese
Surinamese National Song Festival, xvii
Surinamese Philharmonic Orchestra, 37, 50
Surinamese Volksmuziekschool
    (Surinamese Folk Music School), 103
Surinam Music Association (SMA), xxii,
    xxiv, xxxviii, 10, 102
Surinam Music Ensemble (SME), xxiii,
    xxxviii, 92, 98–102
Surinam Remembers Mohammed Rafi, 103
Suripop, xxxviii, 105
susa (play in dance form), xiii, 19, 22
Sut Eye, 93
Swahili music, 71
Sweden, 52, 84, 89, 93
swing, 87, 88
Swingmasters, 64, 86, 88–89, 90
Switzerland, xxvi, 74, 80, 83
Symphonie Macabre opus 7, 48

tablas, xxxvii, 26–28, 29
taboos, 15
Taharga, 102
Taj Mahal, 26
tajuban, 32
Tak, Tjen A, 58, 89
tala, 26
talking drums, xxxviii, 12, 13
Tamanredjo (Suriname village), 33

tambora (drum), 14
tambourine, 28, 142, 146
tango, 56
Tan Sen, 26
Tanta (Aunt), 18
Taptoe (Military Tattoo), 44
Tasha's World, xxxi
Taylor, Cecil, 102
Teheran, 83
terbangen, xvi, 33, 152
terbangen-cilik, 33
terbangen-kencring, 33
T-Group, 104
Thalia (Paramaribo theater), xvii, xxxvii
Thomas, John, 98
Thompson, 58, 89
Thorbeckeplein (Amsterdam), 85
Thunderstorm, 106
timbal (old name for conga in Suriname), 21
timbales, 86, 93
timpani, 56
Tinbergen, Jan, 49
tjapu (percussion instrument), 12, 146
Tjen A Kon, Ricardo, 107
Tjon, Marius, 102
Tjon A Yong (Henny Vonk), 114
TMT (The Music Translators), 91
toasting, 111
toccata, 47
Togo, 13
Tokyo, xxxi, 49
tom-toms, 57
Topijn, 87
Torarica Hotel (Paramaribo), 89
Tosh, Peter, 110
Trafassi, 107–8, 122–23, 131, 133–34
trance, 4, 7
Treaty of Westminster, x
Trekkers, De (brass band), 43
Tri Djokko Muljo, 104
Trinidad and Tobago, xiii, xxxvii, 32, 50, 57, 62–63, 71, 89
Trio (Amerindian tribe), x, 3–4, 7
TRIS military band (Tropical Armed Forces in Suriname), 44

troki (precentor), xxiii
trombone, 41, 51, 69, 82
TROS radio, 96
Troy, Doris, 64
trumpet, xxviii, 38, 41, 50, 56, 59–60, 63–65, 78–85, 87–88, 90–91, 93, 96
tuba, 41, 56–77, 62, 69
Tubantia, xxviii
tuku (style of Winti music), 21
tum drum, xxxii
tumao, tumaun (apinti), xix, 13
Turkey, 82
Turks, xxviii
twelve-tone system, 85
tweneboa (kind of cedar tree), 15
Twinkle Stars, 61, 64, 95, 100, 104–6, 112, 121–23, 134
Typhoon (Glenn de Randamie), xxix, 132, 137–38

Uiterloo, Hugo "Iko" (Lieve Hugo), xxii, xxiv, xxvi–xxvii, 62–64, 109, 120, 123, 128, 132–34, 137, 159
ukulele, 33, 65, 149
Unitas Fratum (Unity of the Brethren/ Moravian Church), 36
United Nations (UN), xiv, 83
United Province (now Uttar Pradesh), xiii
United States, xii–xiii, xxviii, xxxii, xxxiii, 23, 39, 56, 61, 65, 77, 86–89, 110, 156
University of Michigan jazz big band, 86
urban Creoles, 10, 11
Urban Dance Squad, xxxiii, 113
Urdu, xv, 27
Ustad Mohammed Rasheed Khan, xiv
Ustads, 28
Utomo, Lamie and Tjondro, xvi, 120, 129
Utrechtsestraat (Amsterdam), 93
Utrechts Stedelijk Orkest (City of Utrecht Orchestra), 48
Uttar Pradesh, xiii, 25

Valdez, Bebo, 92
Valientsplein (Paramaribo), 59
"Van de regen naar de zon" (From the Rain to the Sun), xxix, xxxiii

Van de Berg, Eric, 102
Van der Kust, "Ray Brooks," 106
Van der Lande, René, 85
Van Dijk (Paramaribo neighborhood), 69
Van Hetten, Iwan, 91
Van Kempen, Michiel, viii, 157, 159
Van Leeuwen, Frans, 100
Van Lier, Sophie, 96
Van Weteringen, Dr. Wilmhelmina, xxv
Van Windt, Glenn, 96
VARA dance band, 84
VARA radio, 78, 80, 96
Vasconcellos, Mario, 89
Veasly, Gerald, 102
Vedas, 28
Veldman, Eddy, 94, 99–100, 102, 106, 133
Venlo (bass player), 90
Vereniging Ons Suriname (Our Suriname
    Union), 21
Vervuurt, Lex, 77, 84, 94
Vienna, 52
Vijent, 68, 70–71
violin, 8, 33–34, 41, 48, 52, 78, 84, 103–4,
    146, 159
Vishnu, 28
Vliet, Toon van, 84
vodu, xix
Volkskrant, 101–2
Volksmuziekschool (Folk Music School),
    xxxvi, 51
Vonk, Henny (Tjon A Yong), 96, 114
Voorhoeve, Jan, vii, 19, 65
Vries, Hessel de, 100
Vrieze, Jopie, 43, 70–71
Vrolijke Jeugd, 65, 66
Vuisje, Bert, 101

Waal, Marlene, 66, 115
Waal, René, 65
wachtensmoede (tired of waiting), xxxv
Wagenwiel (nightclub), 80
Wailer, Bunny, 110
waltz, 61
Wan spraakkunst vo taki en skrifi da
    tongo foe Sranang (One Grammar for

Talking and Writing in the Surinamese
    Tongue), 48
Washboard (music group), 62–63
"Wasmasjine" (Washing Machine), 107
Waterloo (jazz band), 37
Waterloo Ensemble, 96
Wayana (Amerindian tribe), x–xi, 3–4, 7, 8,
    9, 122, 134
wayang (shadow puppet plays), 31, 32
Wayono, 9
WDR orchestra, 101
Weather Report, 101
Webster, Ben, 87, 95
Weill, Kurt, 46
Weinappel, Harvey, 96
Weltak, Marcel, viii, ix
Weltevreden, Eddy, 90
Wessels (conductor, Surinamese
    Philharmonic Orchestra), 43
West Africa, 19
West Bantu, 13, 15
Westerborg, Fred van, 81
Westerkerk (Amsterdam), 37
West Indian carnival, London, 108
West Sudanese, 15
What If, 112
whole-tone scale, 30
WIC (Dutch West India Company), xi
Willem-Alexander (king of the
    Netherlands), xxix
Williams, Dr. Ramon, xxi
Williams, Tony, 100
Willigers, 47
Wina Orchestra, 103
Windt, Glenn van, 96
Winti (Amerindian), 63
winti (music/songs), xxiii, xxxi, xxvi, 10, 43,
    68, 71, 111
Winti (religion), xi, xix, xxiv–xxxviii, 3, 10,
    12, 16, 40, 71, 109
Winti-banjas, 18
Winti kaseko, 62, 67
Winti-poku, 22, 68–69, 109–10
Winti-pré (ritual dance), xxiv, 16–17
Winti songs, 40, 62, 65, 69

Winti spirits, 22, 69
Withers, Bill, xxxii
Woiski, Max, Jr., 93–95
Woiski, Max, Sr., 77, 89, 92, 106, 114
woodcutting, 15
Wooding, C. J., 16, 157
World War II, 73–74, 76, 86

Yakki Famirie, xx, 132–33
Yamore, 9
Yanasei (the other side of life), xxv
"Yankee Doodle," xxxviii, 56
Yanomami (Amerindian tribe), 4
Yoga voor de pianist (Yoga for the Pianist),
   49
Yuang Ling Lu project, 102

Zaandijk, the Netherlands, 99
Zaire (Congo), 72
Zapakara, 78, 89, 94
Zapata Jaw (Nelson Renfrum), 92
Zappa, Frank, 110
Zebeda, Johan, 109
Zeefuik, Denise (Denise Jannah), xxvi, 115,
   127
Zeeland, xvii
Zegelaar, Jules, 79, 82
Zeist, the Netherlands, 46
Zilver Harp (Silver Harp Dutch music
   award), xxxi
Zorg brothers, 69
Zorn, John, 102
zouk, xx–xxi, xxx
Zuiverloon, Waldy, 88

CPSIA information can be obtained
at www.ICGtesting.com
Printed in the USA
BVHW030538270621
609935BV00001B/4